Critical Education in International Perspective

Bloomsbury Critical Education

Series Editor: Peter Mayo

Books in this series explore the relationship between education and power in society and offer insights into ways of confronting inequalities and social exclusions in different learning settings and in society at large. The series will comprise books wherein authors contend forthrightly with the inextricability of power/knowledge relations.

Advisory Board:
Antonia Darder (Loyola Maramount University, USA), Samira Dlimi (École Normale Supérieure, Rabat, Morocco), Luiz Armando Gandin (Federal University of Rio Grande do Sul, Brazil), Jose Ramon Flecha Garcia (University of Barcelona, Spain), Ravi Kumar (South Asian University, India), Antonia Kupfer (University of Dresden, Germany), Peter McLaren (Chapman University, USA), Maria Mendel (University of Gdansk, Poland), Maria Nikolakaki (University of Peloponnese, Greece) and Juha Suoranta (University of Tampere, Finland)

Also available in the series:
Course Syllabi in Faculties of Education: Bodies of Knowledge and their Discontents, International and Comparative Perspectives, edited by André Elias Mazawi and Michelle Stack

Critical Human Rights, Citizenship, and Democracy Education: Entanglements and Regenerations, edited by Michalinos Zembylas and André Keet

Ecopedagogy: Critical Environmental Teaching for Planetary Justice and Global Sustainable Development, Greg William Misiaszek

Education, Individualization and Neoliberalism: Youth in Southern Europe, Valerie Visanich

Hopeful Pedagogies in Higher Education, edited by Mike Seal

Pedagogy, Politics and Philosophy of Peace: Interrogating Peace and Peacemaking, edited by Carmel Borg and Michael Grech

Forthcoming in the series:
Decolonizing American Higher Education: Subaltern Scholars, Professors, and Administrators Speaking Out, Pierre Orelus

Decolonizing Indigenous Education in the US: Beyond Colonizing Epistemicides, Samuel B. Torres

Feminism, Adult Education and Creative Possibility: Imaginative Responses, edited by Darlene E. Clover, Kerry Harman, and Kathy Sanford

Vietnamese Diaspora, Genocide, and Critical Education, Kevin D. Lam

Critical Education in International Perspective

Peter Mayo and Paolo Vittoria

BLOOMSBURY ACADEMIC
LONDON • NEW YORK • OXFORD • NEW DELHI • SYDNEY

BLOOMSBURY ACADEMIC
Bloomsbury Publishing Plc
50 Bedford Square, London, WC1B 3DP, UK
1385 Broadway, New York, NY 10018, USA
29 Earlsfort Terrace, Dublin 2, Ireland

BLOOMSBURY, BLOOMSBURY ACADEMIC and the Diana logo are trademarks
of Bloomsbury Publishing Plc

First published in Great Britain 2022
This paperback edition published in 2023

Copyright © Peter Mayo and Paolo Vittoria, 2022

Peter Mayo and Paolo Vittoria have asserted their right under the Copyright, Designs and Patents Act, 1988, to be identified as Authors of this work.

For legal purposes the Acknowledgement on p. xlv constitute an extension of this copyright page.

All rights reserved. No part of this publication may be reproduced or transmitted in any form or by any means, electronic or mechanical, including photocopying, recording, or any information storage or retrieval system, without prior permission in writing from the publishers.

Bloomsbury Publishing Plc does not have any control over, or responsibility for, any hird-party websites referred to or in this book. All internet addresses given in this book were correct at the time of going to press. The author and publisher regret any inconvenience caused if addresses have changed or sites have ceased to exist, but can accept no responsibility for any such changes.

A catalogue record for this book is available from the British Library.

Library of Congress Cataloging-in-Publication Data

Names: Mayo, Peter, 1955- author. | Vittoria, Paolo, 1976- author.
Title: Critical Education in International Perspective / Peter Mayo and Paolo Vittoria.
Description: London; New York, NY: Bloomsbury Academic, 2021. |
Series: Bloomsbury critical education |
Includes bibliographical references and index. |
Identifiers: LCCN 2021006743 (print) | LCCN 2021006744 (ebook) |
ISBN 9781350147751 (hardback) | ISBN 9781350147768 (ebook) |
ISBN 9781350147775 (epub)
Subjects: LCSH: Critical pedagogy. | Social justice and education. |
Freire, Paulo, 1921-1997–Influence.
Classification: LCC LC196 .M259 2021 (print) |
LCC LC196 (ebook) | DDC 370.11/5–dc23
LC record available at https://lccn.loc.gov/2021006743
LC ebook record available at https://lccn.loc.gov/2021006744

ISBN: HB: 978-1-3501-4775-1
PB : 978-1-3502-1525-2
ePDF: 978-1-3501-4776-8
eBook: 978-1-3501-4777-5

Series: Bloomsbury Critical Education

Typeset by Newgen KnowledgeWorks Pvt. Ltd., Chennai, India

To find out more about our authors and books visit
www.bloomsbury.com and sign up for our newsletters.

Dedicated to the memory of Elza Cortese (1950–2021) and Lilian Farrugia (1925–2020), mother-in-law and aunt of Paolo Vittoria and Peter Mayo, respectively and to the memory of Frei Joao Xerri OP (1947–2021), a good Maltese friend and contact in Brazil (his adopted country) and Rome over the years.

Contents

Series Editor's Preface		ix
Foreword: 'Alternative Ways to Think and to Do Critical Theory and Pedagogy Alternatively'		xiii
João M. Paraskeva		
Acknowledgement		xlv
1	Introduction. Critical Education: An International Perspective	1

Part 1 Education, Markets and Alternatives

2	Lifelong Education/Learning: An Alternative Critical Approach	11
3	Philosophy of Differences and Social Creation: Anna Maria Piussi and Antonia De Vita	21

Part 2 A Critical Reading of the World

4	Gabriela Mistral: Poet of Education	29
5	Ada Gobetti: Education for Resistance and Reconstruction	39
6	Lorenzo Milani and the Schools of San Donato and Sant'Andrea a Barbiana	47
7	Paulo Freire, Globalization and Emancipatory Education	65

Part 3 Education and Migration

8	Towards an Anti-Racist Education and Human Solidarity in the Mediterranean and in the Context of Migrations	79
9	Hegemony, Migration and Misplaced Alliances: Lessons from Antonio Gramsci	91

Part 4 Popular Education, Social Movements and the Struggle for Independence

10	Amilcar Cabral and Paulo Freire: The Struggle for Independence and Popular Education in Guinea-Bissau, *with Amilcar Araujo Pereira*	105

11	Julius K. Nyerere's Signposts for a Postcolonial Education	119
12	Social Movements and Critical Education in Brazil: From the Origins of Popular Education to the Struggle for Democratisation, *with Roberto Leher*	133
Epilogue		157
Notes		169
References		187
Author Index		207
Subject Index		209

Series Editor's Preface

This book series was introduced against an international background that comprised and continues to comprise situations that are disturbing and intriguing. The onset of Covid-19 has thrown into sharp relief arguably the major casualty of this pandemic, an unprepared, failed state. We have been left with a state shorn of the facilities and provisions one would expect of a purportedly 'democratic' entity that dances not only to the tune of capital accumulation but also to that reflecting the concerns of all people under its jurisdiction. The latter is certainly not the case as, with regard to the provision of social safeguards, the state has, in many places, almost been rendered threadbare by its accommodation of nefarious neoliberal policies which leaves everything outside the demands of capital to the market and voluntary organizations. While wealth is concentrated, as a result, in the hands of a few, there are those who are left to struggle for survival in a Darwinian contest that rewards the 'winners' and renders others disposable. Questionable wealth is concentrated in the hands of a few, who take advantage of their network of spin doctors and 'fake news' soothsayers, to play the victim with regard to the pandemic. They and the many policymakers who accommodate them deflect their responsibility onto ordinary citizens and further justify curtailing the state's social spending, to the detriment of the many, 'the multitudes', as referred to by Michael Hart and Toni Negri.

The series was launched at a time when the 'social contract', ideally one which transcends the capitalist framework (as Henry Giroux astutely remarks), is continuously being shredded as several people are removed from the index of human concerns. Many are led to live in a precarious state. Contract work has become the norm, a situation that renders one's life less secure. There is also criticism targeted at the very nature of production and consumption with their effects on people and their relationship to other social beings and the rest of the planet, hence 'questionable wealth'.

They are also difficult times because the initial enthusiasm for the popular quest for democracy in various parts of the world has been tempered by eventual realism based on the fact that strategically entrenched forces are not removed simply by overthrowing a dictator. Far from ushering in a 'spring', the uprisings in certain countries have left political vacuums – fertile terrain for religiously motivated terrorism that presents a real global security threat. This threat, though having to be controlled in many ways, not least tackling the relevant social issues at their root, presents many with a carte blanche to trample on hard-earned democratic freedoms and rights. The situation is said to further spread the 'culture of militarization' that engulfs youth, about which much has been written in critical education. Terrorist attacks or aborted coups allow scope for analyses on these grounds, including analyses that draw out the implications for education.

The security issue, part of the 'global war on terror', is availed of by those who seek curtailment of human beings' right to asylum seeking and who render impoverished migrants as scapegoats for the host country's economic ills. The issue of migration would be an important contemporary theme in the large domain of critical education. This phenomenon and that of Covid-19, as with any other pretext, are availed of by powers acting exclusively in the interest of capital. This leads to a further siege mentality marked by increasing otherizing, scapegoating, surveillance and incarceration. Security extends beyond the culture of fear generated through terrorism to include health issues such as the pandemic, the latter said to be spread by those who, in reality, are the least equipped to work and live safely in their homes, including rejected asylum seekers and other migrants who have been denied citizenship, those who live in restricted and overcrowded spaces or … who do not have a home – period. They face a stark choice: exposure or starvation. Barbarism, in Rosa Luxemburg's sense of the term, is a key feature of this choice and the society in which many live.

The series was introduced at a time when an attempt was made for politics to be rescued from the exclusive clutches of politicians and bankers. A more grassroots kind of politics has been constantly played out in globalized public arenas such as the squares and streets of Athens, Madrid, Istanbul (Gezi Park), Cairo, Tunis and New York City. A groundswell of dissent, indignation and tenacity was manifest and projected throughout all corners of the globe, albeit, as just indicated, not always leading to developments hoped for by those involved. Yet hope springs eternal. Some of these manifestations have provided pockets for alternative social action to the mainstream, including educational action. Authors writing on critical education have found, in these pockets, seeds for a truly and genuinely democratic pedagogy that will hopefully be explored and developed, theoretically and empirically, in this series.

It is in these contexts, and partly as a response to the challenges they pose, that this series on critical education was conceived and brought into being. Education, though not to be attributed powers it does not have (it cannot change things on its own), surely has a role to play in this scenario: from exposing and redressing class politics to confronting the cultures of militarization, consumerism, individualism and ethnic supremacy. The call among critical educators is for a pedagogy of social solidarity that emphasizes the collective and communal in addition to the ecologically sustainable.

Critical educators have for years been exploring, advocating and organizing ways of seeing, learning and living that constitute alternatives to the mainstream. They have been striving to make their contribution to changing the situation for the better, governed by a vision or visions of systems that are socially more just. The ranks of the oppressed are swelling. Hopefully, it is the concerns of these people that are foremost in the minds and hearts of those committed to a social-justice-oriented critical education. I would be the first to admit that even a professed commitment to a critical education can degenerate into another form of radical chic or academic sterility. We need to be ever so vigilant towards not only others but also ourselves, coming to terms with our own contradictions, therefore seeking, in Paulo Freire's words, to become less incoherent.

This series offers a platform for genuinely socially committed critical educators to express their ideas in a systematic manner. It seeks to offer signposts for an alternative approach to education and cultural work, constantly bearing in mind the United Nations Sustainable Development Goals that, albeit difficult to realize, serve as important points of reference when critiquing current policies in different sectors, including education. The series' focus on critical education, comprising the movement known as critical pedagogy, is intended to contribute to maintaining the steady flow of ideas that can inspire and allow for an education that eschews the 'taken for granted'.

In this particular volume, Paolo Vittoria and I bring to fruition work emerging from years of collaboration in critical education. We also revise together papers we originally drafted separately, two of which with a co-writer. The work lends a Mediterranean and Latin American perspective to critical education. We could not cover every segment of Planet Earth as we write best on what we know best. Vittoria has lived and taught for years in Brazil while I have a working knowledge of that context, especially Brazil, because of my many years working on and around Freire's ideas. This is true also of Vittoria's work. In fact, it was Freire's work which brought us in contact in 2005 when we engaged in a symposium on Freire at the University of Rome La Sapienza at the Mirafiori campus. A year later we brought our common Mediterranean background into the equation by jointly delivering a seminar on the relevance of Freire to this specific region to a class of doctoral and laurea students, and other guests, such as the late critical educator, Bruno Schettini, at the University of Naples Federico II. Our collaboration led to a book on critical pedagogy published in Italian in 2017 and launched in various Italian sites. This book contains some material in English from that volume but goes beyond including fresh new chapters. It seeks to bring to light movements and exponents of a critical approach to education not normally given prominence in the English-speaking world. We cover figures such as *noblesse oblige* Freire and Antonio Gramsci, the latter with respect to the theme of migration. We, however, also expose readers in English to the work and ideas of exponents of Italian feminism of difference, namely, Anna Maria Piussi and Antonia De Vita. We also discuss Gabriella Mistral from Chile, Ada Gobetti from Turin, Lorenzo Milani from Florence, Amilcar Cabral and Julius Nyerere from Africa. We also address such themes as anti-racism in a Mediterranean context and grassroots struggles in Brazil especially with regard to the country's leading movement, the Movimento Trabalhadores Rurais Sem Terra (Movement of Landless Rural Workers), otherwise known simply as the Movimento Sem Terra (MST – Landless Peasant Movement). Two chapters are written with two Brazilian writers – Roberto Leher, the former rector of the Federal University of Rio de Janeiro, and Amilcar Araujo Pereira, militant of the Black movement in Brazil and academic at the same Rio university. We are honoured by Mozambican scholar João M. Paraskeva writing the book's foreword and three top social scientists generously endorsing the work. These are Marta Soler-Gallart, from the University of Barcelona and editor of *International Sociology*, Donatella Della Porta, from the Scuola Normale of Pisa, well known for her many studies on such topics as social movements and Raewyn Connell, author of leading sociological works. This book should be of interest not only to readers and practitioners in critical education but also to those engaged in popular education, philosophy, sociology and political science.

Peter Mayo
Series Editor
University of Malta
Msida, Malta

Foreword: 'Alternative Ways to Think and to Do Critical Theory and Pedagogy Alternatively'

João M. Paraskeva

Viral Fascism

Fascism became respectable

Max Horkheimer

One upon a time, in the mid-1930s, Panait Istrati, a Turkish communist writer, visited the Soviet Union. It was a bloody time, an era of a massive carnage. Elected in 1922 as secretary general of the Communist Party, Joseph Stalin soon unleashed a war on dissent, crushing even old close allies. One of Stalin's acephalous acolytes tried to minimize and domesticate such a bloodbath, and convince Istrati that violence against the enemies was part of the revolution, that it was needed for the success of the revolution. In such context, he evoked the proverb, 'You know very well that you can't make an omelet without breaking eggs', to which Istrati tersely replied: 'All right. I understand. I can see the broken eggs. But where's this omelet of yours?'

This graphic story shared by leading public intellectual Slavoj Žižek,[1] shows rather well not only the herculean challenges framing critical theory and critical intellectuals but also the importance of critical theories and pedagogies under the current rampant Ur-fascism[2] which frames 'the fourfold disaster of the contemporary world: the social, economic, geopolitical and environmental disasters.'[3] Peter Mayo and Paolo Vittoria's *Critical Education in International Perspective* constitutes a powerful and timely answer to our modern challenges, so graphically visible in our daily lives. Let's pay attention to some outrageous figures.

Between 1900 and 1999, the United States used 4,500 million tons of cement. Between 2011 and 2013, China consumed 6,500 million tons of cement. That is, in just three years China spent 50 per cent more cement than the United

States consumed in the preceding century.[4] In the summer of 2017, in different states in the United States, for the first time in history, a significant number of commercial planes were prevented from taking off due to high temperatures between 123 and 125 degrees Fahrenheit, at a time when President Trump walked away from the Paris Agreement. By August 2017 and 2018, humanity had already exhausted the earth's natural resources.[5] Extractivism is driving the planet to an unsustainable limit.[6] It seems that we are about to experience an ecological bomb.[7] Globalization globalized the few and localized the rest.[8]

As I write this foreword, in the United States, public debt is over $27 trillion; sixteen million children live below the poverty line, a kid drops out of school every 41 seconds and the racialized 'school to prison pipeline' became domesticated in a nation that is responsible for 25 per cent of the world's prison inmates.[9] The neoliberal incarceration system in the United States is one of 'penal pornography punishing the poor'.[10] In 2014, there were approximately $1.3 trillion outstanding student loans.[11] What is shocking is that, for much lower debt, 'the European Union and IMF promptly tore Greece apart. For comparable or lower sums, recession, austerity measures, personal sacrifice, unemployment, and poverty are imposed on the millions of citizens of indebt countries.'[12] In Texas, one school district reinstated corporal punishment.[13] Betsy DeVos, Donald Trump's secretary of education, sponsored federal funds to arm schools and teachers.

In China, Deng Xiaoping and Xi Jinping's 'Beijing consensus',[14] which 'emphasized the need to uphold and develop a Marxian political economy for the twenty-first century, adapted to China's needs and resources',[15] triggered a new miracle that pumped a new political economy, or as Alain Touraine[16] would put it, a 'new political management of the economy' replicating a coloniality model of 'human, nature and development'.[17] Moreover, the most recent events in Hong Kong and the attacks of cultural and religious minorities speak volumes of how dissent has been *mercilessly* crushed by Beijing.

In Brazil, it looks like the masses have no memory. The nation did not make a U-turn and elected Jair Bolsonaro despite his overt attacks on minorities, LGBT communities and people with disabilities. In India, Narendra Modi's authoritarian impulses escalate 'a belligerent nationalism of the Hindu *rashtra* (nation)'.[18] Rightist and far-rightist groups understood accurately that the need was 'to listen to those voices without agreeing with them; those issues should be articulated without legitimizing them, and recognized without institutionalizing them'.[19]

In Hungary and Poland, the scenario is also frightening. In the former, with Viktor Mihály Orbán's far-right democratic rise to power, the 'cultural classifications have been increasingly biologized and moralized'[20]; in the latter, Andrzej Duda's rightist impulses re-escalated Indigenous nationalist desires and unleashed authoritarian populist policies. In Venezuela, Hugo Chavez's leadership, defeats and conquests interrupted by his premature death are collapsing with Nicolas Maduro under constant attack both internally and externally. Venezuela looks like 'a toothless nation that beheads chickens'.[21] In Madiba's South Africa, xenophobia and inequality are reaching alarming figures. The South African new political bourgeoisie suspended Mandela's promised revolution.[22]

The UK 'bravely' decided on 'Brexit'. They are done with the 'other'. What they ignore is that we all know that they have the privilege to 'Brexit'. As usual, 'the Other' is disposable. Brexit is a vivid racial move.[23] France is in flames with the Yellow Vests revolt, an inorganic movement that demands *quasi* everything, yet somehow in contradictory ways.[24] The recent decapitation of a teacher – Samuel Paty – only added fuel to the fire. In Cataluña, people clearly voted for independence from Spain, and in Andalucia, the far-right Vox, for the first time, grabbed twelve seats in parliament. Recently in Portugal, the far right elected a member of parliament despite its overt fascist claims. Of all of the people in the world without access to safe water, almost 40 per cent live in Africa; 589 million sub-Saharan Africans live without electricity and cook by burning whatever they can find. The expansion of West Bank settlements under every Israeli government became the 'norm'. Israel is probably the only nation in the world without fixed borders. The spectrum of 'abnormality' becomes domesticated. Today, a terrorist attack may still make the headlines of major newspapers but sadly barely constitutes a surprise.

Aleppo, Baghdad, Benghazi, Harare and other African cities, Lampedusa, Lesbos, the US southern border, as well as the overtly disgusting open hunting season on the 'Other', just to mention a few examples, reinforce a 'subjectivity' that should never have been constructed: immigrants, refugees. Massive waves of human beings have the right to freedom and to escape war and hunger under the crumbling 'welfare' of the West. The European Union and United States 'through their 'fortress' politics', centred on the notion of 'security', are the target of current protests regarding this human tragedy (Chapter 9). The migrants trailing from Africa to Europe and marching in caravans from Honduras to the United States demonstrate the failure of both Western dominant and counter-dominant human rights.[25] In a way, the multitude of adults and children marching announces the reconfiguration of a concrete utopia. The utopia of being in a more just world can only be obtained by moving towards the Global North and confronting the beast in the eyes. Like any human being in world, they too have the supreme right to fight for their own lives and existence. Without knocking at the door, the 'Other' has decided to enter and to confront the colonial matrix of power in its terrain. History repeats itself, the first as tragedy, then as farce, as Marx so strikingly said. 'Inconveniently', the 'Other' is now breaking 'abyssal lines' and coming by his or her foot ... and will. Oppression triggers within the oppressed powerful avenues of imagination towards the utopia of perpetual freedom.[26]

The second decade of the twenty-first century is creating a path for a far-right agenda to succeed. The 'masses' are placing their vote on candidates who insult people with disabilities, women and people of colour, as well as unleashed an overt attack against immigrants. Fascism, one would argue, 'became respectable'.[27] Welcome to the real colours of the epistemicide. Democracy is being used to kill democracy.[28] We are facing, Fraser[29] states,

> an hegemonic gap. With a political menu saturated yet limited to progressive and reactionary neoliberalism(s), there was no force to oppose the decimation of working class and middle class standards of living which left a huge segment of the electorate a natural political home; it was only a matter of time before someone would fill the gap.

The global far-right resurgence is the lava of the capitalist new neoliberal volcano. It is the result of a social symptom perpetually ignored throughout the centuries, and it needs to be seen as the continuous materialization of 'the' eugenic framework that festers modernity and solidifies modern Western Eurocentrism – in a word, the Empire. The current authoritarian momentum welds a new nexus between education and political economy and takes this nexus into a different level by kneeling public education and educators into new capitalist modes of production and consequently new conditions of class, gender, race, ethnic, caste, sexual exploitation, inequality and segregation required by market desires.[30] There is no capitalism without perpetual dynamics of exploitation, inequality and segregation. Capitalism and a just society and democracy are both a blunt oxymoron. It seems that both the right and the left of the political realm failed miserably. The state of affairs is so chaotic that 'if the heart could think, it would have stopped'.[31] Democracy, under the neoliberal gaze, is at a critical stage; the entire consulate of modernity is exhausted. The emergence and normalization of such a 'fachosphere' determines – and it is determined (by) – the cruelty of the identical, thus openly unleashing a war on the 'Other'. Peter Mayo and Paolo Vittoria's volume is quite precious as it offers a powerful examination as it 'connects with the quest of challenging the mantra of there being no alternative to the present neoliberal scenario governed by the ideology of the market and which spreads throughout all aspects of people's lives' (Chapter 1).

Under the current social phenomena, fascism became viral. The fear of the 'Other' saturated the common sense, fertilized the topology of the identic(al)[32] and gave a carte blanche to embark on the neo-crusade against the 'new Other'. Such a neo-crusade is a must for the stabilization of what I would best call the 'fourth hegemonic' phase of capitalism, neoliberal tribal populism.[33]

The Eugenic Yoke of the Identical

Globalization is the hell of the identical
Byung-Chul Han

The way dominant and counter-dominant groups have approached the saga of the 'Other' has legitimized the 'non-existence of the Other'. Framing the other in Eurocentric terms speaks volumes of how the onset of the epistemicide and reverse epistemicide[34] frames our classrooms, and it shows the real colours of the cognitive Empire[35] which fosters the terror of the identical.[36] In fact, curriculum, the way we know it, the way we think and talk, is a topology of violence,[37] that is, the violence of the identical, a racialized ideology,[38] is the result of the dominant epistemicide[39] and the reverse epistemicide[40] that opened the floodgates to a spurt of impulses in which 'the negativity of the other gives place to the positivity of the identical'.[41] The identical 'mirrors an ontic need'[42] and to be within the identical is to 'go through hell',[43] the hell of the aphotic, not of the panoptic. If the latter serves to discipline, the former 'constructs an exclusive optic which identifies and excludes as such persons hostile to the system or unfit on its terms'.[44] The identical is the ace of neoliberal globalization that arises 'in a spoiled, perverse and corrupted diversity that opposes alterity'.[45] There is thus an abysmal difference between 'diversity, and alterity'.[46]

The yoke of the identical frames the immunological grid marked 'by the disappearance of otherness and foreignness'.[47] Otherness, Han adds, 'represents a fundamental category of immunology and every immunoreaction is a reaction to Otherness'.[48] The autocracy of the identical triggers what Terry Eagleton calls 'the multiplicity of the not yets'.[49] The identical – and 'the totalitarianism of the same'[50] – is everything and does everything, and, because it produces the other as non-existent[51] it not only never feels itself[52] but also promotes the cult of the contemporary.[53] Globalization is about 'the hell of the identical'.[54] Migration,

Peter Mayo and Paolo Vittoria posit, appears to provide the only way out, often at terrible human costs (Chapter 9).

To worsen the chaotic state in which one is already in, in the fall of 2019, the world saw the emergence of Covid-19 in Wuhan, China. Not surprisingly, with the emergence of the virus, the war on the 'Other' escalates and soon the virus has been defined as produced by the 'Other'. Education is not detached from such malaise, a malaise that has been addressed by the critical movement. As Peter Mayo and Paolo Vittoria rightly argue, 'the manner in which mainstream education contributes to "otherizing" has become a main concern of many critical approaches to education which broaden the area of enquiry to view education and pedagogy in their broader contexts, including different forms of public pedagogy such as advertising, entertainment (especially the film industry), all forms of mass popular culture, elite culture and activism' (Chapter 1).

To evoke one of the great lyrics of the great Portuguese revolutionary singer Zeca Afonso – 'death took to the streets on a day like this' – one could argue also that 'fascism took to the streets on a day like this', a day that relates to an epoch that, as Walter Benjamin would have certainly argued, 'even the dead will not be safe from such an enemy if it wins, and this enemy has not ceased to be victorious'.[55] This sense of 'Armageddon' is quite central in Peter Mayo and Paolo Vittoria's *Critical Education in International Perspective*. As they sharply argue, 'right-wing populist, xenophobic and downright neo-fascist politics is often triggered … by the phenomenon of mass migration' (Epilogue). We are truly facing a paradoxical time, that is, 'on the one hand our current time is marked by huge developments and thespian changes, an era that is referred to as the electronic revolution of communications, information, genetics and the biotechnological. On the other hand, it is a time of disquieting regressions, a return of the social evils that appeared to have been or about to be overcome'.[56]

'El Patron Colonial del Poder'

Let's go comrades, the European game is definitely finished,
it is necessary to find something else

Frantz Fanon

We are witnessing an era of 'random regression symptoms'.[57] Social normalcy was what Theodor Adorno termed as 'retrogressive anthropogenesis', that is, 'social cultural evolution which on the testimony of cumulative growth in productive forces gives the impression of progress, turns out to be the extended act of regression in the history of the species'.[58] We are facing, in Franco Berardi's[59] words, a collapse, which is not simply related with economic and cultural factors; it is also related with 'a crisis of social imagination about the future', that is, 'the imagination of the end is being corrupted by the end of imagination'.[60] The crisis is out of the so-called political, conveniently, and yet, it is profoundly political.[61] It became a 'means of governing in a world that seems to hold together only through the infinite management of its own collapse'.[62] More than ever, it looks like 'society is organized along immunological lines'.[63]

Such a paradox graphically reveals how modernity and the totalitarian cult of a modern Western Eurocentric epistemological framework are maxed out. Modernity was/is a 'misleading dream'.[64] Modernity's final sentence was determined partially by modernity itself and its truly totalitarian cult, which was a cultural and economic napalm that attempted to erase all other epistemological manifestations, that paradoxically ended up being systematically reinforced and strengthened from the belligerent clashes with modernity. If colonialism is a crime against humanity, and colonialism and imperialism had no existence outside of modernity, then modernity is also not innocent in such a crime against humanity. Not because it was inconsequential in dodging genocidal policies and practices, but precisely because its very existence relies on its capacity to perpetuate massive genocide. Peruvian public intellectual Anibal Quijano[65] coined this modern Western Eurocentric system of dominance, *el patron colonial de poder*, the 'coloniality matrix of power'.[66]

The twentieth century 'was the last Eurocentric century'.[67] As Fanon beautifully stated, 'let's go comrades, the European game is definitely finished, it is necessary to find something else'.[68] The eugenicism of Eurocentrism is undeniable, an eugenicism that 'asserts that only Europeans can progress and that Indigenous peoples are frozen in time, guided by knowledge systems that reinforce the past and do not look towards the future'.[69] Modern Western Eurocentric thinking 'is an abyssal thinking, a system of visible and invisible distinctions, the invisible ones being the foundation of the visible ones'. 'The invisible distinctions are established through radical lines that divide social reality into two realms, the realm of "this side of the line" and the realm of "the other side of the line"'.[70] Such abyssal lines – so well unpacked by Peter Mayo and Paolo Vittoria when they insightfully dissected Gramsci's Southern Question (Chapter 9) – constitute the very core of 'the epistemological foundation of the capitalist and imperial order that the global North has been imposing on the global South'.[71] There is no 'incomplete other'.[72] Invisibility and non-existence of the 'one side' are the roots of visibility and existence of the 'other side'. In such a context, not just knowledge, but the very question/answer 'what is to think', is totally compromised.

Welcome to the imperial/colonial zone, a zone that is *par excellence*, the realm of incomprehensible beliefs and behaviours which in no way can be considered knowledge, whether true or false. Imperialism and colonialism are the specific formations through which the West came to 'see', to 'name' and to 'know'[73] Indigenous communities' Eurocentrism – and its abyssal thinking – is much more than a vision of ignorance and fear, and it 'implies a theory of world history', that 'legitimates at one and the same time the existence of capitalism as a social system and the worldwide inequality that accompanies it'.[74] Eurocentrism is the epistemicide and the reverse epistemicide.[75] Eurocentrism is not actually a social theory; it is indeed 'a prejudice that distorts social theories'.[76]

Modernity by itself 'is not only a cultural revolution'[77]; one cannot delink the abyssal thinking from the political economy and culture of the material conditions of the epistemicide underlying the emergence and development of capitalism. It is actually the carburettor of such a system. The very Western modern claim of 'beyond the equator there are no sins' was a kiss of death to the other side of the line.[78] Colonialism is 'the blind spot upon which modern conceptions of knowledge and law are built'.[79] Thus, 'modern humanity is not conceivable without modern sub-humanity'.[80]

Needless to mention is how the educational systems in general, and curriculum in particular, are both profoundly implicated in such an epistemicide. In fact, by identifying particular forms of knowledge as 'official', schooling participates in a blunt epistemicide[81] – a lethal tool that feeds the dynamics of White supremacy and a eugenic Empire.[82] The epilogue in *Critical Education in International Perspective* unpacks the challenges imposed by the 'neoliberal model and its iniquities and contradictions, including the commodification of education', advocating and providing for instances of alternative ways to think and to do education 'with broad democratic popular reach' towards a just 'world we wish to see'.[83]

Alternative Ways to Think and to Do Critical Theory Alternatively

The reason that it is criticized cannot (alone) be the one that emancipates

Boaventura Santos

Along with Lídia Jorge,[84] one would argue that we need an 'alarm state' to challenge and crush such lethal regression, confronting what Giorgio Agamben aptly frames as 'the state of exception'.[85] It is, however, the moment to dare 'to learn to think about capitalism coming to an end without assuming responsibility for answering the question of what one proposes to put in its place'.[86] It is also perhaps the time to question why it has been so difficult to interrupt and smash such havoc. To be more specific, why has it been so difficult to destroy this hegemonic reasoning? Why does the creation of a just society so eloquently unpacked, for example, in the *Bamako Appeal* that 'affirms the solidarity of the people of the north and the south in the construction of internationalism on an anti-imperialist foundation',[87] seem to be unreachable?

In fact, 'it seems that there is no lack of issues that can promote anger, discomfort, and indignation'.[88] The aggressiveness of neoliberal policies has caused serious mutilation to the construction of a robust critical theory and pedagogy. There should be no question about it. The systematic attacks on public education, the financial and cultural strangulation of public institutions, has caused serious difficulties to the critical project. Should not this 'chaos' be more than enough to help the emergence of a dominant critical theory and pedagogy? What more will it take for a critical social theory to be established as a cultural hegemony in the face of this social tragedy? Why did such a reading of the wor(l)d became a great challenge?[89]

To return to Slavoj Žižek again in our discussion, 'is critical theory and pedagogies still actual today?'[90] Why is it so difficult to build a critical theory? This question raised by Santos[91] fuels intellectual restlessness in several leading critical scholars as well, especially those of a more Marxist or neo-Marxist inclination or those who critically engage the tradition in this domain – Michael Apple,[92] Peter McLaren[93] and Henry Giroux,[94] among others. That is, in 'a world where there is so much to criticize, why has it become so difficult to produce a critical theory?'[95] Irrespective of countless noteworthy efforts, conceptual sophistication and notable accomplishments, from 'critical structuralist, existentialist, psychoanalytical, phenomenological approaches', it is unquestionable that critical theories have been incapable of being hegemonic. Why?

Working from and within different epistemological terrains, Peter Mayo and Paolo Vittoria dare to address such questions. In doing so, *Critical Education in International Perspective* is not just another book on critical theory; it also an attempt to do 'critical theory'.[96] The volume offers a rich multiplicity of avenues to better understand the current challenges faced by critical theories, pedagogies and theorists, challenges that 'call for more nuanced approaches' (Epilogue).

Among such rich avenues, I would highlight two, which I think constitute the leitmotif of the volume's insightful critical rationale.

First, *Critical Education in International Perspective* constitutes a clarion call against the dangers of erroneously perceiving 'society as a totality'[97] – one of the critical challenges faced by most critical approaches. For example, the work and struggles led by public intellectuals such as Anna Maria Piussi and Antonia De Vita, and Ada Gobetti and Don Lorenzo Milani clearly demonstrate a crucial 'philosophical conscientism', as Kwame Nkrumah[98] would put it, a 'philosophy of praxis' so well articulated in Antonio Gramsci's understanding of common sense and hegemonic power structures that interact, so sublimely unpacked by collective movements such as the *Plebs League* as well as in Paulo Freire's legacy famously and brilliantly epitomized in his pivotal *Pedagogy of the Oppressed*.

The struggles led by these public intellectuals show us the importance to avoid falling in the lethal swamp of formulating a 'total alternative to the society that exists'.[99] Quite sentient is the point that while the 'objective conditions for revolution were present, however the subjective conditions were lacking'.[100] They acknowledge that 'there is no single principle of social transformation, and even those who continue to believe in a future socialist society see it as a possible future in competition with alternative futures. There are no unique historical agents or a unique form of domination.'[101] This is not a minor issue, and it is one of the most powerful arguments of the volume and so crucial for the success of critical theories and pedagogies.

By framing critical theory and pedagogies historically (Chapter 1), Peter Mayo and Paolo Vittoria not only highlight major movements and figures as well as the accomplishments faced by critical theories and pedagogies but also the challenges and contradictions within the progressive hemisphere within different parts of the world. Such wrangles to overcome systems of dominance, as they document, show rather well how 'any of the concepts that were crucial "no longer have the centrality they once enjoyed" or were internally so reworked and nuanced that they lost much of their critical strength'.[102] As they clearly show, 'critical theory needed to run away from mechanistic frameworks and move towards a major theoretical reconstruction to address the problems of the present'.[103] In this regard, for example, they accurately unpacked one of the most important challenges facing a critical struggle today. The disgraceful perversion of lifelong learning towards the dangerous cult of lifelong earning, which places 'employability – not employment – at the heart of the agenda in the discourse on lifelong learning' (Chapter 2), speaks volumes regarding how the endless historical pandemic of instrumental reason colonizes even counter-dominant terrains. As I have argued elsewhere,[104] the 'objective' nature of reason subsumes its subjective nature. Reason 'become[s] completely harnessed to the social process'.[105] It becomes mechanistic, technical, since it gives up 'its autonomy', and the more ideas 'become automatic, instrumentalized, the less does anybody see in them thought with a meaning of their own'.[106]

The different battles fought by critical theorists and pedagogues within and beyond the Eurocentric platform, for example, constitute a vivid example that there are 'multiple faces of domination and oppression and how many of them have been irresponsibly neglected by modern critical theory, such as patriarchal domination. Thus, since the faces of domination are manifold, the resistances and the agents that lead it are equally manifold'.[107] To be more precise, the book highlights Piussi and De Vita's 'philosophy of difference', Gobetti's 'education as a philosophy of liberation' and Milani's 'Christian-inspired pedagogy', the onto-epistemological and pluriverse anti-racial approaches in the Mediterranean context to address 'massive processes of immigration flows involving, not only people from North Africa, but also people from sub-Saharan Africa' (Chapter 8), Julius Nyerere's *Ujamaa Vijijni* and the power of 'grassroots democracy revolved around Ujamaa' (Chapter 11). All these testify to not just the vitality of pluri-diverse critical approaches in challenging Eurocentric dominant and counter-dominant technical praxis of pedagogy but also the fact that 'it is not possible to bring together all resistances and agencies under a common grand theory'.[108]

Second, and in the light of what I have argued, *Critical Education in International Perspective* attempts to 'contribute to further internationalizing the discourse on critical approaches to education'.[109] Following Darder, Mayo and Paraskeva's[110] political take, and contrary to most of the approaches in the field related with the internationalizing of the critical perspectives, Peter Mayo and Paolo Vittoria acknowledge the importance and legitimacy of powerful non-Western non-Eurocentric approaches. They unpack the rich examples of Mediterranean movements and groups, as well as the contribution of African intellectuals such as Julius Nyerere and Amilcar Cabral to the critical thinking and pedagogies. In doing so, both Mayo and Vittoria unequivocally open up the lethal canon of modern Western onto-epistemological reasoning, challenging the modern abyssal thinking and its abyssal divide.

This volume is a clarion call for valorization of the importance and richness of what Santos[111] calls a radical co-presence of epistemological 'pluri(di)versity'. This places face to face different onto-epistemological perspectives within and beyond modern Western Eurocentric matrixes. As I have examined elsewhere,[112] this radical co-presence pushes Gramsci's philosophy of praxis into another level. All knowledge is co-knowledge,[113] which implies a radical different understanding of learning, one that is neither time- or credit-conditioned nor competitive but which is characterized by sharing and co-investigating knowledge (Chapter 3). As a philosophy of praxis, the radical co-presence is not a kind of 'truth and reconciliation tribunal'. It is the recognition on an equal epistemological term of endless non-Western, non-Eurocentric epistemological platforms that need to sit down face to face on an equal footing with the dominant traditions – with a common aim: to crush the epistemicide.[114] This radical co-presence respects and fosters 'an Indígenous subjectivity geographically rooted and historically placed'.[115] This new philosophy of praxis, said to be the very enzyme of a new and just world, does not happen – nor can it – in the pattern constructed by Eurocentric Western modernity. Echoing Audre Lorde's rationale, such a just world 'cannot be built with the master's tools' that is, 'the master's tools will never dismantle the master's house. They may allow us temporarily to beat him at his own game, but they will never enable us to bring about genuine change',[116] that is, the reason that it is criticized cannot (alone) be the one that emancipates.[117] A new philosophy of praxis is a vivid expression of an itinerant education and curriculum theory and pedagogies, one that paves the way for 'critical and emancipatory multi-citizenship education'[118] (Chapter 7).

In opening up the cannon of modern Western Eurocentric critical reasoning, Peter Mayo and Paolo Vittoria adamantly show that there is not only a 'discrepancy between experiences and expectations – the non-coincidence between experiences and expectations is the great historical novelty of the paradigm of modernity'[119] but also that 'more than a common supra-disciplinary social theory, what we need is a translation theory that makes the different struggles mutually intelligible and allows collective actors to talk about the oppressions they resist and the aspirations they animate'.[120] An itinerant educational and curriculum theory, as I have examined in other contexts,[121] is good, for instance, for translation theory, an alternative way to think and to do critical theory and pedagogy, one that aims precisely at a general epistemology of the impossibility of a general epistemology.[122] In doing so, Peter Mayo and Paolo Vittoria, in a neo-Gramscian manner, show how correct Karl Marx's claim that the social liberation of the individual can only happen if such hope for liberation is available for everyone.[123] *Critical Education in International Perspective* is a vivid example of a radical co- presence towards an ecology of knowledge[124] – the begin-anew, as Antonia Darder[125] would put it – which pushes one towards a post-abyssal momentum, a post-abyssal epistemology. This non-abyssal commitment concomitantly highlights the historical legitimacy of the epistemologies from the South. The volume brings to the fore the importance of non-Western non-Eurocentric onto-epistemological perspectives to address the colonial power matrix.[126]

The volume epitomizes the rich legacy of these onto-epistemological matrixes, underlining the organic reasoning of non-Eurocentric intellectuals such as Julius Nyerere and Amilcar Cabral and their impact in the struggle against world colonialism. Elsewhere, I framed such intellectuals – and many others – as militant intellectuals,[127] intellectual *Naparamas*[128] who constitute the generation of utopia.[129] Complexifying Santos's arguments, I would argue that Julius Nyerere and Amilcar Cabral, together with so many and other non-Eurocentric organic intellectuals, constitute the real demiurges of the epistemologies from the South. Their anti-colonial educational philosophical praxis – or Africana Philosophy, as articulated by Paget Henry[130] insightfully states – is a clear evidence of the power of such epistemologies in the struggle for a just world, epistemologies that – as Kwame Nkrumah[131] would put it – frame, an alternative philosophical conscientism. By opening up the canon of modern Western Eurocentric onto-epistemological matrix, Peter Mayo and Paolo Vittoria insightfully expose – among other issues – the robust vitality and legitimacy of the epistemologies from the South.

The Demiurges of the Epistemologies from the South

No elite, no trouble

Kwame Nkrumah

Education was always one of the priorities of African anti-colonial movements like PAIGC ('Partido Africano para a Independência da Guiné e Cabo Verde') in Guinea-Bissau and Cape Verde (later on PAICV – 'Partido Africano para a Independencia de Cabo Verde'), TANU ('Tanganyika African National Union that became Chama Cha Mapinduzi') in Tanzania and FRELIMO ('Frente de Libertação de Moçambique') in Mozambique. More than a space to improve knowledge, schools such as, for example, Frelimo's 'Mozambican Institute and Bagamoyo School', were seen as a base for the masses to seize power, and teachers and students were militants.[132] Moreover, knowledge was the base of comradeship.[133] The importance of schools is quite clear in Amilcar Cabral's argument:

Set up schools and develop teaching in all the liberated areas. Constantly strengthen the political training of teachers. Persuade parents of the absolute necessity for their sons and daughters to attend school, but organize activity for the pupils in such a way that they can also be useful at home in helping their family. Set up courses to teach the adults to read and write. Combat among the youth, notably among the more mature, the obsession with leaving the country to go and study, the blind ambition to be *doctor*, the inferiority complex and the mistaken notion that those who study the courses will have privileges tomorrow in our land. Protect and develop manifestations of our people's culture, respect and ensure for the usages, customs and traditions of our land. Combat all particularisms prejudicial to the unity of the people. Teach ourselves, and teach others to combat fear and ignorance. Learn from life, learn with our people, learn in books and from the experience of others. Constantly learn.[134]

Julius Nyerere's *Ujamaa* educational programs in Tanzania – something that the People's Republic of Mozambique, People's Republic of Angola and the Republics of Guiné Bissau and of Cape Verde did not follow after independence – were a clear evidence of a different postcolonial move, showing a leader and a social chain to return to the collective nature of African civilization, 'changing the aims and outcomes of education [by] encouraging secondary school leaders to return to the village and engage rural and related agricultural programs of community development'.[135] Although Nyerere's *Ujamaa* educational programs faced severe challenges, namely, the foci on an agrarian collective society within a massive capitalist world (Chapter 11), it is undeniable that some accomplishments were made. For example, Nyerere's Tanzania plays arguably *the* role in the process of independence of Mozambique by supporting FRELIMO apparatuses, among those, FRELIMO's schools not only in Tanzania but also in the liberated zones in the north and centre of Mozambique.

Although Julius Nyerere – also called Mwalimu (i.e. teacher in Swahili) – 'did not write formally about education, rather he spoke about the role of education and higher education in particular in many public addresses',[136] it was quite clear that for Mwalimu, not just education but *Ujamaa* also places a very personal and collective responsibility 'upon the educated to ensure the well-being of other community members'.[137] Mwalimu's educational philosophy, Julie Hatcher and Mabel Erasmus argue, sought to '(a) increase desire for change (b) increase an understanding that change is possible; (c) equip people to make decisions to improve their society'.[138] Quite clear are the parallels between Nyerere and other critical intellectuals, such as Freire (Chapter 11) or even, I would argue, Gramsci. For example, Nyerere's Christian socialist way of struggle against the oppressors echoes clearly Gramsci's 'wars of maneuver vs wars of position'. I would flag also an interesting similarity between Julius Nyerere and John Dewey:

> Both reiterate how developing personal capacities can ensure the advancement of society. They both value the importance of personal experience as the bedrock for further skill development, regard knowledge as a common good to be used to make improvements in daily life, and call for social responsibility to be a buy-product of education. Although they lived in two different eras and on two different continents, Dewey and Nyerere articulate the value of education in social and democratic transformation.[139]

Regarding the life in Tanzania and the United States, Dewey and Nyerere were quite 'clear on the social role of education and called for education to develop civic minded individuals and professionals [a] role that is equally relevant in times of social transformation and social stability'.[140] Thus, it is no surprise that, at the time when community engagement becomes the buzzword for higher education in the West, in general, and the United States, in particular, 'Nyerere's vision of higher education for the 21st century could also be regarded as relevant to the West'.[141] Nyerere's educational vision is well grasped by Nkulu[142]:

> A rural village had its food supplies depleted and its people began starving. The villagers agreed to pool their meager resources and select a few capable individuals to send as messengers to a distant village to purchase more supplies. Nyerere wanted educated Tanzanians to develop abilities similar to those of the messengers from the village: an awareness of everyday life conditions in their society and the ability to reflect critically and to act upon such conditions for the well-being of many, if not all.

The parallels (not submission or alienation) between Western and African intellectuals and intellectualism are also quite visible in the commonalities between Antonio Gramsci and Amilcar Cabral. In a Paulo Freire piece that I had the privilege to co-translate, he defended the view that 'a person like Amilcar Cabral should be studied side-by-side with a person like Antonio Gramsci'.[143] The differences between them, Freire [144]adds, is that Amilcar died possibly older than Gramsci, and he had what Gramsci had not, that is, Amilcar had countless years of war in the bush inside the jungle. Conversely, Gramsci was in jail. Freire[145] encourages all of us to read Gramsci and Cabral simultaneously (see Chapter 10), a study that has enormous importance, and it needs to be done by educators.

Needless to say, within the complex terrain of African epistemologies, *Ubuntu* and *Ujamaa* need to be understood as integral parts of a collectivist model of societal teaching and learning. There is an Africana critical theory and pedagogy. It is quite clear, Constantine Ngara[146] stresses, that we have a complex and dominant 'African paradigm of knowing in the context in which it informs pedagogy from an African perspective'. In other words, 'Africans ways of knowing, not only reflect African world views, but they define *Ubuntu* (Zulu/Ndebele), *unhu* (Shona), *utu* (Swahili)'.[147] Such a collective way of learning (a kind of collective cognitivism) makes the individual less individual, that is, 'the basic knowledge structures that the typical African child brings to school have been collectively constructed and transmitted through a participatory and collectivist model of learning with a community focus'.[148] Within such communalism, so well examined and ferociously advocated by an intellectual such as Kwame Nkrumah,[149] 'there is a variety of unique and interesting Indigenous cultural games, puzzles, and riddles that are available for sharing across the continent to develop children's language, content, and mathematical skills'.[150] Such communalism shows a sharp contrast with Western society. Despite the fact that the Western commonsensical pastoral defends that parents have a responsibility to socialize their children, schools end up assuming that social task – rightly so, one must say – because of the inability of the most parents to perform that task. However, with the focus more and more on irrelevant social devices, such as high-stakes testing, schools have been incapable of addressing their responsibility in the socialization and education of youth for the common good. Western education is not about education anymore. It is about training bodies to live in an increasingly cannibalized market-driven society.

However, in Africa, the education of a child was a collective social responsibility and not just the responsibility of the biological parents.[151] *Ujamaa* was 'villagization'. Both *Ubuntu* and *Ujamaa* needed to be seen as a new ethic of engagement in society and in schools, and within such a social system, the leverage is on society and not on the cult of the 'abstractivity' of the disciplines. It goes without saying that such indigenous ways of knowing 'shape the background cognitive structures, knowledges, and beliefs that a typical African child brings to school'.[152]

Eduardo Mondlane, founder of FRELIMO and whose work deserves more attention from the field of critical theory and pedagogies, challenges the Western eugenic assumption that human reasoning comes from the West. He challenges Western archaeologists, historians and sociologists and their fields of study to produce and develop an egregious historical fallacy. Well before Paulo Freire and others, Mondlane challenges the mind of the colonized as the great weapon in the hands with the colonizer,[153] and the way the ' "africana" education way was assaulted, dismantled, and replaced by an educational system completely out of sync of the africana cultural matrix, detached the African individual from their past, cultural traditions, forcing to adapt to a new colonial society'.[154] With this colonial educational system came 'a new economy which institutionalized new creative forms of exploitation and slavery',[155] a 'new development', one that was always intensely challenged by African people. In this regard, one needs to highlight Walter Rodney's seminal piece 'What if African Refuses Development'[156] – so ignored in our field.

It was Mondlane who right at the emergence of FRELIMO built the famous 'Instituto Moçambicano', in Dar-es-Salam, to educate the masses. He framed the need for a new education with the need to produce and transform the role of the intellectuals. That is, 'in the eyes of the people, education means progress', a progress that needed to be achieved by mastering the 'witchcraft of the white man so that it could be used to liberate the people from oppression'[157] and simultaneously protect and develop the struggle for freedom 'which was the best school on the world'.[158] In Mondlane's eyes, 'the intellectuals were a creation of the capitalist society', and although they are important in the struggle for liberation, they need to assume themselves as revolutionary leaders and consciously defend that 'they can get more of an education in the Revolution than is a university'.[159]

The same powerful impulses one undeniably identifies in Amilcar Cabral. As he argues, 'the underestimation of the cultural values of the African people based upon racist feelings and upon the intention of perpetuating foreign exploitation of Africans, has done much harm to Africa'.[160] In this context, he claimed that the victory against colonialism was only possible by the return to the source, which was much more complex than a struggle against foreign domination. He states:

> The return to the source is therefore not a voluntary step, but the only possible reply to the demand of concrete need, historically determined, and enforced by the inescapable contradiction between the colonized society and the colonial power, the mass of the people exploited and the foreign exploitive class, a contradiction in the light of which each social stratum or indigenous class must define its position. When return to the source goes beyond the individual and is expressed through groups or movements the contradiction is transformed into a struggle (secret or overt) and is a prelude to the pre-independence movement or of the struggle for liberation from the foreign yoke.[161]

Return to the source made Cabral and *Cabralism* a serious challenge to critical traditional theory, not just because of the inherent complex metamorphosis of this process but also 'in the sense that his critical theory is not quarantined to the life-worlds and life struggles of white workers in capitalist societies'.[162] That is, at the heart of Cabral's critical theory, Reiland Rabaka[163] claims, relied is conscious reading that dominance and oppression were beyond the capitalist system and were determined by a world system that urges for the need of a common theory and praxis of liberation respectful of the idiosyncrasies of the oppressed. Angela Davis highlighted how Cabral 'urges us to develop our theories and strategies by directly engaging with the specific economic, political and cultural locations of our struggles'.[164]

Another intellectual whose work deserves more attention is Samora Machel. In one of his masterpieces and his educational philosophy, 'Fazer da Escola uma Base para o Povo Tomar o Poder'[165] (Making School a Base for the Masses to Take Power), Machel argues for an educational system that fosters democracy, collectivism and social responsibility, and that sees teachers and students as militants. It goes without saying that militants do not have a negative base; quite the opposite. In Machel's terms, students and teachers as militants define the real subjects of the educational system engaged, omitted to the construction of the common good. He argues:

> Being a militant like being a teacher, does not consist solely of correctly preparing the lessons, explicating clearly the material and correcting justly the exercises. It is evident that this is part of the duty of the teacher, but it is not enough. This is also done by the bourgeois teachers animated by a professional conscience. In his essence, the militant teacher is s/he who through his/her example and teaching contributes to the formation of a new mentality in the student. The militant teacher is for all a point of reference, a permanent illustration of correct behavior. The militant teacher learns from the student and knows how to orient him/her in the synthesis of experience and liberation of initiative. The militant teacher is an active element in the practice of productive work which mobilizes natural resources and furnishes new ideas to man. The militant teacher is conscious of his limitations and opens himself to self-critique and critique; including that of students. The militant teacher possesses in the highest degree the consciousness of belonging to the working class. The militant teacher is combatant for the victory of our values, a gear in the liberation of the creative initiative of students. The definition of the student as militant also manifests itself as necessary. Even though the central task of the student is to study, this in itself does not distinguish him from a bourgeois student. The characterization

of the militant student is situated in at the level of objectives and methods of his study. The militant student, in studying fulfills a duty to which he was entrusted by the masses to serve it. In him/her, there cannot exist the mythical obsession of the diploma, the hope of high salaries and privileges, the notion that he is part of an elite of future rulers.[166]

Although schools were crucial, Machel argues, they 'need to teach the natives the path to human dignity and the grandeur of the nation that protects them'.[167] That is, he claims, education implied clearly the need to challenge the production and preparation of the oppressed as submissive mental slaves of capitalism.[168] Machel argues that 'teachers should learn amongst themselves. Students should learn amongst themselves. Teachers and students should learn from each other. This signifies a constant exchange of experiences at all levels and efforts at each level to synthesize the experiences.'[169] Moreover, 'collective work, the exchange of experiences, critique and self-critique extends [students and teachers] to the totality of the center and to the lives of each one'.[170] It is, in fact, 'through this process that we will be able to obtain a true mutual understanding, an understanding based on common effort, in the demonstration of the practice of values and limitations of each one'.[171]

Democratic education that implies 'the democratization of the methods of work, founded in the collectivity of our lives, becomes in this domain an inexhaustible source for the everyday replenishment of our unity, of our brotherly ties of camaraderie'.[172] Machel's educational philosophy saw knowledge as the base of societies' camaraderie and defended a collective model of leadership. Leadership, Machel argues,

> is not and cannot be the monopoly of a group, which decides and imposes orientations. Just as the tallest tree takes roots on the ground and always grows from bottom up, the orientations should arise from the sentiment and consciousness of the base, the vanguard acting as the fertilizer, which strengthens and accelerates the process of affirming consciousness.[173]

In 'Producers and Students', Machel connects production as a school 'because it is one of the sources of our knowledge, and it is through production that we correct our mistakes'.[174] Moreover, he claims that 'practice is not enough, one must also know, study. Without practice, without being combined with force, intelligence remains sterile. Without intelligence, without knowledge, force remains blind, a brute force.'[175] Scientific studies were hopelessly detached from the communities and seemed not rooted in the struggle of production. 'To produce [is] to learn'[176] that also allows one to be able to interrupt and destroy colonial historiography, one 'that produced its own knowledge of Africa based on the premise of European superiority and the civilization nature of its mission'.[177]

In Africa, Kwame Nkrumah argues, under colonialism, 'capitalist development led to the decline of feudalism and to the emergence of new class structures'[178] and its consequent new division of labour. This labour stratification is and was a determinant of both the production and the modes of production, and is/was related to the value and uses of value of commodities in a Marxist sense – 'enable [human beings] to produce more than [they] need for mere survival. Production created a surplus'[179] crucial in the equation of the colonial imperial project. As Cabral[180] argues, the definition of classes within one or several human groups is a fundamental consequence of the progressive development of the productive forces and of the characteristics of the distribution of the wealth produced by the group or usurped from others. That is to say, the socio-economic phenomenon 'class' is created and develops as a function of at least two essential and interdependent variables – the level of productive forces and the pattern of ownership of the means of production. This development takes place slowly, gradually and unevenly, by quantitative and generally imperceptible variations in the fundamental components; once a certain degree of accumulation is reached, this process then leads to a *qualitative jump*, characterized by the appearance of classes and of conflict between them.

It would be naïve to infer that there were no class divisions in the anti-colonial period. As Nkrumah[181] unveils, class divisions were quite clear before the colonial occupation and genocide. What was new was that with the advent of colonialism, those anti-colonial class puzzles – led by the local tribal chiefs – were not only reinforced and strengthened but also taken to a different level with the full-blast emergence of a petty bourgeoisie. While the former 'became [important] local agents of colonialism',[182] the latter was quite connected with the intricacies of the finance and quite crucial in the sustainability of colonialism's next momentum: neocolonialism. Cabral is precious in this regard as well. In challenging the supremacy of class division as the key to understand the colonial formula, Cabral poses the following question: 'Does history begin only with the development of the phenomenon of "class", and consequently of class struggle?'[183]:

> To reply in the affirmative would be to place outside history the whole period of life of human groups from the discovery of hunting, and later of nomadic and sedentary agriculture, to the organization of herds and the private appropriation

of land. It would also be to consider—and this we refuse to accept—that various human groups in Africa, Asia, and Latin America were living without history, or outside history, at the time when they were subjected to the yoke of imperialism. It would be to consider that the peoples of our countries, such as the Balantes of Guinea, the Coaniamas of Angola and the Macondes of Mozambique, are still living today—if we abstract the slight influence of colonialism to which they have been subjected—outside history, or that they have no history. Our refusal, based as it is on concrete knowledge of the socio-economic reality of our countries and on the analysis of the process of development of the phenomenon 'class', as we have seen earlier, leads us to conclude that if class struggle is the motive force of history, it is so only in a specific historical period. This means that *before* the class struggle—and necessarily *after* it, since in this world there is no before without an after—one or several factors was and will be the motive force of history. It is not difficult to see that this factor in the history of each human group is the *mode of production*—the level of productive forces and the pattern of ownership—characteristic of that group. Furthermore, as we have seen, classes themselves, class struggle and their subsequent definition, are the result of the development of the productive forces in conjunction with the pattern of ownership of the means of production. It therefore seems correct to conclude that the level of productive forces, the essential determining element in the content and form of class struggle, is the true and permanent motive force of history.[184]

That is, savage colonialism brutally wiped out the African communalist social fabric, in which 'all land and means of production belong to the community [there] was people's ownership [and] labor was the need and habit of all'.[185] With the emergence of colonialism,

> communialist socio-economic patterns began to collapse as a result of the introduction of export crops such as cocoa and coffee. The economies of the colonies became interconnected with world capitalist markets. Capitalism, individualism, and tendencies to private ownership grew [and] gradually primitive communalism disintegrated and collective spirit declined.[186]

Clearly, class-segregated dynamics assumed a paramount role in the struggle against colonialism because colonialism

> increased [the] level of productive forces [that led] to private appropriation of the means of production, progressively complicat[ing] the mode of production, provok[ing] conflicts of interests within the socio-economic whole in movement, [thus making] possible the appearance of the phenomena 'class' and hence of

class struggle, the social expression of the contradiction in the economic field between the mode of production and private appropriation of the means of production.[187]

Colonialism clearly created a fractured dichotomous society between the oppressors and the oppressed, an explosive dichotomy fuelled by capitalist modes of production, the pillar of colonial power dynamics. Such a framework is visible in Machel's critique when he argues that 'the existing of exploiting classes, white or black or any other color, creates an exploitative form of power and state'.[188]

However, although class was a vital category with colonial state power intricacies, it was not the only one. As Nkrumah states, 'the close links between class and race developed in Africa alongside capitalist exploitation'.[189] It is impossible to delink one from the other:

> Slavery, the master-servant relationship, and cheap labor were basic to it. The classic example is South Africa, where Africans experience a double exploitation—both on the ground of color and class. Similar conditions exist in the USA, the Caribbean, in Latin America and in other parts of the world where the nature of the development of the productive forces has resulted in a racist class structure. For race is inextricably linked with class exploitation; in a racist capitalist power structure, capitalist exploitation and race oppression are complementary; the removal of one ensures the removal of the other.[190]

The oppressor–oppressed 'link' can only end drastically. As C. L. R James argues, the slaves 'like revolutionary peasants everywhere, aimed the extermination of their oppressors'.[191] Colonial power saw and fabricated a socio-psychological context that naturalized and legitimized a eugenic fallacy based on the notion that Africans are 'an inferior and backward race with primitive customs, and ignorant people who must be educated by the superior and advanced race with all its goods, customs and knowledge'.[192] Naturally, 'the race struggle became part of the class struggle [since] wherever there is a race problem it has become linked with class struggle'.[193] Race and class issues were not just confined to colonialism. They were explosive within the neocolonial momentum, as well with the ascendency of an indigenous bourgeoisie 'aspiring to ruling class status copying the [way] of life of the ex-ruling class [which] in reality they were [an] imitation [of] a race and not a class'.[194] The same sturdy criticism was flagged by Machel as well. According to him, the struggle against colonialism was also a struggle based on a new concept and practice of power.[195] Such a struggle was not to change the 'established black power in place of white power'.[196] As he argues, the aim of the struggle against colonialism is not to end Africanizing exploitation. The struggle, according to Machel, is between 'the power of the exploiters and people's power',[197] and one 'cannot serve the masses by governing with State powers designed to oppress the masses [that is] to Africanize colonialist and capitalist power would be to negate the meaning of our struggle'.[198] Summing up, in both colonialism and neocolonialism, 'the question is one of power [and] a State in the grip of neocolonialism is not master of its own destiny. It is this factor which makes neocolonialism such a serious threat to world peace'.[199]

It is clear that the colonial arrogance 'to claim a country just by visiting it'[200] leads colonialism to a profound misinterpretation of the power of African epistemes. Frantz Fanon was not that wrong when he stated that the twentieth century would be in the history of humankind, not just for the 'atomic discoveries and interplanetary explorations [but also] unquestionably [due] to the conquest by the peoples of land that belong to them'.[201] The veracity of such a claim is certainly due to a complex combination of issues. One of those issues is undeniably the sagacity of Africana episteme. The so-called colonial economic superiority – that was not apsychological as well – was profoundly incapable of deleting Africana ways of reading the wor(l)d. Paradoxically, colonialism did everything in its capacity to block any chance of the emergence of a well-consolidated Africana intelligentsia. The colonial motto 'no elite, no trouble', Nkrumah argues,[202] was actually a subtle, crude reality of genocide perpetrated by colonialism. He states:

> In Congo in 1960 there was scarcely a qualified Congolese in the country to run the newly independent state, to [be an] officer [in] the army and the police, or to fill the many administrative and technical posts left by departing colonialists.[203]

Patrice Lumumba – another major figure within the epistemologies from the South – was quite sentient of this saga, not just regarding Congo but all African nations struggling against colonialism as well.[204] As he states, when he visited Guine (Conakry), 'only three of these eighteen ministers have studied at a university; the other have finished high school, held jobs, and acquired certain amount of experience [so] the government has brought in French technicians to help in the field of law, economics, agronomy', a reality quite plausible for Congo. A radical cut with the past would be unwise because 'in many areas we still need Belgium's experience'.[205]

The absence of a strong Africana *quadre* was judiciously, yet erroneously, attributed to the colonial imperial circuits of cultural production as a natural consequence of a weak, or a lack of any, form of an African episteme worthy of such name because of a widely acknowledged African lack of development. Walter Rodney and Julius Nyerere, among others, ferociously challenged the colonial fallacy of (under)development. Rodney reverses the issue. In his remarkable work 'How Europe Underdeveloped Africa', the Guyanese theoretician argues that within the colonial imperial framework, development is not just as a one-side set of processes and cannot be reduced to a eugenic economic equation. Rodney claims that

> more often than not, the term 'development' is used in an exclusive economic sense—the justification being that the type of economy is itself an index of other social features. What then is economic development? A society develops economically as its members increase jointly their capacity for dealing with the environment. This capacity for dealing with the environment is dependent on the extent to which they understand the laws of nature (science), on the extent to which they put that understanding into practice by devising tools (technology), and on the manner in which work is organized. Taking a long-term view, it can be said that there has been constant economic development within human society since the origins of man, because man has multiplied enormously his capacity to win a living from nature. The magnitude of man's achievement is best understood by reflecting on the early history of human society and noting firstly, the progress from crude stone tools to the use of metals; secondly, the changeover from hunting and gathering wild fruit to the domestication of animals and the growing of food crops; and thirdly, the improvement in the character of work from being an individualistic activity towards an activity which assumes a social character through the participation of many.[206]

The West created a false nexus between development (and concomitantly underdevelopment) and bad government.[207] Development or underdevelopment is not something abstract or anchored in a single social dynamic showing the same tendencies diachronically and synchronically. Quite the opposite. In the anti-colonialist and anti-capitalist Africana societies, the pace of development was not one of solid systematic and solid growth. Individual and societal development towards greater freedom, autonomy and the common good faced a huge step back with the advent of colonialism and the lethal consequences of this capitalist imperial state. African civilization, like Asian civilizations,[208] showed significant levels of contextualized levels of development – at the social level and the way societies were communally based towards the common good, this is an undeniable reality – with natural ups and downs typical of every historical process. As Rodney[209] argues, 'Africa, being the original home of man, [was] the focus of the physical development of man as such, as distinct from other living beings'. With the advent of colonial capitalism, the entire pace and rhythm of development in Africa – with its natural ups and downs – was not interrupted but wiped out, positively terminated, because of the demands of a colonial imperial project. While during the anti-colonial and anti-capitalist momentum labour and work was in fact the 'key' to the betterment or the *res*public, with the advent of capitalism, Africana civilizations were confronted not just with slavery but also with the division of labour and new modes of production. The informal and formal dynamics at the base of society were dramatically altered with notorious ideological and political consequences:

> Specialization and division of labor led to more production as well as inequality in distribution. A small section of Chinese society came to take a large disproportionate share of the proceeds of human labor, and that was the section, which did least to actually generate wealth by working in agriculture or industry. They could afford to do so because grave inequalities had emerged in the ownership of the basic means of production, which was the land. Family land became smaller as far as most peasants were concerned, and a minority took over the greater portion of the land. Those changes in land tenure were part and parcel of development in its broadest sense. That is why development cannot be seen purely as an economic affair, but rather as an overall social process which is dependent upon the outcome of man's efforts to deal with his natural environment.[210]

The Western commonsensical fabrication of underdevelopment and barbarism – despite the fact that it was in the West that history saw some of the major human atrocities from the Inquisition, crossing the Holocaust to the 1990s Balkanic genocide in Bosnia – was rooted not on an idea of different forms of intellects but precisely on the eugenic idea of no intellect at all from such 'third-world' communities. As Julius Nyerere[211] vehemently argues in the seminal 'Arusha Declaration', the African community's survival relied not only on African epistemological frameworks but precisely on its capacity to preserve them and pass them on to future generations as well. The money and time spent on passing such forms of knowledge to others 'are better spent and bring more benefits to our country than the money and great amount of time we spend on other that which we call development'. This is crystal clear in Machel's reasoning as well. As he argues, 'we must be aware that the new generations are growing up in contact with the old generations who are passing on the vices of the past. Our practical experience shows how children and young people in our own centers can be contaminated by decadent ideas, habits and tastes.'[212]

Moreover, the struggle against colonialism was not subservient to any counter-hegemonic Western epistemologies. Despite the innumerable avenues of support, solidarity and influence from the so-called socialist world in the struggle against colonialism, it is undeniable that it was these informal cultural politics of elderly which allowed the African intellectual leaders to boost their political consciousness. Machel argues that 'no book by Marx ever arrived in my home town, nor any other book that spoke against colonialism. Our books were these elders. It was they who taught us what colonialism is, the evils of colonialism and what the colonialists did when they came here. They were our source of inspiration.'[213] Although subservience towards Western counter-hegemonic perspectives was clearly not the case, the existence of communal ideological interests cannot be undermined. Nkrumah[214] goes actually above and beyond such a position, arguing that the attitude of Africans 'to the Western and the Islamic experience must be purposeful. It must be guided by thought, for practice without thought is blind.' Because of a colonial educational system that refused to incorporate African epistemological perspectives,[215] the survival of African communities relied precisely on its capacity not just to resist colonial epistemologies but simultaneously to continue engaging in reading the word and the (now new colonial) world from an African episteme already in place well before the lethal colonial encounter. However, the struggle against colonialism and imperialism occurred within the very core of the imperial powers as well. Christian states, Lumumba argues, would eventually realize (as they actually did it) 'that it is not at all in their interests to use force to perpetuate a policy that is bound to collapse sooner or later despite all their efforts'.[216] Looking back to the case of the Portuguese colonial Empire, it was clear that the struggles led by anticolonial movements, such as FRELIMO, PAIGC, MPLA (Movimento Popular de Libertação de Angola), MLSTP (Movimento de Libertação de São Tomé e Príncipe) and FRETILIN (Frente Revolucionária de Timor-Leste Independente), made everyday life in its own mainland unsustainable. This unsustainability led to the so-called Carnation Revolution on 25 April 1974.[217] The imperial cultural politics of misrepresentation of the struggles against colonial empires was no longer efficient. The success of an African resistance to and counter-attack against European colonialism was not expected – that is, it was not on the cards. The Empire was lost between the theatres of war in the colonies and the social convolution on the mainland.

The successful African uprisings could be well framed in what Enrique Dussel insightfully called a 'philosophy of liberation'.[218] That is, the old classic ontology of the centre dominated by Europe and the United States is under the gun of the oppressed, which is an irrevocable process. A philosophy of liberation, Dussel claims, 'is rising from the periphery, from the oppressed, from the shadow that the light of Being has not been able to illuminate'.[219] That is, he continues, 'our thought sets out from non-Being, nothingness, otherness, exteriority, the mystery of nonsense. It is, then, a "barbarian philosophy." '[220]

It goes without saying that capitalism imposed a monolithic notion of development, one plagued by deterministic frameworks and irrationalities viciously steeped in class, race and gender segregation dynamics, the very core of the imperial project. Thus, colonization and civilization constitute an oxymoron. Between the former and the latter is an infinite distance.[221] Under the label of underdevelopment, and the urgent need to offer pounds and gallons of civilization, colonialism produced an explosive dialectic 'de-civilizing' the colonizer and subjecting the colonized to 'thingification' (*Verdichlung*). Colonization, Aime Cesaire states, lives on a boomerang effect in that it

> dehumanizes even the most civilized man; that colonial activity, colonial enterprise, colonial conquest, which is based on contempt for the native and justified by the contempt, inevitably tends to change him who undertakes it; that the colonizer, in order to ease his consciousness gets into the habit of seeing the other man as an animal, accustoms himself to treating him like an animal, and tends objectively to transform himself into an animal.[222]

As an eugenic philosophy of practice(s), colonialism relied heavily on dehumanization, de-civilization and brutalization of the oppressed and colonized as well. Fanon taught a great deal in this context. He[223] examines how the success of colonialism was based on the psyche of the colonized. As he argues, 'it is not possible to enslave men without logically making them inferior through and through [and] racism is only the emotional, affective, sometimes intellectuals' explanation of this inferiorization'.[224] As shocking as it might be, Cesaire states, what Hitler did was to apply 'to Europe colonialist procedures which until then had been reserved exclusively for the Arabs of Algeria, the "coolies of India and the 'nigger's [*sic*] in Africa' " '.[225] What is dangerous is how these dehumanizing practices are so connected with the cultural politics of memory lost. That is, Albert Memmi argues, within the social processes of 'thingification' and brutalization, the colonized 'loses memory', not just because of a biological effect but also precisely of a socio-psychological process because 'memory is not purely a mental phenomenon'.[226] More to the point,

> just as memory of an individual is the fruit of his history and physiology, that of a people rests upon its institutions. Now the colonizer's institutions are death or petrified. He scarcely believes in those which continue to show some signs of life and daily confirms, their ineffectiveness. He often becomes ashamed of these institutions, as of a ridiculous and overaged monument.[227]

The struggle against the epistemicide implies a non-negotiable position against eugenicism but above all against 'the repercussions of [such eugenics] at all levels of sociability'.[228] This will help one to understand not only the rumble between race and culture but also the fact that, while race is not the totalitarian category that fuels the wrangling among colonizer and colonized, it is arguably one of the 'crudest element[s] of the colonial structure'.[229]

The success of anti-colonial struggles heavily relied on the strength of African epistemologies that refuse to surrender and to subjugate to the colonial power matrix. These epistemologies simultaneously challenge and destroy the psychological impact of colonialism. They do so by continuously devising strategies of demolishing the colonial mindset that persistently views African ways of understanding and perceiving the social context not exactly as inferior but actually as non-existent.[230] This is because of the incredible incapacity of Western episteme-logic to admit any epistemological framework beyond the Western Eurocentric platform. Respecting and relying on African epistemologies was undeniably an ideological position, a political statement, a matter of social emancipation. Samora Machel unveils this accurately:

> Our political ideology is the result of the combat of the laborious masses explored by their emancipation and was tempered in the armed political struggle of our people against colonialism, imperialism and exploitation for the conquering of and edification of Popular Power. Each victory that we reach, each weakness that we note, find their foundation in the way that we have made the popular masses assume and live out the ideology.[231]

While African communalism and welfare fundamentally based on African epistemological perspectives was raped and silenced because of colonial invasions, it is undeniable that true independence, that is, a true victory against colonialism, Nkrumah argues, requires 'a new harmony [that needs to be] forged, an harmony that will allow the combine[d] presence of traditional Africa, Islamic Africa and Euro-Christian Africa, so that this presence is in tune with the humanistic principles underlying African society'.[232] That is, a 'new ideology is required, an ideology which can solidify in a philosophical statement, but at the same time an ideology which will not abandon the humanistic human principles of Africa'.²³³ According to Nkrumah, such an ideology will be borne out of the crisis of the African conscience, a philosophical consciencism that will give the theoretical basis for an ideology whose aim would be to contain the African experience of Islamic and Euro-Christian presence as well as the experience of the traditional African society, and by gestation, employ them for the harmonious growth and development of that society.

Nkrumah is actually putting forward a drastic social revolution that would be impossible without an intellectual revolution, a revolution in which African 'thinking and philosophy are towards the redemption of society'.²³⁴ Thus, such a philosophy should 'find its weapons in the environment and living conditions of the African people ... [it is] actually from those conditions that the intellectual content of our philosophy must be created'.²³⁵ Needless to mention the role that education plays in such a humanistic principle. After all, he argues, 'practice without thought is blind, and thought with practice is empty'.²³⁶ Fanon²³⁷ argues for the importance of a kind of critical nationalism, one that fosters cultural differences and antagonisms that are at the very root of the real and needed African subjective consciousness.

Fanon's approach or rather 'critical *Fanonism*' helps greatly in this regard. That is, it is through education that the oppressed and colonized will challenge and understand that the dynamics of the so-called new industrialization will rely on them as (disposable) 'parts' of a new mode of production within a system that can only exist by producing massively oppressed bodies and minds. That is, the oppressed and colonized will be 'shocked to find that s/he continues to be the object of racism and contempt'.²³⁸ That is, it is through education that the oppressed and colonized African people not only run away from any mythologized past – so dear for the new elites²³⁹ – but also engage with the possibility and the 'utopistics'²⁴⁰ of the Africa to come, one that 'people [are] impatient to do, to play, to say'.²⁴¹ The task, Cesaire reminds us, is to 'go beyond the past'.²⁴²

Perhaps one of the most important epistemologists from the South whose work and thought have been so unfairly ignored is the great Aquino de Bragança, arguably the great ideologue of FRELIMO and of the anti-colonial movements, and one of the great thinkers of the non-aligned movement. Santos so correctly places him as a world intellectual *avant la lettre* and hails him as 'the' great southern epistemologist. Aquino de Bragança was ahead of his time and showed that a radically different epistemological 'walk and being' is real.²⁴³ Bragança's majestic philosophy of praxis was frontally against the socially constructed monumentalism of both dominant and counter-dominant Eurocentric perspectives.[244] An unconditional humanist, one who understood very well the common contradictions, weakness and strengths of the world counter-hegemonic movement, Aquino de Bragança was an organic intellectual in whose philosophy of praxis he articulated like no one else the wrangles of antifascism and anti-colonialism, and rejected the notion of truth based just on a bunch of intellectuals.[245] In a nation that won the war against five hundred years of colonial occupation, Aquino de Bragança created the Center for African Studies in its capital, Maputo, to precisely produce 'research without researchers'. Instead of hiring foreign researchers, Aquino de Bragança built a team of researchers by having individuals doing research, individuals who never did research. Government employees, members of the army, students and community all started studying their families, their histories. All their energies ended up being the engine of a new social science research, emerging in the new independent Mozambique. It is in this context that the centre produced studies regarding the Mozambican miners working the gold mines in South Africa. Santos defines him accurately:

> The political, theoretical and epistemological positions of Aquino de Bragança converge towards a constant attitude of dialogue, building bridges, weave knots, seek complementarity, let be surprised by reality, refuse political and theoretical dogmatisms, that is try to understand the new with new ideas. Such valorization of the diversity of the social experience and the desire of not undermining it, combined with his concern in showing that the very realities of nations of the Anti-imperial South have been occulted, devalued or twisted when examined through theoretical frameworks developed in nations of Imperial North and even non-Imperial North (such as Marxism) prefigure an epistemological posture very close to what I have been designated by epistemologies of the south.[246]

Aquino's organic intellectuality anticipates and parallels so many approaches so well examined in this precious volume. Aquino's reasoning claims public intellectualism as 'an infinite labor of love', as José Martí[247] would put it; a 'poetic play', as Ada Gobetti's frames; a permanent poetic manifesto for education, as Gabriela Mistral (Chapter 4) so ferociously advocates, one that perceives that the act of thinking is not just theoretical and eugenically reduced to a pale 'τεχνη' (i.e. technique), a cognitive mechanic that praises the mind as a muscle, thus making repetition a pedagogical learning cult.[248] The struggle against this cult has been quite structural within the counter-hegemonic platform within and beyond the Global North. It is also more important than ever, in a world, framed by technological apparatuses, that is facing an unpreceded pandemic (Chapter 5).

Peter Mayo and Paolo Vittoria's powerful and timely volume accurately addresses such North-South wrangles. The book unpacks not just the rich legacy and footprint of the onto-epistemologies from the South and diverse non-Eurocentric epistemological matrixes but also how different onto-epistemological terrains, movements and intellectuals rub against each other providing a more just critical theory and pedagogies. In so doing, Peter Mayo and Paulo Vittoria's volume echoes what the demiurges of the epistemologies from the South so vividly reminded us, that is, the 'colonial epistemicide is not a sclerosis – it renews constantly, it mutates permanently, it keeps changing its inner physiognomy. It mummifies the cultural matrix of the oppressed and in doing so it mummifies individual thought.'[249] Mayo and Vittoria's formidable volume brings to the fore crucial movements and intellectuals and the battles fought within and beyond the Global North's predominantly Eurocentric platform for a just world through a just education and curriculum. At a time when democracy and public values have been hijacked, and in which neoliberalism has imposed itself as a public pedagogy paving a private language, Mayo and Vittoria's critical volume is crucial to remind us not only the historical legacy of critical theories and pedagogies in different parts of the world and what has been accomplished, but especially the challenges we all have ahead of us, so well highlighted in the initial little story of Panait Istrati.

To recapture Slavoj Žižek's question – is the critical matrix actual still? – one would argue *à la* Žižek, 'yes please'.[250] In fact, critical education draws much inspiration, these days, from writers from the 'South' who speak to the 'Global South' (Introduction). Mayo and Vittoria not only reinforce such an argument but also confront us with the strength of a crucial principle. A principle that, as Marx argues,

> will develop new principles to the world out of its own principles. We do not say to the world stop fighting; your struggle is of no account. We want to shout the true slogan of the struggle at you. We only show the world what it is fighting for, and consciousness is something that the world must acquire, like it or not. The reform of the consciousness consists only in enabling the world to clarify its consciousness, in waking it from its dream about itself in explaining to it the meaning of its own meanings.[251]

Mayo and Vittoria argue for a perpetual reinvention metamorphosis paving the way for critical gleaning of concepts in a manner that provides an antidote to cultural and educational imperialism (Epilogue). *Critical Education in International Perspective* is a volume of hope, an alternative way to think and do critical theory and pedagogies alternatively, one that boosts alternative ways to conceptualize the utopia differently towards 'heterotopia'.[252] In this sense and in a Freirean way it 'rejects the view that the conditions of our time determined the limits of what is possible' (Chapter 7). The challenge of heterotopia relies on the fact that one 'needs to reflect what we really are', as Fernando Pessoa[253] would put it. Leo Panitch and Sam Gindin (2006), in their 'Transcending Pessimism', render the issue complex. They shared a story of one of Barbara Kingsolver's remarkable novels in which a woman asks her lover:

> Did you ever dream you can fly?
> Not when I was sorting peackens all day.
> But, really, did you ever fly in your dreams?
> Only when I was close to flying in real life.[254]

Your dreams, Panitch and Gindin rightly add, are 'what you hope for and all of that is not separate from your life. It grows right out of it.'[255] Here lies the strength of a just educational and curriculum heterotopia. Undeniably, as Peter Mayo and Paolo Vittoria argue, critical education approaches can ill afford to avoid the challenge posed by the need to acquire 'powerful knowledge' (Introduction), which is, after all, a political pedagogical challenge. As I have said elsewhere,[256] and as *Critical Education in International Perspective* promises, the struggle continues.

João M. Paraskeva
Marion, MA
4 November 2020

Acknowledgement

We thank Professor Raymond A. Morrow from the University of Alberta, Canada, for providing us with a critical reaction to an earlier draft – the usual disclaimers apply. In the revised verson, we took up a number of points he made.

1

Introduction. Critical Education: An International Perspective

An important corpus of literature and accounts of practice, in different contexts, tackling the education-power nexus, helps enable people to confront and question structures, processes of domination and related attitudes, assumptions, myths and specific social constructions of reality – all of which constitute, to borrow from Michel Foucault, 'regimes of truth'. It highlights approaches, that are varied and whose exponents therefore do not sing from the same hymn book, and involve critical scrutiny of crucial aspects of dominant hegemonic relationships. One recurring and general strain, however, is the development of a critical consciousness.

According to a prolific author in this critical tradition, Henry A. Giroux, these approaches to learning and education more generally attempt to

- create new forms of knowing;
- pose questions concerning relations between margins and centres of power;
- encourage readings of history … that tackle issues of power and identity in connection with questions of social class, 'race'/ethnicity, gender and colonialism;
- refute the distinction between 'high' and 'low' cultures with a view to developing a curriculum that connects with people's lifeworlds and everyday cultural narratives; and
- give importance to a language of ethics throughout the educational process (adapted from Giroux, 2011).

Giroux is from the United States, as are many others – some using the term 'critical pedagogy', others 'critical education' – who appear in the relevant literature on critical approaches to education. The area might *prima facie* have a North American ring to it. The issues it confronts, however, are, globally speaking, widespread. The recurring concern is with the relationship between education and power, hence existing throughout historical periods and across geographical spaces. What is relatively new and post the 1970s is the variety of issues involved concerning critical education. Giroux (2020), for instance, is on record in refuting the claim that he is a founding figure of a movement gravitating around one aspect of critical education, 'critical pedagogy', as there are many figures, from different parts of the world, who have preceded him and carried out work in the same vein, not using the term but adopting a similar critical approach. The essays in this book shed light on several approaches, throughout twentieth- and twenty-first-century histories, adopted to critically address the relationship between education and power and issues concerning social justice.

The approaches to critical education discussed here, by and large, share with other traditions – critical education, critical pedagogy, critical studies in education, critical curriculum studies and so forth – the feature that education is seen not in reductively instrumental terms but according to the broader view of its contribution to the development of a healthy democratic public sphere where questions are raised and assumptions are challenged. It connects with the quest to challenge the mantra of there being no alternative to the present neoliberal scenario governed by the ideology of the market and which spreads throughout all aspects of people's lives, even the most intimate ones.

This is a universal concern as mainstream education is being transmitted worldwide according to the 'technical-fix' model, using the centuries-old approach of colonizing people's ways of learning and attempting to ride roughshod over Indigenous ways of learning, knowing and interacting with the environment. Critical education draws much inspiration these days from writers from the 'South' who speak to the 'Global South'. These include, but are not confined to, one thinker whose ideas, in the pursuit of learning through *conscientização*, are at the furthest remove from the instrumentalist notion of education. This is Paulo Freire, who had spent time in exile in different places, forced to leave his native Brazil by an authoritarian military regime precisely for his propagation of a politically democratic approach to education which was at odds with the type of instrumental education favoured by the country's rulers. His pedagogy of the oppressed (Freire, 2018) was meant to contribute to the democratization of Brazilian society. Critical education, therefore, is not confined to a 'Northern' perspective but openly embraces a 'Southern' one – 'North' and 'South' being relative terms, as old tapestries dating back to the 'Golden Age' of centres of Arab and Islamic culture suggest – the spread of this culture represented as moving down from 'North' to 'South'.

Freire's exposition of his pedagogical views in the acclaimed book *Pedagogy of the Oppressed* was a source of influence in critical approaches to education and society. Ironically, one of his places of exile, and precisely the place where he had this book translated from the original Portuguese, *Pedagogia do Oprimido* (Freire, 2013), was the United States (Freire, 2018). This is where he came in contact with US-ensconced academics and activists and where the basic elements of his radical pedagogy began to creep into US and Canadian thinking, allied as they were with those that belonged to the Deweyean tradition in this part of the world. It also drew on European intellectual traditions, especially the Frankfurt School of Critical Theory, although this raised questions regarding emancipatory politics in view of the 'negative dialectics' of some of its major exponents. Within critical theory, it drew on Jürgen Habermas's view of communicative action and deliberative democracy. It drew insights concerning power/knowledge and moral regulation from Foucault and, of course, it built on Antonio Gramsci's elaboration of hegemony at the heart of education and vice versa. While open to the criticism of being somewhat Eurocentric, critical approaches to education, often owing to the presence of students from 'Southern' diasporas in the 'North', broadened their areas of concern. The influence of the Jamaican-born Stuart Hall and Afro-Americans such as Angela Davis began to be felt. One of the foremost Afro-American exponents of critical education is bell hooks (Gloria Watkins), whose early work such as *Talking Back: Thinking Feminist, Thinking Black* drew substantially from two major early works by Freire, *Pedagogy of the Oppressed* and *Education for Critical Consciousness*.

The more the parameters of critical education began to be broadened, the more one drew on other figures of inspiration from different parts of the world. To give one example, we would argue that radical Italian educators such as Don Lorenzo Milani (to be discussed at length later on) can be regarded as key figures who anticipated many insights associated with critical approaches to education as well as critical sociology of education. The issue of citizenship and people exercising the 'right to govern', rather than to simply be governed, either in a heavy-handed manner or through moral regulation and governmentality, as argued by Foucault, was given ample treatment by Milani and the students at Barbiana. While class politics was the prime focus of their attention, it often was intertwined with considerations regarding racial politics based on observations of what occurred in the United States; the figure of Stokely Carmichael featured prominently in the famous *Letter a una Professoressa* (Letter to a Teacher). This and other aspects of Milani's proposed education and critique of public schooling make him and his ideas congenial to a genuinely critical approach to education. Equally congenial is the work of another Italian, Ada Marchesini Gobetti (Tarozzi, 2017), and her notion of emancipatory education (Gobetti, 1982) pronounced by a person who dedicated her life to teaching after years of engagement as a partisan fighting Nazi-fascism (she was a key figure on the Central Committee for National Resistance). This followed her collaboration with her late husband, the intellectual prodigy Piero Gobetti, an illustrious victim of fascism and its Black Shirt thuggery. Her pedagogical ideas and political activism are given due treatment further on in this volume.

One can go on and include people such as Maria Montessori, who, while not overtly professing a critical education and the notion of education as political, had her schools closed by the fascist regime. The kind of education these schools promoted and the personality they helped develop were considered anathema to those desired by the regime. One can also include Aldo Capitini and his notion of grassroots democracy (Omnicrazia) and Danilo Dolci, with his view of learning through collective community action, into the equation (Vigilante and Vitoria, 2011). This goes to show that critical education is not something new and confined to a specific context. Italy, like many other nations, has had its fair share of those who would qualify as critical educators. Different contexts have their own traditions in this regard. People living within them can draw from other different contexts provided that they do not transplant ideas and projects but 'reinvent' them, in keeping with Freire's own words. The strands and influences are, therefore, many. However, the common goal we adopt in this set of essays is social justice. We would summarize by saying that critical education exists in the context of the collective struggle for social justice and the dismantling of structures of oppression. It entails, among other things, reason, emotion and imagination.

Once more, emphasis is placed on the centrality of politics and power. One cannot see a genuine critical education as simply involving an individualizing approach. It has to be seen in a wider global context characterized by social and human-earth differences and 'North'-'South' imbalances and exploitation. Some argue for a political economy approach to studying education to understand how schools and the rest of the educational system function. The Marxist influence has been very strong here, and one can highlight the contribution of Peter McLaren, from the mid- to late nineties onward, and his colleagues from the UK and Canada (Dave Hill, the late Joyce Canaan, Sarah Carpenter, Alpesh Maisuria and Mike Cole in particular). Following on Gramsci and others, some argue for a focus on the state and education, even allowing for challenging the current mantra that, in this globalizing world, the state has receded into the background. This view has been criticized on the grounds that the state plays a central role in this neoliberal period. It paves the way for the mobility of capital and serves to police the victims of neoliberalism's excesses, pouncing on them rather than the structuring forces at play in these contexts. Others have focused on textual representation and the construction of the students' subjectivity. The degree of state intervention in health issues with regard to Covid-19 is a decisive factor with regard to the incidence of this pandemic within a single nation state (see Polychroniou, 2020). Its great spread, with many casualties, in countries such as the United States and Brazil, when compared to its containment in the very same country which US imperialism sought to destroy over forty years ago, Vietnam, lays bare the ravages of unbridled neoliberal politics – a clear case of barbarism, in Rosa Luxemburg's sense.

The manner in which mainstream education contributes to 'otherizing' has become a main concern of many critical approaches to education which broaden the area of enquiry to view education and pedagogy in their many contexts, including different forms of public pedagogy such as advertising, entertainment (especially the film industry), all forms of mass popular culture, elite culture and activism.

One area of great concern is pedagogy within social-justice-oriented social movements, and here the challenge has also been posed with regard to developing a non-monolithic and non-Western-oriented notion of social movements (Kapoor, 2009; Vittoria, 2016). The domain of popular culture also brings into focus the strong relationship that exists between education and cultural studies in terms of how, in the words of Raymond Williams, cultural products and ideas connect with 'a whole way of life' (Williams, 1982, 239) and with a people's 'structure of feeling' which is felt but is not always articulated by everyone. The realms of complex relations between education and power are infinite, and this is the domain of critical education which can be enriched by the ever-important contributions emerging from different contexts including those of 'food production' in, say, India (Shiva, 2009), the struggle against epistemicide (Santos, 2016) and 'decolonisation of the mind' (Thiong'o, 1986) in the Global South, and the context of 'settler colonialism' and Apartheid in Palestine (Silwadi and Mayo, 2014). It often foregrounds the work concerning people living a bicultural existence and hence the relationship between culture and language, as foregrounded by the Puerto Rican scholar, Antonia Darder (2012), the lead editor in a compendium bringing international perspectives to the fore (Darder, Mayo and Paraskeva, 2015) and a leading critical pedagogy exponent (Darder, 2005). It also foregrounds the neoliberalization of higher education

(Giroux, 2014a) and New Fascist politics (Giroux, 2008) in the age of populism – populism has taken different forms throughout history and in different contexts, which also includes left-wing populism, much augured by the likes of Chantal Mouffe. It foregrounds education against the culture of militarization and the New Right amalgam of neoliberalism and traditional values in the United States and more recently Turkey. The list is not exhaustive.

One ought to highlight, in this context, the critical education work of educators in Turkey who place their jobs on the line because of their stances, including editors of journals in critical education or critical pedagogy; critical education has quite a following in Turkey. Turkish critical educators certainly 'place their money where their mouth is' as manifested by the presence of several of them in the 2013 Gezi Revolt in Istanbul (Gezgin, Inal and Hill, 2014). The different international learning experiences of Occupy Movements provide much grist for the mill for a critical education, well captured in the slogan 'Occupy Knowledge' promoted by Greek scholar and activist Maria Nikolakaki, who directs an international higher education cooperative which has 'critical pedagogy' as one of its main programmes.

Taking our cue from Michael W. Apple, who identifies strongly with critical education, and his work on the curriculum (Apple, 1990, 1995, 2000), a series of questions emerge. There are questions regarding a variety of forms of textualization, not only curricula, to include museums, films, documentaries, re-enactments and so forth. Who benefits? Who suffers? Who is included and who is excluded? Which culture is valorized and at the expense of which other cultures? How are people represented? This represents a call for educators to take sides and not remain indifferent. As Lorenzo Milani would argue, better a fascist than indifferent (Martinelli, in Borg and Mayo, 2007), of course, not to be taken literally. Likewise, we have Gramsci's statement, 'odio gli indifferenti' (I hate those who are indifferent). It re-echoes or is re-echoed in a sentiment expressed in this regard by Gobetti and reproduced in the relevant chapter. All these connect with Freire's well-known statement that being neutral is tantamount to siding with the dominant.

Furthermore, while not eschewing individual learning, much critical education promotes collective learning and action. As Freire would argue, people liberate themselves not on their own but in concert with others. Everything is also to be read 'against the grain', through the different liminal spaces available (see the late Roger I. Simon's 1992 classic). Gramsci's and Milani's readings of Italian history, against conventional sanitized interpretations, are cases in point. What is not said in texts is as important as what is said. What is intimated or possibly understated is just as important, if not more, as what is explicitly stated. Here the work of Palestinian Edward Said and the notion of 'contrapuntal readings' becomes relevant. While highlighting different forms of culture, there is the important caveat that none of these should be romanticized. Critical pedagogical work needs to be open to the criticism regarding its own absences and occlusions.

There is one final point which needs to be made. While the ideological bases of all kinds of knowledge should be unmasked, one ought to be careful not to short-change learners. One of the challenges, in my view, is to grapple with the task of imparting and learning what Michael Young and Johan Muller (2010) call 'powerful knowledge'. There are echoes of Gramsci and his idea of the Unitarian School here. The concern is with a type of education that does not sell the subaltern short in comparison with the ruling classes who can still obtain these skills, irrespective of whether they are offered by established educational institutions, through their materially rewarding cultural capital and what are nowadays referred to as 'invisible pedagogies'. As we shall see, the School of Barbiana's exposure of the situation concerning the Giannis and the Pierinos, sons of peasants and middle-class persons, respectively, underlines this.

Critical education approaches can ill afford to avoid the challenge posed by the need to acquire 'powerful knowledge', which is, after all, the political pedagogical challenge also posed in the 1930s by Gramsci and, much later, in curricular circles, by the likes of Lisa Delpit (1988), with regard to Afro-American schooling in the United States, and Young (2013) in the UK. On the other hand, it has much to offer in terms of complementing this rigour and mastery of powerful knowledge through its emphasis on the politics of education. One can impart this knowledge differently from the way it has been conventionally taught. The classic example concerns how to deal with the colonizing language within a politics of decolonization and provide cognitive justice (Santos, 2016, 2017) to that which is Indigenous. It would be foolish to throw away the colonizing language, say, English, given its current hegemonic status, a point stressed by the rulers of Guinea-Bissau to Freire (Freire and Macedo, 1987), with respect to Portuguese. Hegemony contains the elements of change within its own interstices (Mayo, 2015). In this case, the dominant colonial language needs to be taught and learnt not in a simply technical manner but in a way which involves questions of its role in global politics and social stratification, and as a colonizing force.

These issues cannot be avoided in a genuine attempt at a critical approach to education. The knowledge denounced as 'colonial' or 'hegemonic' can serve as an instrument of political empowerment in a globalizing world. Not learning it would, as Gramsci argued, maintain people in a politically and economically marginalized state (see Young and Muller, 2010, on their probably unintended echoes of Gramsci here). Critical education, no matter how internationally relevant and context conscious, should safeguard against the danger of throwing out the powerful knowledge baby with the ideological bathwater.

Part One

Education, Markets and Alternatives

2

Lifelong Education/Learning: An Alternative Critical Approach

The European Union (EU) has been very busy promoting internationally, and especially within its member states, its EU Agenda for Adult Learning, conceived within the context of its master concept of Lifelong Learning (LLL). This emerged almost ten years following the publication of its much-discussed Memorandum on Lifelong Learning (CEC, 2000). This memorandum was often criticized for being somewhat too economistic in tenor (Bauman, 2005). A follow-up report was expected to be produced ten years after, evaluating the tenets of the document in light of critiques and observed practice. This did not materialize, and instead, we have had a short document on adult learning indicating priority areas. LLL has had quite an international resonance and has been debated in various parts of the world. It has taken over from the earlier United Nations Educational, Scientific and Cultural Organization (UNESCO) master concept of Lifelong Education (LLE).

The Expansive UNESCO Conception

The concept has a relatively long history. When focusing on contemporary contexts where a certain economically inflected version of the concept is hegemonic, it would be useful to trace the concept's evolution or dilution to indicate the specific concerns and interests of the different forces at play at different moments in time. Historical amnesia often serves to render a certain interpretation of concepts as 'common sense', to the total exclusion and subjugation of other alternatives, some yet to be explored in the liminal spaces available while others have been historically repressed.

The UNESCO version of LLE, which attached great importance to adult education and non-formal education, was promoted through a body of literature comprising books and papers by a variegated group of writers (ranging from Liberal to Marxist) with a strong humanistic base. The names of Paul Lengrand (1970), Ettore Gelpi (1985a), R. H. Dave (1976), Bogdan Suchodolski (1976) and Arthur J. Cropley (1980) come to mind, together with the authors of *Learning to Be*, otherwise known as the Faure Report (Faure et al., 1972). Some of these writings had their basis in Scientific Humanism, a philosophical outlook that foregrounds human rather than religious values, with which Julian Huxley, UNESCO's first director general, was associated (see Finger and Asún, 2001, 22).

At the risk of generalizing from among the work of a diverse group of writers, one can say that this movement provided an expansive and humanistic view of the entire process of human learning 'from the cradle to the grave'. They promoted what was therefore an all-embracing concept covering education throughout the whole lifespan and comprising the various sources of learning to which a person can be exposed. And yet, despite this basic underlying tenet, the concept is often used interchangeably with adult education. This tends to confuse the issue. One can speak of inconsistencies in the various uses of the concept, and the same would apply to LLL. This loose usage becomes more frequent these days as the term 'LLL' tends to be more attractive for funding purposes than 'adult education' itself. Funding mechanisms are perfect vehicles for the further inculcation of any ideology that resides in language. The chapter has earlier shown that even the EU is using LLL this way. On the other hand, adult education would, to our mind, constitute a crucial component of any LLE or LLL strategy.

With regard to LLE, Kenneth Wain (2004) refers to two waves of writing in the area, namely, the more evolutionary utopian wave and the alternative pragmatist approach. Wain had argued that the utopian wave can be easily criticized on the grounds that it provides a very optimistic view of a 'common humanity'. Difference is here subsumed under a single model, according to which a common destiny beckons (Wain, 1987, 230). Wain refers to an alternative model of the 'learning society',[1] the particular social conception that necessitates LLE, proposed by those members of the second wave of 'pragmatist' writers who 'are ready to reverse all these tendencies, to take different societies as they are' and who 'are thus ready to argue that there is not any one model of such a society that can be universally imposed, and that the shape any "learning society" will take depends upon an ongoing dialectical relationship between the ideological, economic, cultural, educational features *that it already has*' (ibid.). Wain includes Gelpi among those who favour a pragmatist approach to LLE and the idea of a learning society: an historical and a comparative approach with the emphasis being placed less on the two concepts' future possibilities and more on the actual present day reality (Wain, 2004, p. 19). Gelpi (1985b, 18) once wrote:

> My thinking is that lifelong education, fundamentally, belongs to the history of education of all countries; it is not therefore a new idea. It lies in the Chinese tradition, in Indian Buddhism; it lies within Greek philosophy and within the spirit of the European Renaissance. The real revolution today lies in the *popular demand* for lifelong education, not in the idea itself.

In short, it is not a question of simply moving towards a process or system of LLE but more a question of examining what form LLE takes at a particular time and in a specific context. This position made sense when viewed in the context of UNESCO's universal education policy which had to take cognizance of the fact that, in continents such as Africa and regions such as Latin America, education would not necessarily result in the creation of new and 'expensive' formal structures of learning but would have to entail appreciation and recognition of the many 'learning webs' and non-formal education experiences and traditions that abound in these contexts. The example of Latin American popular education, spearheaded by the towering figure of Paulo Freire, internationally the most heralded popular educator but certainly not the only prominent one, comes to mind. Likewise, experiences such as Indigenous intergenerational 'knowledge transfer' and 'reinvention', involving community elders and other forms of Indigenous knowledge, come to mind with respect to, say, African countries and, for example, 'first nations' communities in the Americas. These were given short shrift by promoters of Western colonial education as part of their so-called civilizing mission. The same would hold for other Indigenous populations such as the Aborigines, Māori, Inuit and Adivasi.

The foregoing paragraphs enhance the expansive nature of the concept as developed within the UNESCO framework. It encompassed a wide range of education modes, settings and 'learning societies'. The writings captured the imagination of many operating in the education and social research fields. In its more pragmatist form, LLE must have appealed to sociologists dealing with issues such as hegemony in its Gramscian sense and the implicit notion of a 'learning society' embedded in Gramsci's affirmation that every relationship of hegemony is an educational relationship. Others, inspired by Habermas, found much purchase in connecting the 'learning society' to the idea of a democratic public sphere in which education plays its part, very much tied to the concept of the 'educated public'.

LLL's Policy Impact

Alas, the older concept of LLE, though bandied about by educationalists and politicians as part of the then trendy education discourse, had little effect on education policy itself. Furthermore, as La Belle (1986) intimates, the concept was already being diluted in Latin America, where it was frequently accorded a 'secondary labour market' economic orientation in certain projects promoted through foreign 'dependency' aid.[2] These were early examples, in 'informally Western colonised' territories, of how UNESCO's expansive philosophy on paper can be distorted. It was a different UNESCO from the one that has existed following the Soviet Bloc's demise. This distortion anticipated what was to transpire on a global scale. This is hardly surprising given that neoliberalism, which would embrace and distort the concept, had its violently repressive 'trial run' in one of these territories.[3]

The LLE movement gravitating around UNESCO faded away in the late 1980s while the concept of LLL had by then already been used by the Organisation of Economic Cooperation and Development (OECD). It eventually was taken up by the EU as a result of the influence of the European Roundtable of Industrialists whose concern was to raise the competitivity of European industry in the face of competition from other areas, including multinational and transnational corporations. The fact that the impetus emerged from industrialists and not educators indicated the trajectory that this concept would take.

Dominant *Doxa*: From Lifelong Education to Lifelong Learning

It would not be amiss to state that LLL constitutes one of the dominant *doxa* in education policymaking worldwide, particularly in the Western world. At face value, it seems like a relatively neutral concept, although very few concepts, if any, are really neutral in policymaking. A closer look at its basic tenets and the way the discourse evolved from the time of UNESCO and the so-called Faure report, *Learning to Be* (Faure et al., 1972), by Edgar Faure and others, indicates that it might well encapsulate all the basic aspects of modern market-oriented conceptions of education.

There is one worrying aspect of the current discourse that often makes it a far cry from the UNESCO espoused concept of LLE. The discursive switch from lifelong *education* to lifelong *learning* is not innocent (Tuijnman and Boström, 2002). It places less emphasis on structures and entitlement, and more on individuals taking charge of their own learning, often at considerable expense. It is an insidious discourse that minimizes the role of the state and leaves everything to the market. Education is therefore turned from a social into an individual responsibility. Policy documents promoting these fashionable ideas should be the subject of constant critical scrutiny by discerning educators – critical educators.

In many uncritical but widely available discourses around the concept, we are bombarded with all sorts of platitudes. Though some critical voices are available (Murphy, 1997; Williamson, 1998; Martin, 2001; Wain, 2004; Borg and Mayo, 2005, 2006; Boshier, 2005; Field, 2010), rarely is education presented as a public good rather than the consumption good that the shift in discourse, from that of UNESCO to the OECD and, to a certain extent, the EU (triggered by the European Roundtable of Industrialists), has brought about. What is most worrying is the now very conventional emphasis on 'employability', on 'learning to earn', which renders what was once an expansive concept of education (LLE), albeit individualistic and liberal for the most part, rather reductionist in scope. This prevails throughout the educational discourse worldwide.

We find it disheartening to hear certain present-day trade union representatives speak more of investment in training of 'human resources', that is, 'learning to earn' and become employable, than of revitalizing that long-standing and historically rich trade union tradition of adult education known as workers' education. In our view, this area represents one of the richest dimensions of the field. It was rich enough to attract quite a range of leading twentieth-century UK-based intellectuals such as Raymond Williams, Richard Hoggart and Edward P. Thompson to engage in and write about the field, notably in such defunct outlets as the *Tutor's Bulletin* for adult educators, some remaining specimen copies of which can be perused at the TUC archives housed in the library of the London Metropolitan University on Holloway Road, London. They wrote not of 'employability' but of employee empowerment and access to various types of knowledge, which allow them to develop beyond being simply producers and, I would add, consumers, these days, to social actors, fully capable of contributing, individually, and most likely collectively, to changing the world around them.

'Employability' is at the heart of the agenda in the discourse on LLL, never mind the fact that employability does not necessarily mean employment, as Gelpi (2002) had astutely remarked in his final book. In Europe, it is particularly fuelled through the European Social Fund (ESF) on which many organizations in adult learning are increasingly becoming dependent. This type of funding places the emphasis squarely on 'employability'. Rather than admitting to the failure to create sustainable employment, spokesmen for industry and policymakers place the emphasis on people lacking the necessary skills – a 'jobs crisis' couched in terms of a 'skills crisis' (Marshall, 1997). The truth is that, in many parts of Europe, youngsters are gaining greater qualifications than their parents ever dreamed of obtaining and yet cannot enjoy their standard of living (English and Mayo, 2012, 119). This has been a recurring battle cry of the many *indignados* occupying various parts of the diminishing public spaces in Europe and across the Atlantic. The whole idea of LLL, as currently promoted, gravitates around the notion of a 'knowledge economy' which might not lead to the level of employment and financial rewards being anticipated, given the global competition for the few high-paying middle-class jobs available (Brown, Lauder and Ashton, 2010).

That there should be some link between adult education and the economy is understandable. It is, however, still worrying to see the dominant, all-pervasive discourse regarding adult education, in the context of LLL worldwide, reduced to simply learning for work. If anything, what we really need are forms of education that enable people to learn to engage critically with work, the kind of education we would expect trade unions to be providing and which has been the staple of workers' education in the past. The narrow 'employability' view of LLL – which attaches lots of importance to old and new basic skills (most laudable) but which ignores the very important notion of 'critical literacy', that is, learning to read the word and the world, as well as its construction through the media (critical media literacy) – ignores the larger, albeit repressed, tradition of adult education that emphasizes the role of the citizen as social actor. It also ignores the role of adult learning as a vital activity within social movements, including labour movements. There is more to adult learning than is internationally celebrated at present.

Furthermore, the discourse is being promoted with great vigour and vehemence in certain industrially developing countries. As Rosa Maria Torres (2013) indicates, LLL, as opposed to LLE, we would add, is very much a westernised concept. It takes the spotlight away, in Latin America, from adult basic education, still a necessity in that region as well as in other regions including southern Europe and the Mediterranean, where illiteracy remains a major factor. It also narrows down the nature of education to skills that suit the agenda of northern states and away from a more holistic, community approach of learning and education as manifest in the discourses of 'southern' states – adult and youth education in Latin America, and community education in other parts of the world.

As for many of these 'developing' territories, there seems to be little recognition of the fact that an increase in investment in adult education or all education for that matter, with economic returns in mind, without a corresponding reciprocal investment in the economic sector, perpetuates, and probably exacerbates, the situation of 'education for export' that has been a characteristic of colonial and neocolonial policies to date.

A Glimmer of Hope?

Hope springs eternal. In this regard, two points come to mind. The first concerns policy transmutations. Hegemonic structures contain, within their interstices, the means for change. Hegemony is incomplete and always in the making. The EU is a classic example thriving on and spreading hegemony. It is not monolithic as an institution. It is full of spaces and epistemic communities that challenge the Commission's views operating 'in and against it', worming their agendas into the programs available, being 'tactically inside and strategically outside' it. Even more, as indicated in Mayo (2019), there are different layers of mediation for a policy before it reaches the ultimate site of practice. These mediating layers of policy movement offer spaces for renegotiation of agendas. We can start with the EU offices and seminar rooms in Brussels. Policy actors are present in various EU epistemic sectors, and they are not homogenous in their views on LLL and what it should comprise. They are (often) guided by their own values when interpreting and perhaps reinventing policy.[4] Then we have the national coordinating body, whose members bring their own values and ideas on LLL to bear on the process of policy interpretation and perhaps transmutation. Then we get to the regional territories, Italy's *territorio* so important in adult education and community *praxis*. Finally, we reach the municipalities. This involves at least four layers of policy movement and interpretation, allowing room for reinventions and hybridization, and, in certain cases, a dose of critical appropriation, unless the gatekeepers want to win favours themselves with Brussels. This can be the case with recent accession countries still learning the tricks of how to circumvent policy. In this case, to adopt a metaphor from sports, and goaltending in particular, it would be difficult to put air past them. The flow, in the majority of cases, is however never straightforward. Structures and agency operate dialectically in unpredictable ways. There are several mediators in the process of cultural transmission, thus offering a glimmer of hope to those working 'in and against' a neoliberal-driven system.

The second point concerns the sustainable development turn in the UN. This brings UNESCO, which has also been using LLL instead of its old LLE in its discourse, back into the debate. The alternative discourse is of a process of LLL which is broad in scope and which necessitates ethical commitments to others. LLL is an important aspect of the UN Sustainable Development Goals (SDGs) (United Nations, 2015). For LLL to be meaningful in this regard, it must be rescued from the reductionist, economic-oriented paradigm, in which it is currently entrapped, to be presented as broader in scope, embracing all forms of intra-human and human-earth relations. It is LLL which derives its first impulse from love for others, humanity and the rest of the cosmos. It requires people feeling rooted in, rather than standing apart from and being ready to exploit, nature. This alternative LLL necessitates an eco-pedagogical approach (Gutierrez and Prado, 2000).

All this lies in stark contrast to the soulless nature of a life centring on the vagaries and volatility of the market, where 'clinical efficiency' becomes the prime value. This market-driven approach is geared towards a world of mechanism, commodification (the Earth as commodity), a collection of items to be bought and sold, as eco-theologian and Catholic Passionist priest Thomas Berry would put it (Berry, 1999, xiii). Money and profit constitute the basic values (ibid.) in a plundering and predatory economy with globalizing tendencies.

This alternative eco-pedagogical notion allows scope for a process of LLL predicated on people being conceived as *relational beings* in harmony with the rest of the cosmos. This would be distinct from an industrially conditioned notion of LLL whereby people are restricted to constantly (re)learning the skills to produce and consume without limits, actions which, needless to say, have repercussions for the survival of Planet Earth *borrowed from future generations.*

This is in line with the United Nations' notion of LLL for sustainable development. It is certainly in tune with the writing of many poets, certainly Romantic poets. One can mention, in this regard, Samuel Taylor Coleridge and his celebration of the 'One Life', in the 'Eolian Harp' and 'The Rhyme of the Ancient Mariner', that somehow connects with the 'Web of Life' invoked by the First Nations people who, as mentioned by Berry, invoke 'all my relations' (ibid.) in this spirit. This conception also echoes the teaching of such contemporary spiritual leaders as Pope Francis (2015). This alternative approach to LLL would be sensitive to ecological issues, averse to the politics of disposability with regard to humans (people removed from the index of human concerns) and the rest of Nature (waste), and therefore in tune with the UN's SDGs; it would involve learning in the context of redefining wealth and human living. Learning in this context would entail

- extending LLE's resonance and scope beyond the anthropocentric framework;
- developing a holistic and bio-centric approach to learning in diverse settings, formal, non-formal and informal;
- extricating ourselves from LLL's Eurocentric hold that reflects Western industrial and technological values;
- helping in the ushering in of an age when not only hitherto undemocratic and hierarchical social relations but also, and most especially, human-earth relations are transformed and wealth itself is redefined;
- learning not only *how* we produce but also to examine *what* we produce and for *what purpose* (developing potentials for qualitative wealth creation; putting ecological (including human) development first);
- learning to integrate economic processes within natural cycles;
- dematerializing and rescaling the economy;
- providing funding for LLL that contributes to a community's green development; and
- fostering LLL for integral development, including green city/bioregional development planning.

(Summarized from (Brian) Milani, 2002)

The SDG-oriented relational aspect of LLL brings to mind social-justice-oriented and ecologically sensitized social movements. These are often criticized for being more focused on single specific issue politics than on a broader politics targeting the structural forces of oppression that span various differences. This conception of LLL entails our confronting single issue politics with a broader politics. The World Social Forum has been providing the right context for many of these movements to coalesce around a collective effort to confront neoliberal globalization. The latter is seen as a powerful, all-pervasive structuring force reinforcing the *Cenozoic State*, that is, life governed by the technical-industrial values of Western Eurocentric culture (O'Sullivan, 2002, 4), as opposed to the *Ecozoic State* characterized by our connectedness to the ecosystem that sustains us (ibid.; O' Sullivan 1999).

LLL in the context of social movements implies an ongoing process of learning and relearning, formally, non-formally and mainly informally. Social movement learning provides an alternative form of LLL with regard to the mainstream. This process of learning projects notions of people not in two-dimensional reductionist terms but primarily as social actors (Martin, 2001). This provides an antithetical view of LLL based not on a view of working *for* the economy, with all the illusions of prosperity involved, but on engaging critically *with* it and society in general, understanding their (society and its economy) underlying contradictions.

Conclusion: Lifelong Learning to Engage Critically with the Economy

While the EU promotes digital and other functional literacies as its much-valued new basic skills (see Message 1 of its Memorandum on Lifelong Learning (CEC, 2000); Cedefop and Eurydice, 2001, 15), critical literacy, the means of 'reading the word and the world' through the critical distance just mentioned, is conspicuous by its absence in the EU discourse. That this term is lacking from the list of 'new basic skills' promoted by the EU is revealing with regard to the transmission model inherent in this particular hegemonic notion of LLL. The alternative LLL approach being proposed would, to the contrary, be based on the use of skills not simply to function in the economy, important though these are, but to interpret and contribute to changing it. This hearkens back, once again, to the old Socratic dictum, as reproduced by Plato in the *Apology*, that an unexamined life is a life not worth living. Also not worth living is a life that does not allow people the possibility of collectively changing it, thus remaking history that includes the history of human-earth relations.

3

Philosophy of Differences and Social Creation: Anna Maria Piussi and Antonia De Vita

In light of the criticisms levelled at what we regard as the neoliberal conception of lifelong learning, carried forward in EU politics and as part of a search for possible alternatives, we consider it important to shed light on practices predicated on respect for the person, differences, creativity and social commitment. In this respect, we consider quite important the thinking of two well-known – at least in Italy, but also beyond (e.g. Spain) – intellectuals, friends and colleagues Anna Maria Piussi and Antonia De Vita. They confront the traditional authoritarian world, particularly the patriarchal world, with a cultural practice that underlines the philosophy of differences and social creation. Anna Maria Piussi and Antonia De Vita espouse an approach towards culture, critical thinking and human and social relations that is completely incompatible with the technocracy characterizing the neoliberal conception of education, incompatible because of its profound sense of humanity.

Let us start with Anna Maria Piussi: she embraced feminism at the end of the 1970s, as a result of not a steadfast ideological commitment but cultural exchanges with two women, Luisa Muraro and Chiara Zamboni. These relations developed in the course of the 150 hours, specifically work in this regard concerning women carried out at the Universities of Padova and Verona. Anna Maria would tell one of us that short courses around a specific theme, in this case women's issues, known as monographic courses, would be held as part of the 150 hours (they were actually more than that) experiment in working-class education (Yarnit, 1980). These are two important figures who, given their inspiration, their standing in the area and the relations they fostered, instilled in Anna Maria the desire to adhere to feminism and the philosophy of differences. The 150 hours was a political-cultural process by which the class of male and female workers engaged in a participative and emancipatory practice that engendered their own education marked by collective learning. It was an autonomous working-class education, unencumbered by the procedures of state-controlled public education.

Interestingly, Anna Maria's initial commitment occurred during this significant moment for the workers' movement, feminism and student politics. This is an important moment which should be a key source of reference for an approach to critical education. Anna Maria's participation in the 150 hours project occurred in connection with a monographic course on women's issues. This and similar courses in the 150 hours experiment had a significant impact on the Italian feminist movement of the period. Anna Maria was both educator and learner in these courses where knowledge and knowing was shared in a process of creation characterized by dialogical and genuinely democratic social relations in the spirit of feminism and, we would add, Freirean pedagogical politics.

Anna Maria is considered a key exponent of the philosophy of differences, one of the '*los pilares sobre los cuales se funda el pensamiento de la diferencia sexual*' (pillars that support thinking regarding sexual differences) (Sánchez-Bello, 2015, 121). Together with Antonia De Vita, Antonia Darder, Ana Maria (Nita) Freire, bell hooks, Joyce Canaan, Shirley Steinberg, Sheila Macrine, Deborah Britzman and others, she is regarded as an important exponent of international critical education.[1] Her ongoing creative and humanizing contribution is in the area of the philosophy and pedagogy of differences at the University of Verona and other universities abroad. The female philosophers (*filosofe*) of *Diotima* immediately come to mind, the classical name deriving from Plato's account, in the *Symposium*, where Socrates speaks about the philosopher of love and Diotima, his teacher. Love, solidarity and the fostering/creation of authentic social exchanges and relations in real life (Piussi, 2003), not artificial 'settings', are at the heart of Anna Maria Piussi's writings. These elements are rooted in not 'market-driven' contexts but, on the contrary, 'life-centred' values (Piussi, 2004). In short, they are human values at the furthest remove from the crude commodification of ideas, the body, creativity and what constitutes the human. This thought extends beyond that concerning women, embracing a broader vision regarding how one goes about one's everyday life (Piussi, 2011): a vision of life, work and society marked not by a quest for power, seen as *dominio* (domination) (Piussi, 2012, 25), but by being in *authority* (as opposed to authoritarianism), rooted in femininity. This vision is therefore far removed from neoliberalism, the patriarchal system and the profit motive. It is far removed from processes that give pride of place to money as the measure of everything and reduce human relations to instrumental ones. Anna Maria's vision is marked by a politics (in the authentic sense of the word) and a primacy of relations governed by a feminine viewpoint capable of rethinking everything, differences included. At the heart of this transformative vision, therefore, lies women's knowledge/s emanating from the subject, relations and experience. They are knowledges placed at the service of all to radically rethink educating, the development of society and the generation of culture. More recently, Anna Maria worked in the context of 'social creation', a concept also promulgated by her important colleague at the University of Verona, Antonia De Vita, a former student of the acclaimed Luisa Muraro. This collaboration is an example of social and work relations engendering further relations in the context of human solidarity.

These elements are central to the processes of social creation which Anna Maria Piussi describes and analyses in her joint work with De Vita (De Vita and Piussi, 2013). These processes of learning and self-learning, often collective learning, create contexts for social solidarity production and political change, such as those, for example, of the social solidarity economy in Italy and the *Madres de la Plaza de Mayo* in Argentina. These processes are extricated from the ideology of capital mobility, where work opportunities are transferred elsewhere, leaving a tragic void in the life of local communities. These creative attempts at retrieving work and recreating life opportunities somehow remind us of the Danilo Dolci-led 'reverse strike' (the 'sciopero alla rovescia') in Sicily. They also recall Dolci's idea of community action and development. The actions involve grassroots social mobilizations outside institutional settings. They are part and parcel of 'democracy from below' that echoes Aldo Capitini and his inspired process of *omnicrazia*, a democracy for all (*omnes*). This is very much in sync with progressive social movements engendering a politics that differs from that of the mainstream. The social movements' politics centres on social justice.

These processes contain an important educative component or dimension. They can be the subject of reflection and documentation in the areas of critical grassroots adult education and critical education in a wider context. They provide a refreshing antidote to the dominant contemporary hegemonic view of lifelong learning, put forward by the OECD and EU, we addressed in Chapter 2.

The concepts that emerge from Anna Maria Piussi's writings, including her collaborative work with Antonia De Vita, help us rethink social and educational relations in a process of hegemony that is not static but dynamic and fluid, therefore marked by constant change. For this reason, the process is transformative. The relations of hegemony, pedagogical relations as Gramsci underlined, are there to be renegotiated. There are affinities here with concepts expressed by Ettore Gelpi (humanistic, critical and radical). This is particularly so because Anna Maria constantly poses the question regarding how the politics and pedagogy of differences can serve to transform structures (made of people) and institutions which are not to be reified. They are not 'a thing' and hence this way of doing politics and pedagogy prevents us from lapsing into 'thingification'. Nothing is monolithic in this regard. This type of pedagogical experience and what she calls *politica prima* has strong ramifications for how we progressively go about adult education and popular education, as evinced by Anna Maria's collaboration with popular educator Pep Aparicio Guadas in Valencia and its surroundings in the Generalitat Valenciana, and with her deceased friend and adult educator, Bruno Schettini, besides many feminists in Spain.

In her fine book on the subject (De Vita, 2009), also the theme of an article she co-authored with Anna Maria Piussi (De Vita and Piussi, 2013), Antonia De Vita provides us with an erudite exploration of the conditions which permit the kind of atomized individualistic approaches to life and its bearing on the capitalist world. She also explores alternative conditions, embedded in alternative social relations, that allow for different and more humanistic types of social relations and social creation. These alternative conditions have the potential to usher in an alternative world which is less exploitative, less predatory and less inhuman. It is intended to foster a form of social and economic organization which has love and solidarity at its core. This is no 'wishy-washy' hippie argumentation. On the contrary, the essay is steeped in a very thorough knowledge of different philosophies and theological insights, including feminist philosophy. In this regard, it is theoretically very grounded and draws on works by Hannah Arendt, Giorgio Agamben, Jürgen Habermas and *noblesse oblige* Luisa Muraro, among others.

It also demonstrates a very deep knowledge of late medieval mysticism, from the Franciscan notion of poverty and its ramifications for economic activity to women's mystic movements of the same period. All this is geared towards an alternative vision of social and economic practice based on what, as we have seen, Indigenous movements would call the 'web of life' and which the English romantic poet, Samuel Taylor Coleridge, cited in De Vita's volume with reference to his popular ballad, 'The Rhyme of the Ancient Mariner', calls the 'One Life', as indicated in Chapter 2. It is the notion of people being rooted in and at one with nature. A piece which Antonia De Vita co-authored with Anna Maria Piussi underlines the notion of social creation shared by both:

> It is the most elementary form of politics, within the reach of everyone. It constitutes a way of life involving daily social relations at work, in the neighbourhood, in the community, in the emotional sphere, and also when thinking. The aim is to make living together more civil. This form of politics enables one to rename reality with a choice of words capable of regenerating it. It is often hidden from public life but demands a shift in priorities: first and foremost, it embraces the politics espoused by social movements. It involves social action which helps create a polis different from the one dominated by political parties and featuring a representative democracy. And yet a rapport can be established with this kind of official politics. In this connection, the unexpected outcome of a case involving the new city council of Milan with regard to the issue of the Roma girls and boys is instructive. (De Vita and Piussi, 2013, 298)

The discussion is not without an appreciable dose of political economy and provides grounded examples of different forms of social creation taking place in Italy, especially in the Veneto area where the author, originally from Puglia, works and lives. These include groups providing different (from the mainstream), including feminist, approaches to philosophy, centring on *Diotima*. The experiences described indicate a different approach to learning which is neither time- or credit-conditioned nor competitive but which is characterized by sharing and co-investigating knowledge. It is also marked by a sense of 'public time', as opposed to 'corporate time' (see Giroux and Searls Giroux, 2004). It is this sense of learning through public time that would be conducive to what Don Lorenzo Milani refers to as 'la pedagogia della lumaca' (the pedagogy of the snail).

The survey, in De Vita and Piussi's writings, of alternative practices includes groups involved in community revival work in the ancient quarter of Veronetta in the medieval city of Verona as well as highly educated persons engaging in agricultural production. This kind of production is characterized by self-management approaches which eliminate intermediaries. This is intended to bring the products of the earth straight to a broad array of people rather than serve as products for a captive niche market of well-to-do persons who can afford what would otherwise be a 'luxury'. The voices and learning experiences of these protagonists in new forms of social creation are foregrounded in long excerpts from interview transcripts. They all provide fresh insights into how transformations in social relations can provide pockets of alternative resources of hope for a better, more human world featuring democratic and community-oriented, rather than atomized, individualistic-oriented, relations of living and production.

This all points to a different way of conceiving of politics and political activity centring on humanized social relations based on cooperation and complementarity rather than competition. The focus is on the conceptions of persons and species as being relational (comprising human-earth relations) and in communion with the rest of the cosmos, as exemplified by the work of contemporaries such as, once again, Thomas J. Berry, Vandana Shiva, Edmund O' Sullivan and Metchild Hart, all previously mentioned with respect to lifelong learning and sustainable development. It is also exemplified by such venerated figures from the past as Francis of Assisi with his 'Canticle of the Creatures' and Samuel Taylor Coleridge. The volume also shuttles between philosophy and economics in the direction of a social solidarity economy.

According to the RIPESS (international network for the promotion of the social solidarity economy), this type of economy fosters respect for men, women and the environment.[2] It returns money to its rightful place, namely, as an instrument that facilitates exchanges rather than financial speculation. It is said to pioneer new forms of exchanges.[3] There are many people working in this field, and we are aware of several Italian authors/activists who are strongly committed in this regard. In many ways, De Vita and Piussi's work makes a very important contribution to the social solidarity economy movement. It does so in a manner that is expansive, embedding this alternative economic vision in a larger vision which is spiritual, cosmic and communal. This vision exalts the notion of love of humanity and the rest of nature in the sense described by Paulo Freire and others (see Darder, 2002), certainly those harbouring that global ecological vision of lifelong learning mentioned in Chapter 2. This vision, shared by both De Vita and Piussi (2013), is geared towards imparting that sense of positive energy for people to continue engaging in acts of social creation that suggest, in the slogan of the World Social Forum, that another world is possible.

Part Two

A Critical Reading of the World

4

Gabriela Mistral: Poet of Education

There are people, making history and becoming recognized historical figures, who often find themselves in contradiction with this very same history. By this we mean that the persons concerned do not adapt to this history but strive to transform it. In this quest to transform, engaging with the contradictions, these persons leave legacies and provide teachings for posterity. This is very much the case with a rural educator, poet, feminist and political thinker adopting the name Gabriela Mistral. She was not one to resign herself to accepting injustice, isolation, inequality and abuse. She has, to the contrary, indefatigably defended, throughout her life, Indigenous peoples and Latin American identities. She engaged in the struggle for a compulsory public education and equal rights for women especially in her own country, Chile. A visionary but concrete and down-to-earth educator, she helped formulate a pedagogy predicated on action and couched in a language that is poetic. In our view, this justifies her appellation: 'poet of education'.

We mentioned, at the very outset, that she *adopted* her name, Gabriela Mistral. This is, in actual fact, a pseudonym reflecting her love of poetry. It derives from the names of two poets she must have greatly admired – Gabriele D'Annunzio and Frédéric Mistral. Her father, a schoolteacher, abandoned her when she was 3 years old. Lucila Godoy y Alcayaga – her real name – was born in 1889 in the small rural locality of Vicuña in Chile. She was raised by her mother, grandmother and her sister. Her sister was herself a schoolteacher who inducted her into the teaching profession. Like her, Mistral would eventually take her first steps into teaching as a teaching assistant, since fully trained teachers were, at the time, hard to come by in Chile, especially in rural areas and isolated ones at that.

Mistral would, from her early days in life, express her indignation at the cultural restrictions of the times. This sense of indignation lay at the heart of her social-political thought and her educational practice. She was a woman of faith, a devout Christian, who was, however, often at odds with official Roman Catholic culture. Her poetry did not go down well with powerful men because they were deemed pagan, socialist and popular. This is one of the reasons why she was often at loggerheads with the Catholic hierarchy and the power it wielded. This power elite must have found it difficult to imagine that a woman, of mestiza origin, poor and hailing from isolated areas at the furthest remove from prominent cultural milieus, would, in 1945, become Latin America's first recipient of the Nobel Prize, in her case the Nobel Prize for Literature. She was awarded this honour, among other things, for foregrounding the languages of Indigenous campesinos/as in schools and squares – rendering them fit for use in what can be broadly called the public sphere. It is an attribute later to be shared with her personal friend and successor, as Chile's second recipient of the Nobel Prize for Literature, Pablo Neruda.

Mistral certainly cultivated the sort of profile that was unorthodox and somewhat disturbing for an educational system that, at the turn of the twentieth century, was marked by discrimination, racism, patriarchy and social exclusion, especially class and ethnic exclusion. These conditions persist till the present day, despite the sense of hope instilled in those harbouring ideas of an egalitarian society, during the brief three-year period of government (1970–3) led by Salvador Allende's Unidad Popular (Popular Unity) coalition. Mistral died thirteen years earlier, thus being spared the savage crushing of this hope, and many of the people who helped generate it, on and immediately after 11 September 1973.

What caused certain people to feel uncomfortable with her ideas was not only her feminism but, above all, the way she interpreted being a woman, engaging with some of the deepest contradictions lacerating Chilean society. This political reading of her country's social reality translates into an educational practice constantly focused on the rights of the most disadvantaged, excluded and forgotten – in short, the main casualties of a politics of disposability. This sensibility is wedded to a political thought and Latin American epistemology inspired by the teachings and literary output of the much revered Cuban poet, José Martí (Mistral, 2017b). She would write that all is in gratitude for and a token of her love of Martí, gratitude for the author in him, gratitude for the inspiration he provided for her work and for the great leadership which he, a son of America, exercised.

At the start of the previous century, Chile was split between Catholic-Conservatives and Lay-Progressives. Mistral, however, did not adapt to this dichotomy. A Christian, she espoused positions that had strong socialist and feminist overtones. In the very first years of her public life, specifically in 1906, she penned a newspaper article which caused a stir in the Catholic Church. Under the heading 'The Education of Women', the article called for a restructuring of the education system on gender grounds. She severely rejected the idea, the normalizing discourse, that women required only a limited education sufficient to manage the household and take care of their children. In her view, education, as a formal system, had to be revamped and this was possible only through a reconceptualization of gender, relations of power, family and society. The educational system required a revolution as a result of which women were to be fully developed as educated beings, something which needed to be universally accepted and not, judging from actual textual evidence, dismissed as the figment of a 'ridiculous fanatic'. With a view to preparing women in a way that broadens horizons and future possibilities, not limited to marriage and home-keeping, Mistral vehemently argued and lobbied for a rethink of education. She conceived of it more holistically, connecting it with other social domains, from the economy to politics. This demonstrates her awareness of education being not an independent variable but a crucial component of a process that entails a broader array of interlocking areas. She advocated an integrated approach. She felt that this would prevent the further deceit of the woman via the false notion of 'protection', brought about by fixed marriages and, worse, to reproduce her own words, 'the sale of one's dignity'.

Hers was a very critical feminist vision based on a rethink of women's social and political organization. Referring to the feminist movement, she was to write that, as elsewhere, the vertebral column is missing as a result of which there is no organization that inspires sufficient faith for women workers, employees, teachers, doctors, Catholics, Liberals, communists and socialists to put forward female candidates to represent them, receive suggestions and address their own issues. In Chile, she states, feminism is at times more an expression of feminine sentimentalism, perfectly invertebrate like a sponge floating in a harmless liquid, than something robust. She elaborates that, in her home country, there are more emotional outpourings than ideas, more bad lyricism than sound social concepts even if a modicum of sense often cuts across like a flash of lightning. She states that there is legitimacy in the aspirations, purity of intentions, bordering on mystical fervour, which enables the women concerned to command respect, but she argues that there is a general lack of acumen in social matters (Mistral, 2015a, 40).

Because of her critical ideas, she encountered great difficulties in establishing herself at the start of her career. This included the attempt to enrol at the *Escuela*

Normal (Teacher Training School). She left school early but engaged in self-directed learning (the approximate term in Latin languages is something freely translated as 'auto-didactic'). The general shortage of specifically educated/trained teachers in Chile, especially in its rural areas, enabled her, in 1910, when she was 21, to work in a girls' lyceum. Attracted to rural education, at a time when the Indigenous cause was not the subject of much debate, she explicitly and vehemently discussed this issue. She did so together with and in the context of Indigenous rights. This was also a time when peasant women were only viewed instrumentally in relation to work. She would openly speak about and to rural women. She spoke of them as persons who needed to emancipate themselves through reading, writing, attending school and educating themselves. This is the cornerstone of Mistral's work. The education question developed out of her thinking on feminism and the defence of the socially excluded. It was merged with such important issues as the rural question and the struggle for an agrarian reform, the latter a perennial struggle in the history of Latin America.

She is on record as having addressed the issue of rural education in a 1954 address to the UN in which she sheds light on small communities without schools. She reveals that one lives, there, without any formal learning. She explains that parents do not send their children to schools in neighbouring localities not only because of the time lost when travelling on foot but also because of the dangers that might be encountered along the way. This recalls the situation of girls who stayed away from the school at Barbiana directed by Don Lorenzo Milani; parents feared potential dangers *en route*. Mistral recommends that, in these situations, there is a need for itinerant schools that move from locality to locality imparting a minimum of instruction: reading, writing, counting. She states that these isolated people show great fervour for these educators and enthusiastically respond to their presence among them. Ever conscious of 'limit situations', as Freire would call them, and practicalities, although she would not, in her heart of hearts, be satisfied with this limited provision, she argued that these schools would be of low cost to the government. There is no need for a fixed place, where the climate is favourable and classes are held in open spaces, she reasoned. She assured everyone that the communal governments, even the poorest ones, will help and the same group of teachers would deliver lessons in different areas. She claims that the itinerant teacher must embody the spirit of a person on a mission, and that it is preferable that these teachers hail from rural zones so that they would have direct everyday experience of living with these people in the midst of nature. Espousing the basic elements of what can be identified as 'popular education', in its Latin

American version, amply treated throughout this book, she advises that, since children help parents with work in the fields during daylight, these lessons would conveniently be held in the evening. The beauty of this, she adds, is that the evening lesson would also reach illiterate peasants often derogatorily regarded as 'hands'. Her recommendation comes with the rider that this literacy work would be complemented by cinema showings (cine forums) and choral singing. She claims that song and cinema enliven the work process and are a source of peasant enjoyment (Mistral, 2015b, 313–14).

A profile of the rural teacher that is Mistral emerges from these reflections on the itinerant schools. These reflections, now commonplace in the literature on rural and popular education and subaltern social movements (e.g. the Movimento Sem Terra (MST)), were quite avant-garde at the time. The profile is that of a rural teacher, without formal preparation, who treats teaching as a vocation rather than a profession, with all the modern baggage which comes with the latter. It is the profile of a person who is also a writer and journalist, besides being a great political thinker, articulating ideas fostering social justice. Mistral was also ahead of her time in that she attached great attention to different means of communication – cinema and television – in a period when their potential was not widely known or appreciated. If it was amazing that Raymond Williams, living in a highly sophisticated society as was British society at the time, could foreground the potentiality of the mass media then, it should be even more significant that an intellectual from rural Latin America would do likewise around or even before the same period. Here is your classic organic and public feminist intellectual *tout court*. We can add to this her status as a great Latin American intellectual alongside José Carlos Mariátegui (La Chira), Simón Rodríguez, Simón Bolívar, José Martí, Paulo Freire and Victor Jara (Chile's much revered but ultimately tragic troubadour, major exponent of *La Nueva Canción Chilena*). Many were intellectuals-cum-educators, and here one must also mention her alongside Latina/o educators who made their mark after her death, such as Paulo Freire and Leonela Realy. She would also have a direct connection with another great Latin American educator, writer and, in this case, politician, José de Vasconcellos.

When José de Vasconcellos served as Mexico's Secretary of Education under the presidency of Álvaro Obregón (1920–4), he invited her over as consultant and collaborator. He promoted popular education and, apart from Mistral, he attracted educators and exceptional artists to Mexico. He helped set up numerous popular libraries and fine arts departments, schools, public libraries and archives. He revamped the National Bibliotheca and directed a mass publishing programme featuring classical works by different authors. He founded the *El Maestro* (the Teacher) review, promoted the school and rural missions and helped stage the country's first book fair. This invites parallels with Spain's cultural groundswell during the Second Republic when Federico Garcia Lorca and Eduardo Ugarte, as leaders of *La Barraca* (the itinerant university theatre company), were directly involved in the cultural mission.

In collaboration with Vasconcellos, Mistral showed her mettle as an educator. She contributed to the Rural Library project, promoting readings for women. Through the help of such media as radio, a key source of education in rural and desert areas worldwide, Vasconcellos helped inspire the spread of literacy among thousands of peasants. He helped establish night schools, with educators devoted to teaching as a mission. Mistral participated in this project.

Referring to both Bolívar and Martí, Mistral exhorted Latin America to not mirror Europe, that is, to avoid becoming a mirror image of its colonizers. She boldly asserted that Latin America was united by two important factors, the language bestowed by God and the sorrow brought upon it by North America, for some its *bête noire*. Of course, it is common knowledge that the language was imposed by the Spanish *conquistadores* at the eventual expense of several Indigenous languages. She defended the mestiza culture undermined not only by colonial violence but also by the spectre of Nazi-Fascism which grew at an alarming rate in Europe. She stated that creolised America had been offended and challenged from the day Germany launched thousands of copies of the most anti-South American book in existence: *Mein Kampf.* She stated that the negation of the mestizos, populating half of America, had never been pronounced before with so much arrogance and ignorance. She added that those who elevated this work to the status of a 'Sacred Scripture' expressly added insult to the injury meted out to the mestizo peoples by the Fuhrer (Mistral, 2015b, 205). Owing to her clear anti-fascist stance, she could not exercise, in 1932, the role of Consul in Italy. Her situation had become untenable.

It ought to be said that her vision for Latin America, despite her poetic ways of expression, was not, in any way, romantic; it was not sweetened or naive. She was, as a matter of fact, very critical with respect to the then existing (probably persisting) social and economic relations. Here lies her greatness: on the one hand, she provides an exquisite poetic language, full of metaphors and profound sensibilities; on the other, she projects a rigorous and complex political vision as she proves capable of comprehending situations not in their immediacy but in their historical context within a wider constellation of social relations. For example, referring to Chile, she considered essential an agrarian reform which would serve as an example to other countries. She states that if Chile was to prove capable of carrying out a real reform (by 'real' she meant a reform carried out with great courage and without fear, a reform which would last fifty and not five years), the example will be taken up by other agrarian countries in Latin America ('... which country is not Agrarian?', she asks). She states that, though considering the reform necessary, certain people fear it because of the spectre of fifteen bloody years in Mexico, going on to underline that it would entail civil work of massive proportions (Mistral, 2015b, 113). Of course, there was also the Monroe Doctrine to be reckoned with, as her compatriot, Allende, and many Chileans, would discover at the cost of their own lives, decades later.

Here public life is characterized on one side by her preoccupation with educational politics and on the other by her concern for children's learning, their rights, the defence of minorities, women's emancipation, Christianity, the Nueva Escuela (New School) and Latin American thought. These were the many concerns and facets of social engagement of a teacher and political intellectual with an all-consuming passion for social justice.

In 1926, the Council of the League of Nations selected her for an important role in the administrative council of the International Educational Cinematographic Institute which had been established in Rome.[1] Her concern for women's issues was very much in evidence when France denied women the right to vote; Mistral denounced the decision. The text 'El Voto Femenino' (The Feminine Vote) was produced in 1928. She inveighed against socialists and radicals who did not put their money where their mouth is, verbally supporting women's suffrage when in opposition and then reneging on their promise once in government. She insisted, throughout her life, on women's right to vote and also to contest the elections, otherwise women would only vote for men. If this were to persist, that is, voting only for men, women would remain in a subaltern position, virtually disenfranchised.

In the 1930s, the Frente Popular (Popular Front) was formed in Chile. It united communists, socialists, unions and the Radical Party. This led to Mistral's personal friend, Pedro Aguirre Cerdá, lawyer and educator, to become President. His slogan was *Gobernar es Educar!* (To Govern Is to Educate!) The Popular Front relied on the support of intellectuals such as Neruda, a great admirer of Mistral. She actively participated in the Front's political programme which promoted public education and schooling besides providing opportunities for teachers to be employed. As with the situation in Mexico, this political development presented Mistral with a great opportunity to put into effect many of her ideas. Included were ideas concerning an education which would not be a carbon copy of foreign and colonial models but would emerge from and respond to the country's own realities, hence, a popular education.

As evinced by her ideas and writings, Mistral provides us with a process of political thinking that is concrete and analytic, which does not give lip service to poetry and the imagination, a point which draws her close in spirit and educational orientation to later US educational philosopher, Maxine Greene. Mistral exalts the imagination in one of her last texts 'Imagen y palabra en la educación' (The Image and Word in Education). She writes that

> 'all the first years of childhood are rich in imagination, although there are many fathers and teachers who do not allow much room for flights of the imagination which they even oppose. When they are told that fantasy among children is something positive, that it is a good thing that they can invent stories, an important element in their physical and other development and in their life, they (fathers and teachers) express doubts about or do not believe in all this. (Our translation from the Spanish original: Mistral, 2015a, 120)

A great and effective social communicator, whose language was embellished by vivid metaphors, and who worked patiently and persistently, Mistral would eventually become an important point of international reference also at a diplomatic level: Advisor to the International Institute of Intellectual Cooperation in 1920; Consul in 1932, the first Chilean woman to be appointed to this position; Honorary Member of the Pan-American Society of Brazil in 1937; 1945 Nobel Laureate, already mentioned; winner of the Literature Prize in 1951; in her capacity as Consul to New York, she represented Chile, in 1953, at the UN General Assembly. The rural teacher rose from poverty, in her country's hinterland, to being a great critical educator not only within the confines of different schools for the marginalized and poor but also in the grander public arena, both nationally and internationally, allowing her to leave her mark among several rural children and among the many other people whose lives she touched. She also left a considerable legacy for popular and a social justice education in different countries, such as her own Chile and Mexico, and in important international forums, notably those connected to the United Nations. Not one for compromising, Gabriela Mistral ranks with Paulo Freire as one of the greatest voices of human emancipation to emerge from Latin America. Like Freire, her sense of emancipation was mainly expressed as occurring through education, connected with other sectors.

She passed away on 10 January 1957. Her spirit lives in her poetry, writings on different social topics, the struggle for emancipation among Latin American women and other marginalized groups and her legacy for a critical education for greater social justice. The best way to remember her is through her verses. One of her poems, 'La Maestra Rural' (The Rural Teacher) highlights the qualities that can be found in the educator of campesino/a children.

Adrienne Joyce Wood Royo summarizes Gabriela Mistral's poem by outlining the eight qualities the rural teacher ought to possess. It is in many ways a poetic manifesto for teaching in rural areas and for teaching in general. For Mistral, Royo states (2007, 76), these eight qualities are

> considered essential in a great rural teacher: 1) purity; 2) poverty; 3) optimistic spirit; 4) sweet demeanour; 5) unpretentiousness; 6) ability to facilitate knowledge; 7) trust in God; and 8) possess a clear vision of her mission. These eight points are wrapped up in the last stanza in which Mistral emphasizes that the long and lasting impact of a good teacher extends beyond her life.

The lasting legacy lies in the seeds the rural teacher sows in her students passed on to future generations. As Royo (ibid., 75) explains, 'those that she instructed may still come by her tomb and may continue to transmit their education to future generations, as they carry the dust of her remains on the soles of their feet to wherever they go, "¡Y el cuidador de tumbas, como aroma, me cuenta, / las plantas del que huellan, sus huesos, al pasar!"' (*Our translation*: the cemetery's custodian tells me that, as one passes by, the scent from the plants marks the presence of her bones!).

The dust of Gabriela Mistral's remains ought to be carried on the soles of our feet as we gain inspiration from those who, in the words of Cuban educator, Leonela Realy, are hijos or hijas (sons and daughters) of Latin America with its popular, critical education tradition forged in the struggle against colonial remnants and social marginalization.

5

Ada Gobetti: Education for Resistance and Reconstruction

A Partisan

Ada Gobetti (1902–1968) was a partisan, actively engaged in the resistance against Nazi-Fascism. A notable public intellectual and fighter in her own right, she was wife and companion to one of Italy's intellectual prodigies of the period, Piero Gobetti. Both were protagonists in the struggle against fascism. Her thinking on education emerged from her political engagement and experience in the Resistance movement (she formed part of the central committee of the National Resistance Movement). Her ideas were expressed in her work as a journalist who wrote columns in *l'Unità*, the newspaper Antonio Gramsci founded, and *Paese Sera*. They are also found in such outlets as *Educazione Democratica* (Democratic Education) and particularly the review *Giornale dei Genitori* (Parents' Newspaper) which she founded.

Writer, journalist and literary scholar, who published a book on Alexander Pope (Gobetti, 1943), among others, Ada represents a pedagogical voice hardly studied in depth in the Italian cultural firmament, let alone the international critical pedagogical circles to which she ought to belong. A superb communicator, she proved capable of fascinating readers with the harmony of her language and elegant prose which can be simple without being simplistic, devoid of superstructures that can serve to obscure meaning. A graduate of the University of Turin, that same university which Piero Gobetti and Gramsci attended (both Ada and Piero contributed to the *Biennio Rosso* (the Red Years) marked by the workers' occupation of factories), Ada was disposed to profoundly explore issues concerning social justice and human dignity, raising pertinent and often disturbing questions. There is an intimate connection with the words she chooses, in her articles, essays, books and translations.

Of great interest is her correspondence with Piero Gobetti, published by Einaudi in 1991, with the title *Nella tua breve esistenza: Lettere 1918–1926* (In Your Brief

Existence: Letters 1918–1926) (Gobetti and Gobetti, 1991). The volume consists of letters that are quite evocative and at times dense. The dialogue, of epistolary proportions, starts with a letter by Piero, a gentle invitation for her to collaborate with him in the review, *La Rivoluzione Liberale* (The Liberal Revolution). There is much in the voice, tone, dialogue and writing that betrays aspects of the personality of this profound activist and political thinker; she encounters love with a kindred spirit. There are passages marked by torment that emerges from the struggle for intellectual independence, a sign of existential and psychological angst on Ada's part. At the same time, we notice the extent to which she felt the impact of Pietro's charisma; her tremendous admiration for him is there for all to see. This feeling was mutual. They got to know each other in 1918 when she was just 16. Italy then went through a difficult period arising from the end of the First World War. It would generate a general sense of disorientation that would culminate in the fascist seizure of power. In her literature, Ada has the merit of having narrated Italy in a manner that was true to life. She wrote about family relations and the troubles of youth. She wrote about an Italy, eventually riven by fascist violence, that calls for a form of political, cultural and educational resistance. This engagement by Ada is present not only in her collaboration with Piero but also in her journalistic activity, which included articles frequently published as exchanges with readers. While Piero was the recipient of her letters, her articles were targeted at a wider public. This called for a different style. In this day and age, we seem to have lost this distinction between public and private. We use social media with a certain ease and indiscretion, sending out messages and other forms of communication visible to all our contacts. This was not the case two decades ago when communication could be private, reserved for a specific recipient, rather than made public. Ada would not adopt the style of a letter when writing in newspapers where she engaged in correspondence with her readers. Her writing, in this regard, is fluid, direct at times, almost conversational, as though she takes the reader into her confidence. At the same time, it was eloquent, elegant and researched – a pleasure to read. Ever since she was a child, she kept a diary, like other children of the period. This provided her with her first steps into cultural engagement, developing her narrative skills. This style of writing about herself, describing and analysing her vicissitudes, would culminate in her most well-known book, *Diario partigiano* (Partisan's Diary) (Gobetti, 1996, 2014). In a direct manner, reflective and at times bordering on the sentimental, she narrates, in this work highlighted by Benedetto Croce, her experience as an intellectual and active resistance woman. Her life of political and educational engagement comprises writing, thinking and action.

In 1925, the fascist regime would brook no intellectual activity that ran counter to its dictates. Piero fled into exile in Paris. He, however, was soon to suffer a severe beating by fascist thugs. This violence is said to have precipitated his death at a young age (25 years). This naturally caused Ada great grief, an indelible wound. This painful period in her private life was exacerbated by the widespread repression spread by the very same regime that caused her husband's death, a repression marked by an absence of civil, social and intellectual liberties. Ada, however, would not surrender but immersed herself in the struggle for regime change, placing her life on the line as an active partisan.

We Are All Educators

Ada relentlessly pursued the struggle for freedom. Her anti-fascism translated into engagement in clandestine activity against the regime; she risked summary execution, if apprehended. *Diario partigiano* is dedicated 'to my friends, both near and far, to those of twenty years or of only an hour' (Gobetti, 2014, 32); it is a work of solidarity, social justice and a testimony to her battles and ideas concerning education. It is the mark of a fighter with a gentle soul.

Ada Gobetti was not only a public intellectual. She took on the role of an organizer, strategist and director of operations within resistance cells. Even here, thought and action were combined in her political work and ideas on education. She served as a moral and organizational fulcrum for many partisans, particularly those of the Justice and Liberty Brigade, very close to the Action Party.

Her active militancy in the anti-fascist resistance marked not only such aspects of her educational thought as those connected with freedom, democracy and social justice but also aspects of actual educational practice. Educational experiences emerged directly from the social conscience of the labouring classes. There was also the educational dimension of people's self-organization, a recurring feature of working-class projects at the time, as evinced by the writings of Gramsci, among others. This is a feature of what is generally referred to, in this book, as popular education, which, in her writings, also included civic education (Gobetti, 1967).

> The education of children and youth is today uppermost in the minds of the Italian people: at least that part of the Italian population that is conscious of its own responsibility and its duty towards future generations. For some time now, we have been witnessing the formation of a pedagogical conscience not only

among teachers, professors or those who make of teaching their profession. We find this also among the working classes, in popular environments, wherever workers carry out their struggle for democracy, peace and progress. (*Our translation from* SCUOLA ED EDUCAZIONE, in LA VOCE DELLA SCUOLA, 1953, *Our translation from* Gobetti, in Leuzzi, 2015, 7)

The partisan struggle's code name was Ulysses, meant to capture a sense of this Greek mythological figure's proverbial courage and roles as explorer and traveller, immersed in a quest to know the world.

Ada's extraordinary sense of what Freire would call 'epistemological curiosity' made her study and devote attention to history. This engagement led her to defend the rights of women. Ada would have a directive role not only in partisan circles but also at an institutional level when she was chosen as vice-mayor of Turin, soon after the city was liberated from fascism.

Education and Women's Organization

Ever the active champion of women's rights, Ada was invited to participate in a women's organization for resistance in the struggle. Its name would literally be translated from Italian to English as 'Groups Defending Women and of Assistance to those Fighting for Liberty'. She objected to the term 'assistance' and wrote that her preference was for 'Liberty Volunteers'. This objection was predicated on the idea of solidarity rather than assistance (*assistenzialismo*). Her intellectual struggle for women's emancipation and solidarity was ongoing and was a key component of her political engagement. She would write in *l'Unità*, in response to letters concerning working women:

> It is evident, from the letters that arrive daily at the *Giornale dei Genitori*, those who are most disturbed, ill-equipped and uncertain regarding their children's education are precisely those mothers who have renounced everything to dedicate themselves exclusively to the family. And yet, despite having to face sometimes dramatic difficulties, those who have a job are more balanced, less discontented, and do not wish to return to the traditional roles. (*Our translation from* Gobetti, in Leuzzi, 2015,)

It is clear how Ada regarded paid employment as the basis for women's emancipation. She was aware that one cannot do without those who have primary responsibility towards their children, namely, adults. Thus was born *Il Giornale dei genitori*.

She often describes the role of a parent as requiring knowledge. This means that one not only dedicates oneself to the child in an ongoing process but also acquires the competences (the craft knowledge) to do so. Parents need to be ever so culturally prepared to carry out this difficult task. *Il Giornale dei genitori* was intended to help parents overcome the outworn conception of controlling and training the child. It was meant to enable them to allow children to express themselves, to be listened to and to engage in dialogue; it is for this reason that she stressed the importance of parent education.

Quite significant is a story, penned under a pseudonym, titled 'Story of Sebastian the Cock' (Gobetti, 1963). It advocates an education that allows us to be ourselves. The cock Sebastian is the rebel, who wants to be himself, an adventurer with the courage to express his own ideas. The story was illustrated by a refined designer and very able radio engineer, Ettore Marchesini, with whom Ada engaged in marriage, her second marriage, in 1937.

Education for Democracy and the Constitution

Dialogue, consisting of open and reciprocal communication, was considered by Ada as an important pathway to construct a nucleus attentive to the growth of children, allowing space for development and autonomy. It is a relational dialectic in which affections, interests and opinions are shared, one in which these children do not feel lonely and abandoned. It is not only physical absence which generates solitude but especially lack of communication, empathy and expression:

> Generally speaking, there is little talk in our families. Each one is taken up by different commitments, stays as little as possible at home and, when there, does not speak; radio, left indiscriminately open and, at times, television, break the silence. This way one unlearns discussing things, loses the habit of communicating ideas, sharing opinions; we become strangers, distant. And children and adolescents, who will, at all times and different places, feel the need to speak to clarify things, expressing their own consciousness, feel lonely and abandoned. (*Our translation from* NON LASCIAMOLI SOLI [Let's not leave them alone], *Unità*, June 1955. *Our translation from* Gobetti, in Leuzzi, 2015, 80)

Her criticism is levelled not only at parents who are little disposed towards dialogue but also at those people, involved in pedagogical work, she polemically calls 'addetti ai lavori' (insiders in a specific field) who fail to understand that the new pathway for a free society needs to be built on a schooling system that helps realize the basic tenets of the Constitution. To this end, the teaching of history is key for new generations to be able to read the present critically and in a profound manner. Of great contemporary relevance is the health crisis we are going through. This renders imperative the need for health education. Ada wrote about this in 1959, though it seems as if she were writing now:

> Parents' reluctance to admit that their children have certain health issues, especially when it comes to contagious diseases, is a sad sign of ignorance and lack of civic awareness: this evidently arises from an instinctive reluctance to embrace laws and regulations from above … at the basis of all this, there is evidently a conception of sickness as something for which they are to be blamed or made to feel ashamed which brings about diffidence not only towards laws but also towards science. (*Our translation from* Malattie e pregiudizi [Sickness and Prejudices], in l'*Unità*, 5 February 1959. *Our translation from* Gobetti, in Leuzzi, 2015, 100–1)

This prescient and extraordinary insight, provided more than sixty years ago, finds its echoes today when public health has suddenly become the key concern of our life, with the onset of Covid-19. This should always have been the case but it had to take a pandemic of this magnitude to drive the point home to us. Ada's relevance lies not only in this aspect of public education but also with regard to education through play, a very relevant topic in these times dominated by technology. Even then, in the 1950s and early 1960s, Ada was worried that television would deny children opportunities for natural and spontaneous play, so important for social and cognitive development.

This is what she had to say on the matter:

> The child also plays with different material, of all types. The child utilises, demolishes, transforms, puts together … they are indispensable for those spontaneous types of play in which the child freely expresses her or his own tendencies and freedom. (*Our translation* from Gobetti, in Leuzzi, 2015, 81)

She goes on to add:

> Children of thirty or fifty years ago used to read more not only because they had few other sources of distraction but also because the book and the newspaper represented, for them, the only means of being in contact with civilisation and the culture of the world in which they lived: they find this contact and awareness much more easily, through cinema, radio, television. To deny the cultural and educational possibilities of these technical means is as absurd as to deny the

advantages derived from motorised travel on the grounds that exaggerating its use would result in one's unlearning how to walk. (*Our translation from* Gobetti, 1958, 171)

The contemporary relevance of Ada Gobetti is remarkable. Quite striking is her ability to understand aspects of childhood, adolescence, parenthood and politics – so very pertinent today. One can engage in dialogue with her on the basis of the insights derived from reading her works. We allow the final word to her, a woman immersed in her time with her sights firmly set on what constitutes our contemporary world and what lies beyond, a future we might imagine or anticipate but for which we cannot legislate. This is a sort of ode to a life full of love expressed with intense lyricism:

> I wished many well in more or less an intense manner. This does not mean that I indiscriminately wished everyone well. I hated fascists and, although humanly speaking, I comprehended and had compassion for the individuals, I had no hesitation in struggling against them. I hate all forms of neutrality. I would love to continue to live because life is beautiful despite everything and, though I suffered a lot, I was also very happy. I believe I should thank all those who wished me well. To these I say remember me not by providing commemorative talks but by continuing the work I started. Echoing Dante 'I recommend to you the journal in which I live' [play on Dante's '*Sieti raccomandato il mio Tesoro*']. I know that this quote sounds ridiculous. I did this on purpose to make you laugh because it is with laughter, a bit tender, somewhat ironic, that I take my leave. (*Our translation from* Ada Marchesini Gobetti: l'abitudine all'azione. Video documentary by Paolo Mieli for Rai Storia)[1]

This is a fitting concluding comment by an activist, committed (to social justice) public intellectual and critical educator who deserves all the recognition she can get not only in her own country but throughout the world. Here is a woman who embodied praxis, put her life on the line when called on to do so and dedicated a significant part of her time to thinking critically about education. She regarded education as an essential ingredient for that sense of genuine democracy which she cherished and for which she fought.

6

Lorenzo Milani and the Schools of San Donato and Sant'Andrea a Barbiana

This chapter[1] provides a critical exposition and analysis of the work of an acclaimed Italian educator, Lorenzo Milani, and ideas that emerged from his experiences in two Tuscan localities. His work is well known in Italy and many parts of Southern Europe. Despite the translations of his works into English and Spanish, in the early 1970s, and their use in sociology of education classes in the UK,[2] he seems to have had a very limited impact on the Anglo-North American dominated critical education field. The chapter revisits his ideas, indicating their contemporary relevance and the signposts they provide for a critically and sociologically engaged pedagogy.

It can be argued that there are figures from various parts of the world who can be looked up to as paragons in the field of critical education. Writing about critical pedagogy, but this can apply to a social-justice-oriented critical education in general, Henry Giroux writes that '[critical] education is fundamental to democracy and that no democratic society can survive without a formative culture shaped by pedagogical practices capable of creating the conditions for producing citizens who are critical, self-reflective, knowledgeable, and willing to make moral judgments and act in a socially responsible way' (Giroux, 2011, 3). Lorenzo Milani, an educator, writer and priest from Tuscany, is one of Italy's most heralded critical educators. His writings and teachings would be worth revisiting in search of signposts for a critical education.

Some of Lorenzo Milani's writings and others with which he is strongly associated, such as the *Letter to a Teacher* (henceforth *Lettera*), have been translated into and published in English. Despite this, Milani has been given scant attention in the English-speaking world, except for an Open University (UK) course in Sociology of Education, 'Schooling and Society' (E 202) that started in 1974 and foregrounded the *Lettera*. This chapter will highlight some of the main features of Milani's critical approach to education, starting off with a biographical introduction.

Biographical Introduction: Lorenzo Milani (1923–1967)

Lorenzo Milani[3] hailed from Tuscany and was born into a very privileged family in Florence. Milani's father was a university professor, his grandfather an acclaimed archaeologist and his great-grandfather an internationally renowned philologist. Milani's parents were atheist. The parents went through the motions of conveniently marrying in the Catholic Church – they were Jews and feared fascist persecution. Milani had his mortifying moments such as when, at the time when he was an art student, he was pulled up by a woman for eating white bread in an alley inhabited by poor people or when, still at school, he would ask the family chauffer to drop him off at some distance from the institution, so that his school mates would not see him being afforded such treatment (Fallaci, 1993, 13, 14). Milani defied his family by joining an art academy instead of the 'taken for granted' university. Nevertheless, his family background gave him the confidence to speak his own mind. It was probably through painting that he drew closer to the Catholic faith. He eventually decided to receive holy confirmation and, years later, joined the seminary, being ordained priest in 1947. Milani's solidarity with the oppressed was strengthened by his reading of the Gospels. After a short spell at Montespertoli, he was sent to the mainly working-class- and peasant-inhabited San Donato di Calenzano where he led an evening 'popular school' for adults, which, he insisted, had to be devoid of all religious symbols to attract people of different political persuasions (Simeone, 1996, 99). Milani regarded conversion as an act of grace and not something that can be taught (ibid.). His classes dealt with a range of subjects many of which concerned class politics and oppression. Invited speakers were challenged by the course participants who were encouraged to prepare the topic beforehand. This and his own unorthodox approach to religion and pastoral work proved too much for influential figures in the San Donato community and sections of the clergy. He was 'exiled' to an obscure locality, Sant'Andrea a Barbiana, a fate he accepted as part of God's 'grand design' (Milani, 2011). Barbiana lacked basic infrastructural amenities; the only road, leading to the settlement of a few households, ended a kilometre away. There Milani developed his best-known educational project, a full-time school for 'drop outs' (read: *respinti*, pushed out) from the public school system and developed an alternative radical pedagogy.

He also wrote his controversial *Esperienze Pastorali* (Pastoral Experiences), which created a furore in Catholic circles and was removed from the bookstores at the behest of those high up in the church hierarchy. Milani also co-wrote, with his students, a series of letters including the *Lettera* and the letters in defence of the right to conscientious objection to military conscription (Milani, 1991). He was struck by Hodgkin disease and died at the age of 44.

'68 and All That!

The *Lettera*, written in reaction to two Barbiana students being denied access to a teacher preparation school (Gesualdi, 2007, 7), had some influence on the '68 movements in Italy. The iconic Italian intellectual Pier Paolo Pasolini called it a ' "wind of vitality", a book that provokes laughter following which tears come to one's eyes. ... The specific subject matter of *Lettera a una Professoressa* is the school but, in reality, it [the book] is about Italian society, present Italian life.'[4] The book served as a kind of 'manifesto' in the struggle for reform of the Italian educational system. Milani's influence was great among those who opted for a conscientious objection to military conscription. The works invited comparison with Paulo Freire's (see Mayo, 2007a). What seems plausible is that both Milani and exponents of strands of critical education drew from the critique of bourgeois institutions that emerged from France. It is well known that Milani was *au courant* with French literature on which certain critical educators drew.

Radical Christianity

Like Freire, Milani's pedagogy is Christian-inspired. As for Freire, one can safely say that two strands characterize his work, namely, Christianity and Marxism, which is typical of his Latin American context and Liberation Theology. Milani's main underlying sources are the Gospels. While Gramsci's works were read at the school (see Borg and Mayo, 2007, 115), there is no evidence of Marxist thinking as an important underlying source. Milani's attitude towards socialism was ambivalent. He criticised the Italian Communist Party (PCI) and the Catholic Church for vying with each other and, consequently, selling young working-class people short in the various Italian localities with which he was familiar. In his view, they placed more emphasis on entertainment, such as carnival balls

(Milani, [1997] 2004), than on education, with a view to swelling membership in the PCI's case or winning over souls in the Church's case.

Milani had no problems with socialism as an ideology, despite his occasional reference to the excesses of 'actually existing socialism'. In fact, Milani is on record as having said that democracy and socialism are the noblest political systems granted to humanity (Milani, 1988a, 25). He considered socialism 'the highest attempt of humankind to give, already on this earth, justice and equality to the poor' (ibid., 26). In the *Lettera*, Milani and his pupils express an almost cynical attitude towards parties in Italy. They do not differentiate between the dominant parties in Italian political life (the 'graduates' political parties), which allow representatives of the dominant social classes to legislate on behalf of the poor. 'But we have to get into Parliament. The whites will never pass the laws that the blacks need' (Borg, Cardona and Caruana, 2009, 107). The inference here is that even those parties that ostensibly represent the interests of the working class and the socialist and communist parties were the preserve of the dominant classes. The authors also state that working-class and peasant-class people, who made it through the formal education system, against the odds, and entered parliament, were often 'embourgeoised' in the process. In the words of Edoardo Martinelli, one of the eight authors of the *Lettera*, Milani's dreamt not of the 'liberation' of people from farming but of a liberated farmer content with living a sober life (Martinelli, in Borg and Mayo, 2007, 113). The focus here is on helping to raise the collective political and cultural level of a class rather than on individual 'upward social mobility' that would not end the exploitative relationship itself.

Gender and Ethnic Difference

It would appear that the kind of critical education promoted at Barbiana was predominantly male-oriented, even though women were also involved in the text's preparation (Gesualdi, 2007, 10). The imagined target of the critique is a woman teacher (see Galea, 2011). It was originally meant as a protest letter addressed to the very same woman teacher who had denied the two Barbiana students entry to the magisterial school (a teacher education institution). Lorenzo also spoke, albeit in a strong moralizing tone, about the dignity of women within what he denounced as a society gripped by the consumer culture ideology. One must also recognize his efforts to persuade parents from the region to send their daughters to the school at Barbiana. These efforts were frustrated as a result of the mentality that prevailed in the contexts where Milani worked. There was also fear of the dangers lurking in the areas around the road leading to Barbiana (recall the situation in rural areas of Chile in Gabriela Mistral's time). These are the sort of dangers that, the authors of the *Lettera* insisted, would have scared off those very same teachers from the public-schooling system who had flunked them.

> Not even one girl came from the town. Maybe it was because the road was hard. Maybe it's the mentality of the parents. They think a woman can live her life even if she has a chicken's brain. Males do not ask them to be intelligent. (Borg, Cardona and Caruana, 2009, 39)

Yet, we come across illustrations indicating that girls attended this school (Milani, [1997] 2004, 74–6), albeit a minority; they were probably from the same village and not from the town. They appear in illustrations such as that capturing an open-air geography lesson. This lesson involves help with reading provided by some of the youths of San Donato, thus indicating that links between the two schools, those of Barbiana and Calenzano, remained strong. We are also shown a rather sex-stereotypical lesson on 'cutting and sewing' (an 'all girls' class).

Overall, however, the attempt was to develop a school enriched by different identities. Italian society was at the time hardly the multi-ethnic society it is today. And yet this writing and other episodes from Milani's life seem to suggest a strong awareness of social differentiation within the power structure:

> Because there is nothing as unjust as trying to create equality among those who are not equal. (Borg, Cardona and Caruana, 2009, 155)

Lorenzo Milani's sense of human solidarity extended beyond national, class, gender and ethnic boundaries. The notion of 'patria' is given short shrift in his and the students' writings. It is also the object of repudiation with respect to its invocation, throughout history, which provided the licence for predatory incursions on defenceless foreign territories. Students were sent to different territories abroad where they would mix with people of different ethnicities, something unlikely to have happened in and around Barbiana or Italy at that time.

Metaphors chosen to describe the discriminatory nature of the power structure in Italian society suggest parallels with undemocratic race relations in the United States. The reference to Afro-American struggles, and to Stokely Carmichael, from the Civil Rights and Black Power movements, also indicates that the range of solidarity among oppressed groups included solidarity with ethnically subaltern groups. An Albert Schweitzer collaborator, who visited the school, was pulled up for her patronizing European 'missionary' treatment and representation of Africans (Martinelli, in Borg and Mayo, 2007, 114).

Blood, Sweat and Tears

One also notes the regime of austerity and discipline imposed by Milani at his school. This reflects the austerity of Milani's life as a cleric and his seminary preparation in Florence. The approach would certainly not go down well with those accustomed to modern-day theories regarding the role of play in human learning and development. As with Gramsci, this austerity is based on the notion that working-class students need to work hard, shedding 'blood, sweat and tears', to acquire that which comes almost naturally to middle-class children (the 'figli di papà', daddy's children), through their cultural capital and habitus. These privileged children consider such institutions as the universities and parliament, each sustained through public funds via direct and indirect taxation of workers and peasants, as their natural preserve. This explains Milani's emphasis on rigour and on alternative ways of educating pupils which makes them experience a sense of ownership of the learning programme and see learning as preferable to working long hours in the labour-intensive fields.

Milani was to write, with regard to the school schedule, that city people are amazed at the amount of time involved – twelve hours a day, 365 days a year. Before Milani arrived at Barbiana, the children observed the same tiring schedule to provide city people with wool and cheese (Milani, 1988b, 54). Any watering down of curricula for underprivileged groups is likely to keep them immersed in their position of social subordination. If anything, they require even more rigour to make up for the fact that the ruling classes obtain this knowledge and pass it on to their offspring not only through schools but also through their cultural milieu. Working-class children and members of other subaltern groups, such as certain ethnic minorities, do not enjoy this privilege and require more time to master this knowledge.

Education, Politics, 'Class Suicide' and Social Justice

Critical educators have helped educators develop sensitivity to the politics of knowledge (Freire, 1985, 80). Echoing Freire, they insist that education is not neutral and involves educating for either domestication or liberation, being either on the side of the privileged or the oppressed. In his 'Letter to the Military Chaplains', Milani forcefully reveals his option:

> If you persist in claiming the right to divide the world into Italians and foreigners, then I must say to you that, in your view of things, I have no Fatherland. I would then want the right to divide the world into disinherited and oppressed on one side, and privileged and oppressors on the other. One group is my Fatherland; to me the others are foreigners. (Milani, 1988a, 19)

He believed in a committed educator, one who takes sides: 'Better a fascist than indifferent!' (Martinelli, in Borg and Mayo, 2007, 113). Echoing Amilcar Cabral, Freire argued that revolutionary activists, and therefore revolutionary educators, need to commit 'class suicide'. They must unlearn and renounce their privilege to work on the side of the oppressed. Don Lorenzo Milani came close to the idea of a person committing class suicide. He renounced his own privileges being careful not to live above the level of his impoverished parishioners. He denounced his own education which reflected his country's imperialistic ambitions: 'I jumped with joy for the Empire!' He denounced the element of deceit as information was withheld from their young impressionable minds. They (the pupils) were not informed that poisonous gas was used against a defenceless people in Ethiopia who, with hindsight, appeared to Milani to claim the moral high ground since they had done nothing to the Italians. In short, he denounced the school for its imperialist propaganda, predicated on lies and misinformation, and which prepared them as pupils and young citizens for the horrors that were to transpire during the Nazi-Fascist period (Milani, 1988b, 65).

Milani went a step further and held the social class to which he belonged responsible for the horrors of the imperialist wars (ibid., 62). Despite being a Jew, which rendered him and the rest of his family liable to persecution by the fascist state, he was also a member of that same bourgeoisie that was responsible for the terrible turn of events in Italian politics. The commonly held view is that this class acted this way to safeguard its privileges. This no doubt was to have, in his mind and that of others, lasting effects. The letters to the military chaplains and the judges have pedagogical implications for the way we read and teach European history. It is the sort of reading history against the grain intended to dispel myths and undermine the degree of sanitization and 'white washing', for instance, concerning the *Risorgimento* (see Aprile, 2010), which has extended beyond Italian shores. The Barbiana focus was on the search for a 'just war that does not exist'. This general reading of history is intertwined with Milani's reading of the history of the social class to which he belonged. The relevant comments express his revulsion at the lengths to which this class would go to defend its privileges.

In his later years as a priest, when visibly conscious of the fact that resources were limited and wary of the emerging consumerism at the time, Milani chose a life of sobriety, austerity and poverty, a practical renunciation of the life to which he was born and in which he was bred: 'He did not live his sober life as a form of penance, abstinence or simply Christian living but as a way of embracing the values and pleasures that can be satisfied and learnt only through poverty' (Martinelli, in Borg and Mayo, 2007, 112). And yet the earlier reference to the 'graduates' political parties' would once again suggest that Milani and the Barbiana students would recognize the limits of 'class suicide'. They seem to doubt whether people from wealthy families can, despite their allegiances and ethical commitment to the subaltern classes, break away from their 'habitus'. Like most critical pedagogues, however, Milani must have seen traditional educational institutions as bourgeois institutions and conventional teaching, marked by 'banking education', as serving to support the status quo through 'cultural invasion' and the 'cultural arbitrary' (Bourdieu and Passeron, 1990, 31) of the dominant social sectors.

Repetition and ultimately exclusion was the case with the compulsory schooling of students from subaltern social strata in Italy during Milani's time. The *Lettera* is written from Gianni's standpoint and in a tone of anger that results from the recognition of the school's 'symbolic violence' to reproduce class hierarchies. And yet, the *Lettera* shows that anger on its own does not lead to transformation. It can result in spontaneous outbursts and resistance (e.g. Willis's 'lads') which lead nowhere. It requires careful guidance and collective channelling into what, for want of a better expression, can be called productive action.

The Barbiana school did not fail students (Scuola di Barbiana, 1996, 80), failure having been identified by the *Lettera*'s authors as the school authorities' weapon to separate the Giannis from the Pierinos. The authors regarded this as anti-constitutional (ibid., 61). Everyone was entitled, according to the Italian Constitution, to several years of education that were not to be spent repeating the same class. Repetition and ultimately exclusion was the case with the compulsory schooling of students from subaltern social strata. What is ostensibly a 'fair' public education system, intended to provide opportunities for all citizens, according to the terms of the Italian Constitution, is in effect a subtle way of reproducing the class system on the basis of a contestable notion of 'meritocracy' (Borg, Cardona and Caruana, 2009, 82).

This book was therefore written as a clarion call for parents to organize themselves in a process of participatory citizenship intended to democratize public institutions such as schools.

> Disarmed. The poorer parents do nothing. They do not even imagine that these things happen. On the contrary, they feel moved. (Ibid., 55)

These schools are funded by the product of their own labours through taxes that many of them cannot evade, including such unfair consumption taxes as those imposed on basic necessities such as salt. What renders their situation ludicrous is the fact that they pay for the salaries of teachers (Scuola di Barbiana, 1996, 68) who, instead of educating their children, act as judges who flunk them and push them out of the system.

> The Tax System. The curious thing is that the stipend used to throw us out is paid by us, the excluded ones. (Borg, Cardona and Caruana, 2009, 86)

In contrast to Gianni, we find Pierino, the doctor's son (ibid., 51), who enters school with a significant head start, who finds the scholastic experience a natural extension to the home culture, who moves easily through the various grades and who 'found himself in the quinta class at nine years of age' (ibid., 69). Unlike Gianni, whose father 'went to work at a blacksmith when he was 12 years old' (ibid., 80), Pierino can afford to have less formal schooling since he can avail himself of the materially rewarding 'cultural capital' derived from home (ibid., 48).

For this reason, Milani helped develop a full-time school at Barbiana, including weekends. Like Bourdieu and Passeron (1990), the *Lettera*'s authors state:

> You say that Pierino, son of the doctor, writes correctly. Of course you say so, he speaks just like you do. He is part of the firm. (Borg, Cardona and Caruana, 2009, 42)

The text's authors demonstrated the school's social class bias through a national award-winning piece of empirical research (Gesualdi, 2007, 9). They identified, through a survey, the professions of the fathers of those children who grow old in the elementary school. The survey showed that 'by failing the older ones the teachers have also hit the poorest ones' (Borg, Cardona and Caruana, 2009, 71). In a memorable line, the authors compare the public school to a hospital that treats the healthy and rejects the sick (ibid., 43). In doing so, they denounce the teachers for their conditions of work. They allege that teachers work fewer hours than they ought to, and should, as a result, be denied the right to strike, although they suggest other forms of resistance and actions, to support the teachers' claims, that do not harm children, for example, Gandhian-style non-violent resistance.

The authors argue that teachers spend the extra hours giving private tuition to the Pierinos who can pay for such a luxury, widening the gap between the Pierinos and the Giannis.

> In the morning they are paid by us to teach all equally. In the afternoons, they take money from the richer ones in order to teach their young gentlemen differently. In June, at our expense, they preside at the tribunal and they judge the differences. (Ibid., 82)

> The old intermediate school sharpened class distinctions chiefly through its timetable and its terms – short hours of schooling and long holidays. The direct effect of these structures is a school '… cut to measure for the rich'. (Ibid., 20)

Following Milani, the boys advocated the establishment, across Italy, of a provision of after-school education (ibid., 100). For this reason, the School of Barbiana entailed long hours of study throughout the week, including weekends.

The Worlds of 'Having' and 'Being'

The school at Barbiana was a community school intended to belong to the world of 'being' rather than 'having'. There is no method and there are no techniques involved in providing this alternative education. In his controversial *Esperienze Pastorali*, Milani claims that those who enquire about the secret of success at Barbiana ask the wrong question.

> They should be preoccupied with not what one has to do to teach but how one should be in order to teach. (Our translation from Milani, 1996, 80).

Freire spoke about reinventing his political pedagogical approach and not trying to apply it cargo-cult style. Milani was adamant that the Barbiana experience would not be reproduced elsewhere. It was an experience related to place and context. It started at Barbiana and was to end at Barbiana. Milani had a free hand in that he was dealing with pupils already cast out of the system and who saw the time spent there as an alternative to hard messy work in the fields: 'school will always be better than shit' (Borg, Cardona and Caruana, 2009, 36). This is not the situation that obtains in a conventional public school system where teachers are constrained by a curriculum, syllabuses, time restrictions and other situations connected with increasingly corporate time. One has to reinvent the Barbiana approach within the 'limit situations' (Freire, 2018) of the pedagogical setting. Furthermore, the School of Barbiana related education to life, without remaining there. The *Lettera*'s authors argued for an education that had to be culturally relevant rather than alienating (see Martinelli in Borg and Mayo, 2007, 110) We are told, in the *Lettera*, that

> Gianni did not know how to write the 'to have' verb. But he knew many things about the world of adults … During the Gym exams the teacher threw a ball at us and said, 'Play basketball.' We didn't know how. The teacher looked at us with disdain: 'Unfortunate children.' … He told the headmaster that we did not have 'physical education' and he wanted to make us do a re-sit in September. We were all capable of climbing an oak tree. Once we'd be up there we wouldn't hold on and we'd chop down a branch weighing a tonne with an axe. Then we'd drag it on the snow up to the doorstep of our home and put it at mother's feet. (Borg, Cardona and Caruana, 2009, 52)

Foreign-language teaching and acquisition constitutes one example of the manner in which Milani insisted on relating learning to life. He sent his pupils abroad to work in various cities and earn enough for their upkeep while they resided there; he secured funds for the Barbiana students to cover their travel expenses. This was intended for them not simply to cross borders and broaden their horizons but also to learn foreign languages as spoken by the native speakers. In public schools, working- and peasant-class students often failed tests, the contents of which had no bearing on the kind of life lived within and outside their region. The *Lettera* authors say, the French learnt by Pierino, which enabled him to pass the state exam, would not allow him to find the way to the toilet in France (ibid., 45).

The Question of Knowledge

As with Freire, the starting point is always that of human beings 'in the "here and now"' (Freire, 1970a; 1993, 85). Likewise, Milani used events or developments within the community that captured the students' imagination and used them as motivating factors for lessons. They constituted the 'occasional motive'. Martinelli (in Borg and Mayo, 2007) discloses that, when he entered the classroom at

Barbiana, he saw Don Milani and the rest of the class analyse skeletons in what was an anatomy lesson. The immediate motive, the key point of departure for his pedagogical activity, was provided by the fact that the floor of the society, which stood adjacent to the church, caved in. Bones were discovered as a result. The more profound and long-term motive, as he explained in the letter to the Judges, with reference to his pedagogical practice, was to avail himself of this particular event to capture the pupils' interest and thus gradually lead them, once they had become so motivated, to tackle the core areas of the disciplines. A few bones were sufficient to enable one to learn how to use vocabulary and texts dealing with anatomy and physiology (Martinelli, in Borg and Mayo, 2007, 110).

In remaining there and not moving beyond, one would be engaging in 'basismo' (a form of populism), as they would say in Latin America (Freire, 1994). In watering down curricula on the pretext that it renders them closer to life, one is again short-changing students, denying them mastery of certain areas which prove crucial in terms of economic and political success. Young and Muller (2010) argue along similar lines. They critique different forms of progressive discourses on education for providing what can be a watered-down version of education. They advocate a future curriculum scenario (ibid., 16) that is flexible in widening and traversing boundaries. This curriculum, however, also retains some sharp contours around key disciplines (profound motive) recognized as 'powerful knowledge'. Young and Muller argue that 'access to powerful knowledge is a right for all not just the few' (ibid., 24). More specifically, they provide an argument for a future curriculum scenario, called Future 3 (Future 1 is characterized by strong classification, in Bernstein's sense, and bold disciplinary boundaries, while Future 2 is characterized by weaker classification and hybridization). Future 3 is characterized by 'boundary maintenance as prior to boundary crossing' (ibid., 16). This scenario allows for some flexibility in the broadening of and crossing boundaries but retains some fixed ones around key disciplines that constitute 'powerful knowledge'. We would argue that this would be in keeping with the Milani approach. The point to register regarding Milani's approach is that remaining at the level of the 'occasional/immediate motive' (no matter how stimulating and 'true to life' this can be) can lead to superficiality and denial of access to the kind of knowledge that really matters in the real world. One therefore needs to take the major step into venturing towards the 'profound motive'. The 'occasional motive' is just a conduit that gradually takes the learners into the heart of those disciplines containing knowledge that is really useful in the outside world. This is what justifies the effort of attending a school, no matter how unorthodox it is in its over-all approach (e.g. the Barbiana school), rather than simply learning from life itself.

It is the school which educates in the sense suggested by the Barbiana experience. It is intended to take learners to that higher level and not simply confine them to the drift of life. In short, moving from the 'occasional' to the 'profound' motive is the means to 'take … students beyond their experience and enable them to envisage alternatives that have some basis in the real world?' (Young, 2013, 107). Anatomy, physiology, history and writing skills in the native language constituted some of the knowledge regarded as powerful enough in Italian society and beyond to require in-depth mastery at the Barbiana school.

As for language, this acquisition of the knowledge and style involved was to occur alongside the learning of other languages, which perhaps required less rigorous application. 'Better to learn many languages badly than simply one well' – this was Milani's maxim (Fallaci, 1993, 361–2; Batini, Mayo and Surian, 2013, 36) which, of course, is not to be taken literally. He was adamant in advocating the proper learning of one or two languages and acquiring a more rudimentary knowledge of other languages where the focus, in the latter case, is mainly on widespread communication with people from different countries or contexts rather than on idiomatic and grammatical correctness.

Dialogue and Not Mortgaging the Child's Future

The students had to move from that stimulating but still basic level (the occasional motive level) to a non-specialized curriculum, not to mortgage the child's future.

> If he has a passion for a subject one should forbid him to study it. Tell him that he is limiting himself or that he will not be rounded out. There's lots of time later to close oneself in specialisation. (Borg, Cardona and Caruana, 2009, 98)

Like Martin Buber, Paulo Freire and other critical educators, Lorenzo Milani believed in dialogical exchange and the Friday conference at San Donato provided an excellent example. Workers and peasants prepared the material beforehand to avoid being ostensibly 'passive' listeners. They were encouraged to engage the speaker and Milani often pulled up the speaker for a lack of adequate preparation and communication (Milani, 1970, 37). Milani practically formalized the 'students-teachers' role at Barbiana for logistical and pedagogical reasons. He introduced peer tutoring realizing that pupils often learn better from their own peers with whom they share the same social class and broader cultural background, and therefore language.

It has been argued that one enhances one's learning by communicating what is learnt to others. At the Barbiana school, those who did not keep track were helped to learn by their peers who, in turn, enhanced their own understanding of what was learnt through the effort involved in conveying it to others. It confirms an approach advocated and used by many others including Maria Montessori and variations of which can be traced as far back as the 'monitorial system' adopted by John Lancaster in eighteenth-century England. In a school which adopted the motto 'I Care' (Milani, 1988b, 56), the students engaged in a pedagogical experience in which they were both teachers and learners. Milani himself tutored the first group of students. As students increased in number – there were around forty students in one particular summer – he adopted peer tutoring as a key pedagogical tool. This pedagogical approach allows for the emergence of what Lev Vygotsky would call 'zones of proximal development'.

> There was only one copy of each book. The boys used to crowd around it. It was hard to notice that one was a bit older and was teaching. (Borg, Cardona and Caruana, 2009, 36)

Older students could spend a whole morning teaching their younger counterparts.

> The following year I was a teacher. That is, I was a teacher for three half-days a week. I taught Geography, Mathematics and French to the prima media class (Ibid., 37)

This must have served as a tremendous source of motivation for the students, once degraded and therefore demoralized by the public schools, to now be 'elevated' to the status of and esteemed as teachers. It is hardly surprising that they would prefer these experiences to the messy ones encountered in the fields (ibid., 36). Furthermore, it also brings to mind a measure one of us has seen adopted in adult education centres to confront the stigma of literacy classes. In this case, all are learners and teachers at the same time. An authentic dialogical approach necessitates the sharpening of listening and observation skills. In *Esperienze Pastorali* (Milani, 1977), Milani states that he owes everything he knows to the workers and peasants with whom he carried out schooling. He states that it is he who learnt from them that which they believed to have learnt from him and asserts that he only taught them to express themselves while they taught him to live and that it was they who led him to think those thoughts that are expressed in the book (paraphrased from Milani, 1996, 76). Milani also believed in a directive form of education. Allowing his students to indulge in the alternative laissez faire pedagogy would have been a case of utter irresponsibility on Milani's part, given the age of the students at Barbiana and Milani's concern for their future in a society where knowledge is power. Teachers would do well to heed this before lapsing into 'romanticized' versions of 'child-centred' learning.

Autonomy

Milani, however, believed in the older students' autonomy. When he left San Donato and took up residence at Barbiana, the Friday conference continued to be carried out by the youths of San Donato. He assisted them from afar by establishing contact with potential speakers (Milani, 1970, 147–8). The emphasis on exchange of views and learning from each other in the learning settings, which Milani helped create together with community members (at San Donato) and his students (at Barbiana), throws into sharp relief the collective dimensions of knowledge. This approach remains relevant in an age when we are bombarded with such phrases as 'self-directed learning', 'individualized modules' and the ideology of competitive individualism. Not only did pupils 'care' but their caring also took the form of a collective pedagogical experience in which they were both teachers and learners.

Furthermore, the afternoon lesson at Barbiana centred on the facts of the day as reported by the local newspaper. Here the newspaper constituted a very important teaching resource, as at San Donato di Calenzano (Simeone, 1996, 105). This lesson combined knowledge of current affairs with the teaching of such skills as critical literacy. This represents an attempt to read the world through a critical engagement with this world's construction via the media.

> I also knew well the historical period in which I lived. That is the newspaper that, at Barbiana, we read every day, aloud, from top to bottom. (Borg, Cardona and Caruana, 2009, 49)

Current events and controversies were followed carefully, articles were engaged with collectively and their underlying ideological positions were identified and unveiled. This exercise in critical literacy often provoked collective responses by the students under their mentor's guidance (Borg and Mayo, 2006). The same applied to the 'Letter to the Judges' in which Milani constantly refers to discussions with his students on the issues raised, including historical issues (Scuola di Barbiana, 1996, 123). The Barbiana pupils not only read but also wrote the world and did so collectively and critically (Taylor, 1993). In keeping with the 'I Care' motto, the class did not proceed to the next stage in the learning process until each and every pupil mastered the last one. Rather than fail pupils, the school gave priority to the child who fell backward:

> However, whoever lacked the basics, who was slow or unmotivated, felt that he was the favourite one. He was welcomed just as you'd welcome the first in class. It seemed as if the school existed solely for him. Until he understood, the others did not move ahead. (Borg, Cardona and Caruana, 2009, 36).

The authors warned against tracking practices as suggested by a member of the Christian-Democratic party, who, in a speech in parliament, unabashedly argued: 'Why on earth should those who are intellectually gifted and motivated be humiliated in a school where it is necessary to clip their wings, in order to keep them at the flight level of those who by nature must necessarily proceed slowly?' (ibid., 88). Being true to the message of the Gospels, an important source of reading at the Barbiana School, Milani and his students opted for an education in which, once again, one learns not to have but to be and be for others. This attests to Milani's belief in ethics being 'powerful knowledge', as mentioned by Young (2013, 108) who draws on Immanuel Kant's urging of people to 'treat everyone as an end in themselves and not as a means to your ends'. This standpoint adds credibility and forcefulness to the arguments developed throughout the *Lettera*.

Certainly teachers play an important role in providing a social justice education predicated on an option for the poor and less privileged members of society. Teachers are not the only important players here; nevertheless, their role remains crucial. While Freire provides edifying images of teachers, whose conditions he sought to improve when he was Education Secretary in São Paulo, one comes across a different image of teachers in the *Lettera*. These are persons who flunk students, assessing them on skills they did not enable the students to acquire. The authors humorously point to the teacher's inane assertion that writers are born and not made, to which they retort: 'But in the meantime you earn your salary as a teacher of Italian' (Borg, Cardona and Caruana, 2009, 137).

In fact, the students indicate that writing is an art which needs to be learnt. The *Lettera* provides insights into the systematic way through which students engage in collective writing, which drew interest from different parts of the region (Corradi, 2012, 13–16). The students at Barbiana were encouraged to place all their random ideas on sheets of papers from which a systematic ordering and sifting through occurred by means of collective discussion until some key non-repetitive ideas remained. This allowed for a coherent piece of writing. They eliminated superfluous words, redundancies and overly long sentences, and were careful not to have more than one concept in a single sentence (Borg, Cardona and Caruana, 2009, 139).

Lessons from Lorenzo Milani and the San Donato/Barbiana Experiences

The School of Barbiana experience provides an alternative form of schooling from which teachers in the public school system can learn. Much depends on the attitude that the teachers develop, as indicated by Milani when stating that it is more a question of how one must be rather than what one must do. Teachers can provide such an alternative education by

- calling for and engaging in an 'after school' programme which is provided to everyone and not just those who can pay for it;
- encouraging peer tutoring; enabling students to learn collectively and 'to be' for themselves and for others; relating education to life; starting with the 'here and now' and moving beyond to higher-order thinking;
- engaging with learners in a critical reading of the world as manifest in its day-to-day reality but also through its construction via the media;
- *calling for* an inclusive curriculum relevant to the different pupils and a school which does not fail students and push them out but ensures that the constitutional right of everyone to enjoy a number of years of public schooling (that does not involve repetition) is respected and safeguarded.

The fact that some pupils from the Barbiana experience ended up as teachers indicates that they had faith in the emergence of a type of teacher who was different from the one the *Lettera* portrays in a negative light. They had faith in teachers concerned with social justice and whose mission is to improve opportunities and experiences for those who have traditionally suffered in a socially differentiated system. The School of Barbiana sought to inspire this type of teacher. And the verb 'calling for' in the list of qualities just provided indicates that many of the challenges cannot be faced by teachers on their own. As many critical pedagogues would argue, they can only be faced by teachers within a movement or an alliance of movements, involving people from other walks of life, including the parents called upon in the *Lettera* to organize themselves, clamouring for reforms in the state school system. These are the sort of reforms that would help revitalize an important sector of the public sphere.

7

Paulo Freire, Globalization and Emancipatory Education

Introduction

Paulo Reglus Neves Freire (1921–1997) is surely one of the most cited and iconic figures in the contemporary education literature. His work becomes all the more relevant in an age when, in view of the intensification of globalization, and the mobility of capital, education is often equated exclusively with the development of the so-called human resources [sic] (see the critique in Gelpi, 2002). This is a feature of some of the dominant policy documents in education such as the Lisbon objectives with regard to the EU member states, discussed in Chapter 2.

Intensification of Globalization and Neoliberalism

In an interview with Roger Dale and Susan Robertson (2004, 151), the Portuguese sociologist and legal expert Boaventura de Sousa Santos states: 'Neoliberalism is the political form of globalization resulting from US type of capitalism, a type that bases competitiveness on technological innovation coupled with low levels of social protection.' He goes on to state: 'The aggressive imposition of this model by the international financial institutions worldwide not only forces abrupt changes in the role of the state and in the rules of the game between the exploiter and the exploited ... but also changes the rules of the game among the other kinds of developed capitalism' (de Sousa Santos, in ibid.).

We have seen how, since the early 1980s, neoliberalism provided the dominant hegemonic discourse surrounding economic development and public policy (Burbules and Torres, 2000). Recall that it was very much a feature of the Pinochet regime's ideology in Chile,[1] Thatcherism, Reaganomics (Pannu, 1996), the International Monetary Fund's (IMF) and World Bank's structural adjustment programs in much of the industrially underdeveloped world (Boron and Torres,

1996; Mulenga, 1996; Pannu, 1996) and the World Trade Organization's (WTO) polices that would also affect educational 'services' (Rikowski, 2002). It is now also a feature of parties in government that have historically been socialist (see Ledwith, 2005, for a discussion of British labour politics on this). The presence of this ideology on either side of the traditional political spectrum in Western democracies testifies to the *hegemonic* nature of neoliberalism. This point is worth keeping in mind with respect to dominant discourses on education and their social-democratic trappings.

The presence of the neoliberal ideology in education, as well as in other spheres of activity, can easily lead one to think and operate within the logic of capitalist restructuring. As a result of this process, once-public goods (education among them) are converted into consumption goods, as the 'ideology of the marketplace' takes hold. Neoliberal strategists advocate increasing privatization and related cuts in public spending on social programs, leading to the introduction of user charges and cost recovery policies. Popular access to health, education and other social services would therefore be curtailed. Neoliberal policies also lead to public financing of private needs. The onus for social and economic survival is placed on individuals and groups. The debate on rights and responsibilities is rationalized, with 'self-help' being advocated for those who end up as the victims of these policies.[2] These policies also lead to a decline in real incomes. The whole question of 'choice' becomes a farce as people who cannot afford to pay for educational and health services are fobbed off with an underfunded and therefore poor-quality public service in these areas (Mayo, 1999a). Neoliberalism also entails a deregulation of commodity prices and the shift from direct to indirect taxation (Boron and Torres, 1996; McGinn, 1996; Pannu, 1996).

Its orthodoxy also includes, as indicated by Mark Olsson (2004, 241), the opening of borders, floating exchange rates, abolition of capital controls, liberalization of government policy, developing integrated private transnational systems of alliances and establishing, within countries, central banks that 'adopt a market-independent monetary policy that is autonomous of political interference' (ibid.). With respect to the United States, Henry A. Giroux refers to the economist William Greider who argues that neoliberalism proponents 'want to "roll back the twentieth century literally" by establishing the priority of private institutions and market identities, values and relationships as the organizing principles of public life' (Giroux, 2004, 107).

The foregoing exposition is, in the main, a set of features of one particular kind of globalization, often referred to as hegemonic globalization (Dale and

Robertson, 2004, 148). This is not the only kind of globalization in existence. There is also 'counter-hegemonic' globalization (de Sousa Santos, in ibid., 150) or 'globalization from below' (Marshall, 1997). This 'consists of resistance against hegemonic globalization organized (through local/global linkages) by movements, initiatives and NGOs, on behalf of classes, social groups and regions victimized by the unequal exchanges produced on a global scale by neoliberal globalization' (de Sousa Santos, in Dale and Robertson, 2004, 150). They include social movements from the South and North playing a major role in monitoring compliance of governments regarding such targets as, for instance, the UN Millennium Development Goals (MDGs, now replaced by the Sustainable Development Goals, SDGs) and advocating for more and better aid (in the early 1970s, the wealthiest nations had committed themselves to 0.7 per cent of their gross domestic product (GDP) to be reserved for international aid), 'justice in trade' (fair trade) and debt write-off as key to the attainment of the proposed and alternative goals. It also entails different movements, previously identified with a rather fragmentary identity and specific issue politics, coming together 'on a scale previously unknown' (Rikowski, 2002, 16) to target global capitalism and the meetings of the institutions that support it, such as the IMF, World Bank and the WTO, thus invoking 'an anti-capitalism of real substance and significant scale' (ibid.).

The foregoing exposition of the two types of globalization[3] within the context of an all-pervasive neoliberal politics (one cementing and the other confronting neoliberalism) is central to the use of Freire as an antidote to the current dominant discourse in education characterized by the emphasis on technical rationality and marketability and which presents this discourse as having no alternatives.

Freire's Antidote

Freire rejected the view that the conditions of our time determined the limits of what is possible. He recognized developments within capitalism witnessed during his lifetime (the intensification of globalization and neoliberalism), for what they were – manifestations of capitalist reorganization to counter the tendency of the rate of profit to fall, owing to the 'crises of overproduction' (Allman and Wallis, 1995; Foley, 1999). Understanding the contemporary stages of capitalist development according to what they represented was a crucial step for Freire to avoid a sense of fatalism and keep alive the quest for working to attain a better world driven by what Giroux calls an anticipatory utopia prefigured not only by critique of the present but also by an alternative pedagogical/cultural politics (Giroux, 2001). 'The fatalism of neoliberalism, buttressed by the propagation of an "ideology of ideological death"' (Freire, 1998b, 14), was a key theme in Freire's later writings. It was intended to be the subject of the work he was contemplating at the time of his death (Araujo Freire, 1997, 10). Freire could well have been on the verge of embarking on an exploration of the conditions that the present historical conjuncture, characterized by neoliberalism, would allow for the pursuit of his dream of a different and better world. Alas, this was not to be.

Ideology

Freire's respective works are embedded in a Marxian conception of ideology based on the assumption that 'the ruling ideas are nothing more than the ideal expression of the dominant material relationships, the dominant material relationships grasped as ideas; hence of the relationships which make one class the ruling one, therefore the ideas of its dominance' (Marx and Engels, 1970, 64) Not only does the ruling class produce the ruling ideas, in view of its control over the means of intellectual production (ibid.), but the dominated classes produce ideas that do not necessarily serve their interests; these classes, that 'lack the means of mental production and are immersed in production relations which they do not control', tend to 'reproduce ideas' that express the dominant material relationships (Larrain, 1983, 24).

Freire sees popular consciousness as being permeated by ideology. And this is crucial to dismantling or unveiling 'common sense' (used in Gramsci's sense of the term) thinking deriving from neoliberalism. In his earlier work, Freire posited the existence of different levels of consciousness ranging from naïve to critical consciousness, indicating a hierarchy that exposed him to the accusation of being elitist and of being patronizing towards ordinary people (Kane, 2001, 50). In his early work, Freire reveals the power of ideology being reflected in the fatalism (see Rossatto, 2005, on this) apparent in the statements of peasants living in shanty towns who provide 'magical explanations', attributing their poor plight to the 'will of God' (Freire, 2018, 163). Nowadays, this fatalism expresses itself in the cynicism regarding alternatives to anything within the market ideology; this is often referred to as the loss of utopia.

Freire provides a very insightful analysis of the way human beings participate in their own oppression by internalizing the image of their oppressor. As with the complexity of hegemonic arrangements, underlined by Gramsci and elaborated on by a host of others writing from a neo-Gramscian perspective, people suffer a contradictory consciousness, being oppressors within one social hegemonic arrangement and oppressed within another. This puts paid to the now hackneyed criticism that Freire's notion of oppressor and oppressed is so generic that it fails to take into account that one can be an oppressor in one context and oppressed in another. The notion of the oppressor and contradictory consciousness suggests otherwise. This consideration runs throughout Freire's oeuvre ranging from his early discussion on the notion of the 'oppressor consciousness' to his later writings on multiple and layered identities (Freire, 1997) where he insists that one's quest for life and for living critically is tantamount to being an ongoing quest for the attainment of greater *coherence*. Gaining coherence, for Freire, necessitates one's gaining greater awareness of one's 'unfinishedness' (Freire, 1998a, 51, 66) as well as one's ability to see through the ideology that provides a mystification of the existing economic and social conditions. This includes the ideology of neoliberalism.

Emancipatory Resources of Hope

Freire accords an important role to agency in the context of emancipatory activity for social transformation. He explicitly repudiates evolutionary economic determinist theories of social change and regards them as being conducive to a 'liberating fatalism' (Freire, 1985, 179), a position to which he adhered until the very end, stating, at an *honoris causa* speech delivered at Claremont Graduate University in 1989, 'When I think of history I think about possibility – that history is the time and space of possibility. Because of that, I reject a fatalistic or pessimistic understanding of history with a belief that what happens is what should happen' (Freire, in Darder, 2002, x). His notion of history as possibility challenges the so-called end-of-history thesis.

Love

Freire was concerned with more than just the cognitive aspects of learning (ibid., 98). He regards educators and learners as 'integral human beings' (ibid., 94) in an educational process that has love at its core (ibid., 91). Just before he died he was reported to have said: 'I could never think of education without love and that is why I think I am an educator, first of all because I feel love' (in McLaren, 1997, 38).

The humanizing relationship between teacher and taught (teacher-student and student-teacher, in Freire's terms) is a relationship characterized by love. It is love that drives the progressive Freire-inspired educator forward in teaching and working for the dismantling of dehumanizing structures. And the entire process advocated by Freire is predicated on the trust he had in human beings and on his desire to help create 'a world in which it will be easier to love' (Freire, 1970a, 24; see Allman et. al., 1998, 9). This concept has strong Christian overtones as well as revolutionary ones. Freire 'did not hesitate to recognize the capacity of love as an indispensable condition for authentic revolutionaries' (1970b, 45).

Education in Its Broadest Context

The terrain for education action is a large one in Freire's conception. Throughout his writings, Freire constantly stressed that educators engage with the system and not avoid it for fear of co-optation (Horton and Freire, 1990; Escobar et al., 1994). Freire exhorted educators and other cultural workers to 'be tactically inside and strategically outside' the system. Freire believed that the system is not monolithic. Hegemonic arrangements are never complete and allow spaces for 'swimming against the tide' or, to use Gramsci's phrase, engaging in 'a war of position' (Freire, in Escobar et al., 1994, 31, 32). In most of his work from the mid-1980s onward, Freire touches on the role of progressive social movements as important vehicles for social change, movements that can contribute to what is referred to 'globalisation from below'. This particularly applies to social movements having an international character. It also applies to the kind of invigorating social movements that emerged in Latin America (Vittoria, 2016, 46) in the last years of Freire's life – such as the Movimento dos Trabalhadores Rurais Sem Terra (MST) in Brazil, to be discussed in the volume, and the Frente Zapatistas in Chiapas with its 'internet war' (confronting hegemonic globalization, especially NAFTA, and at the same time availing itself of some of its media as a form of 'globalisation from below') – that have strong international support in other parts of the world.

Freire himself belonged to a movement striving for a significant process of change within an important institution in Latin America and beyond, namely, the radical current within the Latin American Catholic Church. As Education Secretary in São Paulo, a position that allowed him to tackle education and cultural work in their broader contexts, Freire and his associates worked hard to bring social movements and state agencies together (O'Cadiz, 1995; O'Cadiz et al., 1998). These efforts on behalf of the Partido dos Trabalhadores (PT) continued to be exerted by the party itself in other municipalities, most notably the city of Porto Alegre, in Rio Grande do Sul, where the PT had been in government in the late 1980s and 1990s, and presumably the other municipalities and states where the party won the elections in the fall of 2000. There were also high hopes that these efforts would be carried out throughout the entire country once the PT leader, Luiz Inacio 'Lula' da Silva, won the federal presidential elections, though perhaps too much was expected of Lula who, in the words of many Brazilian sympathizers, won the government but not the state.

The last years of Freire's life were exciting times for Brazilian society with the emergence of the MST (Tarlau, 2019), a movement that makes global connections with Indigenous movements worldwide. The movement allies political activism and mobilization with important education and cultural work (See ch. 4 in Kane, 2001). The movement is itself conceived of as an 'enormous school' (ibid., 97). As in the period that preceded the infamous 1964 coup, Freire's work and thinking must also have been influenced and reinvigorated by the growing movement for democratization of Brazilian society. In an interview with Carmel Borg and me, Ana Maria (Nita) Araujo Freire states:

> Travelling all over this immense Brazil we saw and cooperated with a very large number of social movements of different sizes and natures, but who had (and continue to have) a point in common: the hope in their people's power of transformation. They are teachers – many of them are 'lay': embroiderers, sisters, workers, fishermen, peasants, etc., scattered all over the country, in favelas, camps or houses, men and women with an incredible leadership strength, bound together in small and local organizations, but with such a latent potential that it filled us, Paulo and me, with hope for better days for our people. Many others participated in a more organized way in the MST (Movimento dos Sem Terra: Movement of Landless Peasants), the trade unions, CUT (Central Única dos Trabalhadores), and CEBs (Christian Base Communities). As the man of hope he always was, Paulo knew he would not remain alone. Millions of persons, excluded from the system, are struggling in this country, as they free themselves from oppression, to also liberate their oppressors. Paulo died a few days after the arrival of the MST March in Brasília. On that April day, standing in our living-room, seeing on the TV the crowds of men, women and children entering the capital in such an orderly and dignified way, full of emotion, he

cried out: 'That's it, Brazilian people, the country belongs to all of us! Let us build together a democratic country, just and happy!'

(Nita Freire, in Borg and Mayo, 2007, 3)

Freire insisted that education should not be romanticized and that teachers ought to engage in a much larger public sphere (Freire, in Shor and Freire, 1987, 37). This has been quite a popular idea among radical activists in recent years, partly also as a result of a dissatisfaction with party politics. The arguments developed in these circles are often based on a very non-Gramscian use of the concept of 'civil society'. In his later work, however, Freire sought to explore the links between movements and the state (Freire, 1993; O'Cadiz et al., 1998) and, most significantly, movements and party, a position no doubt influenced by his role as one of the founding members of the PT.

Freire argues that the party for change, committed to the subaltern, should allow itself to learn from and be transformed through contact with progressive social movements. One important proviso he makes, in this respect, is that the party should do this 'without trying to take them over'. Movements, Freire seems to be saying, cannot be subsumed by parties, otherwise they lose their identity and forfeit their specific way of exerting pressure for change. Freire discusses possible links between party and movements. The question to be raised is: how can such an alliance have a global dimension?

> Today, if the Workers' Party approaches the popular movements from which it was born, without trying to take them over, the party will grow; if it turns away from the popular movements, in my opinion, the party will wear down. Besides, those movements need to make their struggle politically viable. (Freire, in Escobar et al., 1994, 40)

One further question would be, how would the forces of globalization, through such means as Structural Adjustment Programmes, place pressure on a party in government to make it toe the line in terms of paying its debts and cutting down on its social expenses, the kind of expenses to which the PT was committed, before getting into power at the federal level, a position it eventually had to forfeit following the 'Golpe Branco' against Lula's successor, Dilma Roussef? To what extent were the Lula governments and the other newly elected left leaning governments of that same period in Latin America victims of this process?

Freire explores links between the party and movements within the context of a strategy for social change. At the time when he was still alive, the PT enjoyed strong links with the trade union movement, the Pastoral Land Commission, the MST and other movements and exercised a leadership role when forging alliances between party, state and movements in the municipalities in which it was in power. Alas, this no longer seems to be the case. The Participatory Budget project in Porto Alegre, an exercise in deliberative and participatory democracy, provides some indication of the direction such alliances can take (Schugurensky, 2002). Furthermore, this alliance must take on an international character if it is to contribute effectively to globalization from below and the World Social Forum would be a perfect example of this type of effort.

Praxis

The discussion has veered towards a macro-level analysis, as is expected in a discussion on globalization. But the global must interact with the local, which includes the kind of micro-level activity that allows people to unveil ideology in order to gain the type of political awareness necessary to work collectively and internationally for social transformation. It would be opportune therefore to dwell on the micro-level context of education with an emphasis on concepts that lie at the heart of the pedagogical relation as propounded by Freire. He regarded *praxis* as one of the key concepts in question. Praxis becomes a constant feature of his thinking and writing. It constitutes the means whereby one can move in the direction of confronting the contradiction of opposites in the dialectical relation of oppression (Allman, 1988, 1999). It constitutes the means of gaining critical distance from one's world of action to engage in reflection geared towards transformative action. The relationship between action-reflection-transformative action is not sequential but dialectical (Allman, 1999). Freire and other intellectuals, with whom he has conversed, in 'talking books', conceive of different moments in their life as forms of praxis, of gaining critical distance from the context they know to perceive it in a more critical light. Exile is regarded by Freire and the Chilean Antonio Faundez (Freire and Faundez, 1989) as a form of praxis. The idea of critical distancing is, however, best captured by Freire in his pedagogical approach involving the use of codifications, even though one should not make a fetish out of this 'method' (Aronowitz, 1993) since it is basically indicative of something larger, a philosophy of learning in which praxis is a central concept that has to be 'reinvented' time and time again, depending on situation and context.

Authority and Freedom

Freire emphasized the notion of authentic dialogue throughout his work, regarding it as the means of reconciling the dialectic of opposites that characterizes the hierarchical and prescriptive form of communication he calls 'banking education'. Knowledge is not something possessed by the teacher and poured into the learner who would thus be conceived of as an empty receptacle to be filled. This would be a static use of knowledge. Freire insisted on a dynamic process of knowledge acquisition based on epistemological curiosity involving both educator and educatee who regard the object of knowledge as a centre of co-investigation. Both are teachers and learners at the same time since teachers are prepared to relearn that which they think they already know through interaction with the learner who can shed new light on the subject by virtue of insights including those that are conditioned by his or her specific cultural background. The learner has an important contribution to make to the discussion. Having said this, Freire warns against *laissez faire* pedagogy that, in this day and age, would be promoted under the rubric of 'learning facilitation' [*sic*]. This is the sort of pedagogical treachery that provoked a critical response from him. In an exchange with Donaldo P. Macedo, Freire states categorically that he refutes the term 'facilitator' (although he had used it earlier in such pieces as the essay in *Harvard Educational Review* concerning the literacy process in São Tome and Principe), which connotes such a pedagogy, underlining the fact that he has always insisted on the *directive* nature of education (Freire, in Shor and Freire, 1987, 103; Freire and Macedo, 1995, 394). He insists on the term 'teacher', one who derives one's *authority* from one's competence in the matter being taught, without allowing this authority to degenerate into *authoritarianism* (Freire and Macedo, 1995, 378): 'Authority is necessary to the freedom of the students and my own. The teacher is absolutely necessary. What is bad, what is not necessary, is authoritarianism, but not authority' (Freire, in Horton and Freire, 1990, 181; Freire, in Shor and Freire, 1997, 91).

Emphasis is being placed, in this context, on 'authority and freedom', the distinction posed by Freire (see Gadotti, 1996) who argues that a balance ought to be struck between the two elements. In *Pedagogy of Hope*, he argues that the educator's 'directivity' should not interfere with the 'creative, formulative, investigative capacity of the educand'. Otherwise, the directivity degenerates into 'manipulation, into authoritarianism' (Freire, 1994, 79). Referring to this aspect of Freire's work, Stanley Aronowitz is on target when stating that 'the educator's task is to encourage human agency, not mould it in the manner of Pygmalion'

(Aronowitz, 1998, 10) The encouragement of human agency is a key feature of the work of Freire.

Globalization and Planetary Consciousness: Ecopedagogy

Needless to say, Freire has had his critics over the years. Some have argued that his vision is anthropocentric, a fair comment on Freire's work, especially his earlier work, although it has to be said that the institute to which he helped give rise, now the Paulo Freire Institute, is working hard within the context of the Earth Charter in the area of ecopedagogy (Gutierrez and Prado, 2000; Gadotti, 2005). The issue of ecopedagogy (see Misiaszek, 2021) is central to an emancipatory process in this age of the intensification of globalization that is said to have a devastating impact on the planet, since the quest for manipulation and control of nature, as we have seen in this book, continues to have a global reach in these 'cenozoic', as opposed to 'ecozoic', times (see O'Sullivan, 1999). Freire has also been the target of criticisms by feminists concerning what bell hooks regards as his 'phallocentric paradigm of liberation' (hooks, 1993, 148), although hooks would always affirm the validity of Freire's work in a process of liberation, and she draws extensively from his work (hooks, 1989). Quite relevant here is Freire's work concerning multiple and contradictory subjectivities (Freire, 1997). Feminist literature is quite instructive in its exaltation of life-centred values as opposed to market-driven values, the former being the kind of values, espoused also by environmentally conscious activists, which enable people to confront the forces of hegemonic globalization with their 'ideology of the marketplace'. There are others who find contradictions in Freire's pedagogical approach (Coben, 1998). Of course, unless the educators are well prepared, there is always the danger of having a travesty of Freirean pedagogy (see Bartlett, 2005, for a discussion on the limits and possibilities of Freirean pedagogy; see also Stromquist, 1997).

Globalization and Migration

Despite these criticisms, Paulo Freire stands out as one of the towering figures of twentieth-century educational thought. The above elements such as authentic dialogue, the unveiling of ideology, love for other human beings (and other species in the universe) and, we would add, a concept of knowledge that crosses borders (this involves one's striving to transcend mental borders) become crucial for an emancipatory education in an age characterized by the intensification of globalization. In the IVth Paulo Freire Forum in Porto, Portugal, one of us referred to these concepts within an attempt to suggest signposts for a critical and emancipatory multi-citizenship education (Mayo, 2005). After all, such an education becomes all-important in the context of one important feature of the intensification of globalization – the migration of 'Southern' populations, victims of a rapacious Eurocentric colonial process, to the 'North'. One of us focused on the Mediterranean in this context. In this and earlier work (Mayo, 2004a, ch. 5), possibilities for the reinvention of Paulo Freire's ideas in this regard were explored. We both focus on the notions of love for all human beings, authentic dialogue in understanding the cultures of those constructed as 'other' (which includes respect for their religious sentiments and the recognition of their ancestral contribution to the development of so called Western civilization) and the use of praxis (that entails recourse to political economy) to reflect on the global colonial process that has led to the plight of people abandoning their ravaged country of origin to settle within southern European shores. This process of praxis would hopefully lead to greater solidarity between people from both sides of the equator who have been relegated to a precarious existence as a result of increasing neoliberal policies. These, we argue, should constitute important features of a critical multi-ethnic and anti-racist education in these intensified globalized times. It is an education which projects the image of the immigrant as 'subject' and not 'object', a full-blooded citizen with multiple and enriching subjectivities and not a deficit figure ripe for Eurocentric missionary and 'assistencialismo' intervention. We return to this theme in forthcoming chapters.

Conclusion: Reinventing Freire

Freire has provided us with a huge corpus of literature containing ideas that can inspire people committed to the fostering of greater social justice in an age when concerns with social justice are placed on the backburner or eschewed altogether as education, like health and other important elements, is constantly turned from a public to a consumption good (from a social to an individual concern). It is now left to others to make creative use of his theoretical and biographical legacy with a view to making sense of the 'glocal' contexts in which they operate. And, as Freire has said, time and time again, they should do this through a process of reinvention and not transplantation.

Part Three

Education and Migration

8

Towards an Anti-Racist Education and Human Solidarity in the Mediterranean and in the Context of Migrations

Like all regions of the world, the Mediterranean is in the grip of globalization, a process strictly connected with capitalism and characterized by a continual economic reorganization and the constant search for new markets. It makes more sense, in this particular historical conjuncture, to use the phrase 'intensification of globalization' given that capitalism has always been global and globalizing. We live in a period marked by mobility at different levels at a time of increasing delocalization of production and the intense movement of capital. We are witness to a constant process of worker mobility or dislocation across and beyond the Mediterranean. People from the 'South' move towards the 'North' in search of new work and life opportunities. Migration constitutes an important and dramatic feature of life in and around the Mediterranean.

Alas, we find ourselves in the midst of a continuous tragedy with regard to migration from the 'Northern' shores of Africa towards Europe: figures released by the International Organisation of Migration (IOM) beggar belief. For instance, 2015 was marked by 3,771 deaths and people dispersed throughout the Mediterranean, and 2014 registered 3,279 deaths. Arrivals by sea around 2017 were 996,645. This tragedy is exacerbated by an entire human waste disposal industry, to echo Zygmunt Bauman, an underworld undertaking reaching murky depths, involving speculation and a lucrative venture that marks the worst forms of human depravity in which people's belongings and dignity, as well as well-being, are sacrificed on the altar of greed and corruption, where syndicates of those trafficking in human misery hardly give a toss for the sanctity of human life. What ought to have been a system of inter-ethnic and human solidarity has degenerated into a dispositif, or more aptly, dunghill of corruption, double-crossing and modern slavery.

How do we therefore analyse the phenomenon of migration? As was declared in the 1997 Civil Forum Euro-Med:

> Immigration represents the emerging aspect, probably the most evident, of the wide process which characterizes more and more the whole planet – globalization. Migrations represent more than a phenomenon, a historical certainty that can be found today, though with different features, in all countries and, in particular, in the most developed [*sic.* read: industrially developed]. Migration phenomena are becoming more and more important within the Mediterranean basin. (Fondazione Laboratorio Mediterraneo, 1997, 551)

In this document, migration is deeply connected to globalization and to a structural change as far as movements across the planet are concerned, also following the routes carved by capital flows. Though a historical certainty of our age, migration, paradoxically, helps generate social uncertainty and therefore a source of anxiety, given that the necessity to sever oneself from one's roots is, more often than not, the result of poverty, misery, violent civil wars, wars with neighbours that are likely to escalate as resources shrink through climate change, unliveable conditions caused by the same climate change and unemployment, the last mentioned the staple of countries in the 'South'. The scourges of xenophobia and racism that are ever on the increase in Europe and elsewhere are major obstacles to confront in the areas of culture (as a way of life), politics and education. Countries in Europe's 'southern region' are engulfed in a massive process of immigration flows involving not only people from North Africa but also people from sub-Saharan Africa. They leave behind them countries ravaged by internal strife, inter-ethnic wars and lack of work opportunities.

They struggle across the Sahara and other hazardous areas to reach the coasts of North Africa where they face the terrors of a destabilized Libya and, if they emerge unscathed from there, face the equal terror of having to cross a sea the likes of which they had never encountered in their landlocked place of origin. Some say they would rather take a chance there than continue to live in what they perceive as the 'hell on wheels' that is Libya where they can be subject to all kinds of oppressions including forms of slavery. They are often placed on rickety boats, surpassing normal capacity limits with hardly any space between them than in a handful of playing cards. Suffocation and dehydration, and the prospect of the boat capsizing, are constant dangers. With a good dose of fortune, some manage to reach Malta, Lampedusa, the rest of Italy, Greece and Spain, aspiring to obtain a better life.

This situation gives the Mediterranean the appearance of a 'Rio Grande' (Malabotta, 2002, 73). The spectre of the violent process of colonization reappears to haunt Europe (Borg and Mayo, 2007, 179). Europe's former empire is striking back in a manner different from that intended by Stuart Hall (2017) when using this phrase (he uses the phrase with regard to the Task Force in the Falklands/Malvinas War in 1982). All this is facilitated by the economic concerns of industrialized countries who require a certain amount of labourers for certain undertakings. These cannot be catered for by members of the local labour market and at a 'cost-effective' price, despite the high levels of unemployment among them (Apitzsch, 1995, 68).

There has been a change of experience in this region. Many of its countries have moved from a situation of mass emigration to one of massive immigration; they moved from being *exporters* to *importers* of labour power.

Architectural images and demographic make-ups of 'North' Mediterranean cities have undergone significant changes. We have been witnessing a transmutation of Mediterranean cities. While the population becomes cosmopolitan, the architecture is a melange that allows the old to coexist with the new. The global interacts with the local in a state of hybridization. One can imagine a scene in which Giotto's Campanile shares its space with Macdonald's 'Twin Golden Arches' with a minaret in the background. In a number of 'southern' cities in Europe, the cupolas which represent historical bulwarks of Christianity against Islam now coexist with the latter's buildings. They did coexist previously but in a different manner. Several minarets of the past served as bell towers, as was the case in Spain after the so-called *reconquista*. One can point to the Giralda in Seville, a similar situation in Valencia or a mosque transformed into a Catholic Cathedral in Córdoba – la Mezquita. Of course, you encounter the obverse in places such as Turkey, more so now that the Hagia Sophia has been turned once again from a museum into a place of Muslim worship, and that part of Nicosia currently under Turkish control – Selimiye Mosque, Nicosia.

This coexistence of symbols from different monotheistic religions, the cause of much conflict in the past, a coexistence you would easily associate with Palestine, is becoming an important feature of the skyline of an increasing number of cities in 'Southern' Europe. Wary of romanticizing this scenario, we need to remark that tensions and conflicts have been re-emerging. The case of Christchurch in New Zealand, quite recently, is a stark reminder that these tensions continue to simmer beneath the surface of multiculturalism. Cases of xenophobia and, more precisely, Islamophobia, are very much in evidence. The roots of this form of racism can be found, among others, in the anti-Islamic crusades which have left their indelible mark in the region, in its political conjuncture and its cultural contradictions. Cultures that, for centuries, were marked by deep-seated antagonistic dispositions towards each other now have to coexist in the same mixed geographical space. This space is seriously threatened by a conflict between fundamentalist religious interpretations of different stripe. Much has been made of the so-called clash of civilizations, as proposed by Samuel Huntington, without little cognizance of the historical fact that they contributed so much to each other, as Edward Said explained in his critique of this thesis. Arabs, Islam and Persians, for example, contributed so much to science, art, mathematics, universities and legal systems in the so-called West, to mention a few areas. There are fundamentalisms on different sides though we tend to associate this term only with one sector. The main constructed dichotomous confrontation is that between one belief system and the West, the latter often taking the form of the defence of the Occident, never mind the hybrid nature of many different cultures. Post 2002, in several countries of 'Southern' Europe, the dichotomy also takes on the issue of colour. There have been cases of blatant racism against not just Arabs and Muslims but also the African *tout court*. In short, there have been signs of 'white supremacy' on the part of Europeans from this region whose posture as 'white' is even questionable. Not that this should matter as defending 'white supremacy' is, in our book, a despicable act, creating this artificial distinction between 'higher' and 'lesser' beings. While the United States has been, since slavery, in the grip of white supremacist wanton killings (lynching, police beatings, etc., with laws and institutions to prevent Blacks from gaining political power), we come across cases of wanton killings even in 'Southern' Europe.

In April 2019, Malta registered a case of wanton killing of an African migrant, from the Ivory Coast, for which two members of the country's armed forces have been charged. They are alleged to have gone out on a 'safari hunt' in search of stray animals as game. It is alleged that, not having found any such poor victims, they turned their attention to African migrants, wounding one and killing another in cold blood. It is the sort of killing that evokes the example provided by Paulo Freire (2000, 2004) in his posthumous book, *Pedagogy of Indignation* – the wanton killing of a Pataxo Indian, Jesus Galdino, who was burnt alive while sleeping in a bus shed. Freire turned this event into an opportunity for reflecting on the nature of education and its effect on people. What is so awry about education today to cause the perpetuation of such horrendous acts? This Brazil murder followed on the La Candelaria massacre, by off-duty policemen, of a group of street children gathering in a particular area in Rio.

Situations such as these, fuelled by hate speech against the poor and destitute, often in the form of migrant communities, lead us to reflect on the role which education can play in this regard. It is always a dependent variable. It can only contribute to change in concert with others and not on its own. One of the major challenges for educators, in this context, is to encourage participants in various projects to cross their mental and cultural borders – become border crossers – to use a phrase popularized by many, notably Henry A. Giroux (1992), in educational thought. Border crossing, in this regard, involves unadulterated knowledge and awareness of the cultures of others, religion included. Probably the most important feature of a critical approach to education, in this context, an anti-racist critical approach, is that of developing a learning process predicated on what Freire calls 'authentic dialogue', a complex dialogue in which one queries: who dialogues with whom and from which position of relative power and relative powerlessness? (Wright, 2009). We argue, from a Freirean perspective, that authentic dialogue is a way of permitting different cultures, forming our society, to become an integral element in the education process and of participants to *listen* to and understand others. We use 'listening' in the sense expressed by Frere in *Pedagogy of Freedom* (*Pedagogia d'Autonomia*), where he states that 'listening' is different from 'mere hearing'. It means being open to the words of the other, his, her or their gestures, their differences. Freire reminds us that this does not mean that we are reduced to becoming part of the other as this would be not 'listening' but self-annihilation (paraphrased from Freire, 1998b, 107). Dialogue, in this sense, can cut across spaces and places, transforming them. It constitutes a fundamental practice for a genuine democracy. This a crucial political requirement where democracy takes on a particular significance, entailing social and civil conviviality and an ongoing struggle against marginalization, exclusion, prejudice, violence and racism – a clear opposition to an unethical and capitalist way of life predicated on these oppressive elements and aggressions.

Dialogue, even in its political interpretation, is conceived of not as a way of garnering the consent of the masses but more as an experience and expression of conscientization. In this particular historical conjuncture, marked by a lack of solidarity, violence and xenophobia, which intermesh with economic interests and financial speculation, the space for authentic dialogue is reduced considerably. It is derided by many as 'utopian' and useless in a society sold onto a pragmatic view of life tied to economic interests. This makes it imperative to persist in our efforts. We need what Giroux calls an Educated Hope. Otherwise we might well give up on the idea of education altogether. We return to Freire:

Dialogism must not be understood as a tool used by the educator, at times, in keeping with his or her political choices. Dialogism is a requirement of human nature and also a sign of the educator's democratic stand.

There is no communication without dialogism, and communication lies at the core of the vital phenomenon. In this sense, communication is life and a vector for *more-life*. (Freire, 1998a, 92; original Portuguese in Freire, 2005. 74)[1]

The different situations of conflict in this region, which can cause multi-ethnic tensions, would lead us to cross boundaries in various ways. Many regions of 'Southern' Europe are marked by the diffusion of Christianity, notably Roman Catholic and Greek Orthodox. We regard it as important that in a distinctly multi-ethnic environment, schools and other educational sites foster an understanding of different religions. We need to learn democracy by doing it, by living a democracy, to echo John Dewey. This is not easy and entails some basic elements: participation, respect for difference, confrontation of ideas and not sanitized exchanges, authentic dialogue itself. One needs to be rigorous because there is always the danger of constructing stereotypes, caricatures of the cultures involved. The complexity of the situation can easily be ignored as we lapse into facile and reductionist social constructions of the other (Fondazione Laboratorio Mediterraneo, 1997, 51). Antonio Gramsci is again instructive here. He is at pains, in his critique of popular novels and other literary works, to emphasize the importance of learning different ethnic groups' context of origin and not simply their present borrowed or adopted one. He argues that we must gain sound knowledge of the conditions in the context which compelled people to leave in search of pastures new, not to lapse into homogenizing people and groups and perpetuate stereotypes (Gramsci, 1975, 2201 Q. 23 note 9; Gramsci, 1977, 178; Forgacs and Nowell–Smith, 1985, 305). He feared the reproduction of these stereotypes and ossified views of different people, according to regional provenance, and, by implication, country provenance, in teacher education programmes (Apitzsch, 2016, 26; original in Gramsci, 1975, 2314 Q. 27 note 1).

The study of different religions, therefore, needs to be carried out with due seriousness. Educators need to make an important effort to furnish students with a fair account of different cultures and religions. We are using education here in its broadest context, including the mass media. This media, that are an example of what Giroux calls 'public pedagogy' (Giroux, 2001, 75), necessitate preparatory courses and continuing professional development (CPD) ones targeting those who are employed, or aspire to be employed, in this sector. The 1977 Civil Forum Euro Med declares: 'Mass media are invited to present a correct image of religions or cultures, resorting, where suitable, to experts in the matter' (Fondazione Laboratorio Mediterraneo 1997, 51).

With regard to Islam, for example, several mistaken concepts abound in the Western world, including countries forming part of the 'North' Mediterranean. (Elsheikh, 1999). To foster greater conviviality and give rise to genuine dialogue among people of different ethnicities, with different cultures, knowledges, wisdoms and learning traditions, we require an effort to learn and understand the other in her, his or their own terms. The migrants' trajectory from their place of origin to the point of settlement is characterized by not only mobility of labour power but also what one of us calls 'portability of culture/s' (Mayo, 2019). We need a truly critical literacy, in Freire's sense of 'reading the word and the world' (Freire and Macedo, 1987), to cross the frontiers of the discursive location in which we are presently immersed. It helps us read critically and subversively the various texts that impinge on our sensibilities and our way of constructing images of alterity (the various sound bites on audio-visual media, YouTube, news outlets, dailies, online information flows, cinematic representations, digitally mediated technologies, documentaries, etc.) and narrative environments. A critical task of deconstruction and unlearning of privileged narratives is necessary here. We consider critical literacy, including critical media literacy, key to confront the politics of (mis)representation and distortion that reflect deeply embedded dispositions towards others, often antagonistic and revealing a sense of what Edward Said calls 'positional superiority'. These would have been reinforced throughout a long historical period.

In many Mediterranean contexts, we are exposed to a cultural heritage that is Eurocentric and which reflects a colonial legacy especially deriving from 'glorious' imperial centres such as Spain. More generally, it throws into relief, as just mentioned, the crusades against the Ottoman Empire. A critical approach in this context would involve confronting, through unsettling questions in a problem-posing manner, the much-heralded heritage. We can raise questions concerning the extraction of gold and silver by Indigenous slaves in the Americas under Spanish overlords and the atrocities this process generated in terms of mass massacres and maiming through use of mercury in the pits by people 'said to have no soul 'and 'destined for perdition in the life beyond' (see Galeano, 2009). The things of beauty, in our heritage, said to be 'a joy forever', to quote John Keats, often have a human genocidal tragedy lurking beneath.

Furthermore, this heritage often consists of exotic and demonic representations of alterity. In these regions, alterity pertains to a variety of people, including the much-despised Saracen, the stock character in several traditional spectacles in

Sicily and other places, in pageants, marionette shows, popular lore and dances. Alterity becomes the target of a certain type of construction linked to what Edward Said (1978), once again, famously refers to as Orientalism. The intricate hair setting of a slave from Africa, carved in marble, connects with the rest of the church's or palace's ostentatious baroque setting. St. John's Church in Valletta, Malta, furnishes us with a classic example.

It denotes the sense of positional superiority of those who commission the representation. It is the kind of distorted representation about which Frantz Fanon (1963) writes, in *The Wretched of the Earth* – the type of French construction of the colonial subject in North Africa, the Algerian or North African in general. According to Fanon, universities promoted this type of construct for more than twenty years (before he wrote this text), basing their view on a purported 'scientific proof' (Fanon, 1963, 296), a situation similar to the construction of the Calabrian peasant as an innately deficient person prone to 'criminality', as promoted by Cesare Lombroso and his followers in Italy.

In an approach to critical education, however, it is important to engage with the politics of representation that are present in various aspects of the cultural and artistic patrimony in this region. This applies also to popular culture, so crucial in education, in community activity, in research concerning traditions, in oral and written expression, and in the imaginary of popular wisdom which is often set against that which is official and hegemonic. It is in the popular that we find what Gramsci hailed as 'the popular creative spirit'. Gramsci is prominent among those who consider popular culture as a class-based political process. It is the space where many who belong to the subaltern classes express their point of view and their reading of the world. This is not to be confused with romanticized versions of the popular often depicted by people who know little of the actual life of the industrial worker or the peasant and their surrounding communities, the sort of criticism Gramsci levelled at the writers of popular literature who provided exoticized views of southerners (his writings on Fr Bresciani's *nipotini* ... progeny). These false or contradictory views at best connect with 'common sense' and are not the product of serious, rigorous and careful study. Common sense spells danger as it often carries out the ideological function of rendering popular culture banal and folkloristic, disconnecting it from actual historical processes.

On the basis of a serious vision, devoid of any banality, we can identify significant cultural aspects from the popular. One needs to show prudence, for example, with respect to traditional folklore manifest, for instance, in the Sicilian marionettes with its confrontation between the crusader knight and the predator, often a Saracen and of dark, swarthy complexion. When we expose immigrants to aspects of 'Southern' Euro-Mediterranean popular culture, often traditionally appealing to westernised tourists, we could be unwittingly reproducing racist elements embedded in them. Our popular culture is, alas, replete with elements that can denigrate aspects of immigrant cultures. How do we engage the popular in a manner that avoids this and, much to the contrary, shows genuine respect for the culture and history of immigrant individuals and communities?

Cultural productions, at the level of the popular or of that classified as 'highbrow', can serve as codifications, in the Freire sense. As codifications, they can enable people to step back from what they know and re-experience the ordinary extraordinarily (Shor, 1987).

This provides room for critical reflection on our 'common sense', to adopt once again Gramsci's term appropriated from Alessandro Manzoni. This common sense is rooted in such areas as our cultural and folkloric traditions. Once more, they are conceptions that accumulate and are consolidated over a long historical period.

We would love to focus, here, on a type of cultural production that can serve as an educational means to help people from a host country in 'Southern Europe' develop a politics of solidarity with those coming from the 'southern' shores of the Mediterranean and other parts of the world. We refer, as an example, to theatre as a means to promote and enhance social conscience. The sphere of social theatre furnishes us with much grist for the mill for social justice awareness and commitment in the Mediterranean. Beside the Spanish Second Republic theatre of Federico Garcia Lorca and his *La Barraca* group and Berthold Brecht and his Berliner Ensemble, we can think of the more recent anti-oppressive theatre associated with the Freire-inspired Augusto Boal and his Mediterranean equivalents such as the *El Warsha* group in the Middle East or the Teatro Giolly in Italy. Boal's Theatre of the Oppressed, in the Brazilian animator's view, cannot be an 'equidistant' theatre that refrains from being politically involved. It is not a neutral theatre in the same way that Freirean pedagogy is never neutral – all this is based on the assumption that taking this posture is tantamount to siding with the dominant. For Boal, the theatre of the oppressed is a theatre of struggle (Vittoria, 2018). It is a theatre of oppressed, for the oppressed and carried out by the oppressed (Boal, 1993). True to his Freire inspiration, Boal sends classical theatre rules spinning as space and time for popular participation are created. The communicative potential is explored for the purpose of enacting a social and political theatre.

Theatre thus becomes a vehicle for radical learning at the level of community. The social theatre (Perina, 2008) can serve as a pedagogical means to promote greater interethnic solidarity and understanding. Quite stimulating and instructive, in this regard, was a theatre representation carried out during a conference on education in the Mediterranean held in the autumn of 1998 at Sestri Levante in Liguria, Italy (Mayo, 1999b). The players formed part of a theatrical company from Genoa, the major city in the area. The act consisted of a juxtaposition of scenes representing the different realities of migration, from both past and present. The situations concerning Italians emigrating to Argentina, the United States and other countries, and the situations concerning in-migration among Italians from 'South' (the Meridione) to North of the Peninsula were juxtaposed against those concerning Africans, including Arabs, and Eastern Europeans looking for a better future in Italy. Dialogues, monologues and singing featured throughout scenes that were intense and moving. There was a dialectical movement between past flashbacks (redemptive memory, in Walter Benjamin's phrase) and present with the hope of that which is 'not yet' – a society marked by an inclusive and inclusionary democracy.

Reference can also be made to the theatre workshop carried out by the il Giolly association involving Israeli, Palestinian and Italian youngsters. Each group created, according to its cultural points of reference, their perceived image of the typical family in each of the three cultures (Vittoria and Mazzini, 2011). The workshop adopted the theatre-image: a particular technique adopted in the Theatre of the Oppressed based on non-verbal communication to develop forms of perception. Use is made of the body, physiognomy, distances and colours. The purpose is to amplify one's language-mediated vision, breaking the signifier-signified nexus – for example, through a smiling face or the shedding of tears. In the specific case of the theatre-laboratory, the contrasts between the image of the Palestinian family and the Israeli family, created by the respective antagonistic groups, were significant. The typical Palestinian family involved two groups, one consisting of males and the other of females, in a circle, with their eyes set on each other and with similar quiet postures. The image was produced, by and large, in a similar manner by both Palestinians and Israelis. On the other hand, the typical Israeli family was identically produced by both groups: contrary to the Palestinian family, the Israeli family was shown consisting of fewer people, all with different looks cast in different directions, because each one was involved in a different activity (sport, work, TV, etc.).

The visual perception was identical for both groups; however, the significance attributed by the two groups to the same image differed; one was the direct opposite of the other. What for Palestinians signified 'solidarity' (circle, looks, quiet) meant 'group conformism' and 'massification' to the Israelis. In contrast, what signified 'egotism and individualism' (each one isolated, taken up by one's own activity) to the Palestinians meant 'freedom, individual expression' for the Israelis. The images revealed a different way of interpreting the same reality by two antagonistic groups – a different, diametrically opposite interpretation attributed to a similarly perceived reality (Vittoria and Mazzini, 2011).

Conclusion

To conclude, we would like to indicate a few challenges among many we consider important for a critical and anti-racist pedagogy in this part of the Western world: avoid the deficit image of the immigrant; not to limit ourselves, as educators/learners, to, once again, 'assistencialismo'; regard the immigrant as 'subject' of the education process and society; take seriously the politics of representation/image of the Other; raise awareness of how the political system classifies persons on the grounds of ethnicity, nationality or type of immigrant (refugees, asylum seekers, 'economic' migrants, guest workers, etc.); raise awareness and understanding of the cultures of others, including their religion, if any; recognize, as autochthonous members of the population, the need to acknowledge the contribution, direct or otherwise, of others to the development of our assumed culture; be made aware of and recognize the contribution of non-Europeans to the development of 'western civilisation' (avoid the 'debtor's syndrome' – Elsheikh, 1999, 38).

Finally, there is a pressing need for an anti-racist education at different levels – at school, adult education settings, among members of the armed forces, the police force (recent incidents in the United States make this rather urgent), immigration officers, members of the judiciary, journalists, health workers, social workers and teachers. The list is not exhaustive. There is also a need for a rethink of immigrant detention centres such as the so-called centres of temporary hospitality in Italy. What is their social role? Are they simply manifestations of the 'carceral state', their title simply a euphemism? Can they be developed into educational spaces for inclusion or relocation? Or are they, to the contrary, part of the state's repressive apparatus?

We require, as indicated in this chapter, an education based on authentic dialogue taking account of the power dynamics involved. We need an education engaging popular cultures, including established local ones, subaltern ones and those which are present in the immigrants' 'portability of cultures'. Immigrants bring with them not only labour power but a variety of subjectivities. This is, however, not enough: it is important that these forms of expression and educational practices are grounded in a critical-historical perspective on education. This is meant to help us avoid the risk that they translate simply into a set of accumulated techniques void of any authentic and well-thought-out attempt at social change. We therefore, in typical Freirean fashion, refer to not a neutral culture, and a neutral dialogical education, but a political education. It is an education reflecting a preferential option for the oppressed, wherever they are. What we call for is an education based on *praxis* where theory and practice, action and reflection, are related in a dialectical manner.

It needs to be a critical antidote to the hegemonic neoliberal discourse exasperatingly full of pragmatic technicism, competitivity, individualistic overtones and productivity, besides goals and objectives set by international organizations that ride roughshod over contextual, biological and social differences. It is necessary to understand the educational-cultural context without ignoring the economic and political aspects. We feel that, out of the different communities, social movements, plurality of wisdoms and sensitivity, an education can emerge that is anti-racist, foregrounding human solidarity and interpersonal subjectivity.

9

Hegemony, Migration and Misplaced Alliances: Lessons from Antonio Gramsci

The spectre of colonialism has returned to haunt Europe with a vengeance. The old continent's former colonies and protectorates are points of origin for several flows of migration. They are mainly directed to this continent which is viewed as the colonial *Eldorado*, the constructed outlet for 'the good life'. Migration has become the principal concern in the region, not least because of the tragedies surrounding it, turning the Mediterranean Sea into a 'graveyard'. This partly results from the barriers erected by the same 'old continent' through its fortress and nationalistic policies that serve to pit workers against workers on the basis of ethnicity and national origins, despite the right to asylum affirmed by the 1951 Geneva Convention. The Geneva Convention also allows for possible instances of 'irregularity' in recognition of situations that lead to 'forced migration'. This necessitates a call for policies that should be international rather than national (so much for the 'receding' of the nation state in a time of intensified globalization), since we are dealing with international, global phenomena.

Concerns with and fears of waves of immigration often lead to misplaced alliances between people on the basis of an ideology that obfuscates the reality that both immigrants and 'autochthonous' workers are members of an international class exploited by international capital and the international ruling class that benefits from it. This ideology induces people to engage in strange alliances involving those whose class interests are economically opposed. They engage in the belief that the interests of the dominating class are very much their own class interests. As the history of the First World War indicates, 'nationalism' is not to be underestimated as a powerful force in creating alliances that pit worker against worker on the grounds of country affiliation, irrespective of the contradictory class interests involved. One writer who expressed views along these lines is Antonio Gramsci. He expressed such concerns in the context of a national politics within an equally migratory Mediterranean context, in his case an 'internal' national migratory context ('South' to 'North', island to mainland or 'il continente'). We shall argue in this chapter that his writings on the Italian migratory contexts of his time, and the strange alliances to which these migrations gave way, have relevance for the present context of migration across the Mediterranean.

The French historian Ferdinand Braudel (1992) declared that 'exchange' was, for a long historical period, a prominent feature of life in and around the Mediterranean basin – the *longue durée* (long term). Despite different wars and national and international antagonism, before the onset of Western imperialism, all manners of goods and services were exchanged. People bartered and traded in one large regional *suk*. The nature of the exchange is, however, different these days. As far as people are concerned, it is not an exchange of and among equals. This applies to migrants crossing over to Europe from and through North Africa, after having negotiated the Sahara and Libya itself (the 'Tijuana of the Mediterranean') where all sorts of hazards are encountered, as described by Derek Lutterbeck (2012) who, through interviews with Somali immigrants, tracked the movement of Somalis from Mogadishu via the Sahara and Libya to Malta. His account certainly captures a sense of the tragedy surrounding what we would call, following Zygmunt Bauman (2006), 'the human waste disposal industry'.

He provides vivid accounts of not only the hazards encountered when crossing the desert and rough seas in rickety boats but also the callousness of people along the way. Included here are people, either acting alone or through smuggling organizations, on both sides of the 'North'-'South' Mediterranean divide, who traffic in human misery, hardly valuing human life.

The European Union's (EU) fortress policy with respect to denial of visas and travel opportunities is compelling immigrants from sub-Saharan Africa (SSA) and more lately from Egypt and Syria, and other countries facing the scourge of religious persecution, fleeing the situation in their country, to pursue some of the most hazardous routes to get to Europe.

The European Union, through its 'fortress' politics, centring on the notion of 'security', is the target of current protests regarding this human tragedy. Parallels with the Mexico-US border situation are invited. While people from South and Central America use sewers to cross over to the United States, people from Africa are risking their lives by selling all their possessions to make the journey, in the case of SSA migrants, across the Sahara to Libya and then be crossed over by unscrupulous *coyotes*, who apparently do not care a toss about human lives.

These situations are rendered more desperate by the failure of the fellow EU partners of frontier countries or islands such as the Canary Islands, Lampedusa and Malta to assist in responsibility sharing. These islands are left to cope with the disproportionate demands (in relation to size and population density) placed on them as first port of call for migrants who cross over from North Africa with a view to reaching Italy or other places in Europe. Alison Gatt (2014) calls for a comprehensive responsibility-sharing mechanism among the EU member states in general. This is a global situation which requires international and not national solutions, a point underlined in several chapters of Xuereb (2013). Possible solutions include, as indicated in a newspaper interview by Maltese lawyer-activist Neil Falzon, issuing international humanitarian visas to ensure that people can safely exercise their right to asylum. Constant reference is made, throughout the various chapters, to the Dublin II Regulation according to which immigrants were to have their asylum-seeking application evaluated by the state through which they first entered the European Union – hence the pressure on Malta, a frontier country with respect to North Africa. This begs the question regarding the European Union and its 'Fortress Europe' politics: Where is the much spoken of (in EU discourse) 'solidarity'? (Mallia, 2012).

It is goods that generally circulate freely and, even here, some qualification is necessary. It is goods from certain countries and within certain regional arrangements (e.g. the European Union) which transfer smoothly. Ask Palestinians who cannot carry goods from one part of Palestine to the other as they negotiate checkpoints. Some who carry goods which are not Israeli but Palestinian, from, say, their parents' home in one part of the country to the other, can well have their goods confiscated at checkpoints. This is part and parcel of settler colonialism within this Mediterranean country. It is part of a global imperial system as a result of which some people are accorded the right to move freely and exchange their goods in the process while others are left stranded or forced to risk life and limb as victims of what Bauman (2006) calls the 'human waste disposal industry'. *The Guardian* reported in 2013 that no less than twenty thousand people drowned in the Mediterranean during the previous two decades. In not more than a week, in 2016, around 1,100 people including children and toddlers drowned off the Libyan coast in what was dubbed the biggest tragedy in the Mediterranean since the Second World War – so many people were therefore eliminated from the index of human concerns.

The reasons which compel people from primarily SSA and Middle East and North Africa (MENA) regions to leave their homeland are many. They would include the effects of neoliberal structural adjustment programmes, civil wars fuelled by a Western-based arms industry, involving the sale of conventional weapons especially during the post-Cold War period; exacerbation of Indigenous conflicts often involving rape with the female victims being disowned by their family; the attempt among women to avoid female genital mutilation; and evading religious fundamentalism, which has taken on sinister forms with the emergence of first Al-Qaeda and then Boko Haram, Shabab and Isis, the latter displaying their ruthless hand in the transit country of Libya. This will lead to even greater migrations from SSA and MENA in the forthcoming years, as little intervention takes place to protect the thousands of victims involved, unless one can trade 'blood for oil'. There are also the negative effects which subsidies for farmers in Europe and North America can have on African farming; climate change and its negative ramifications; the spread of fatal diseases such as Ebola decimating families, Indigenous groups and communities; an impoverished environment (the ransacking of Africa); a colonial ideology whereby West is presented as 'the Best'; the quest for better employment opportunities ... and one can go on, perhaps falling prey to Western stereotypes and monolithic constructions of 'Africa' (see Wright, 2012). Life in and throughout Africa and among Africans is much more complex than any set of ideas would make us believe, prone as people are to essentializing. Handel Kashope Wright's (2012) title from *Macbeth*'s dagger scene "Is this an African I see before me?' seems very apt in this context.

There is, however, one major global reason that cannot be discounted, no matter how simplistic or complex is the argument made. The economies of highly industrialized countries register shortages in the amount of labour power that is required, and this has to be 'imported' often at a cost which can undercut any claims for high remuneration by locally based workers and their representatives on the basis of national or regional 'demand and supply' politics (Apitzsch, 1995, 68). This kind of politics can be undermined by a greater 'reserve army' pool available through the process of uneven levels of global industrial development, endemic to the capitalist mode of production. This plays into the hands of unscrupulous employers, and also governments, on the lookout for ways and means of depressing local wages. It is this quest, on the part of capitalism itself and its representatives, to depress wages that renders members of the 'autochthonous' working class vulnerable, rather than the spectre of immigrant labour. This is crucial for any discussion concerning alliances between capital and labour in the present historical conjuncture.

Couched differently, the main reason for massive migration from South to North and East to West is the quest for low-cost labour by corporations and other businesses alike that serves as a 'push-and-pull factor'. As David Bacon (2008) argues, hegemonic globalization makes migration necessary.[1] Meanwhile, the same victims of this process are rendered 'illegal' and criminalized for responding to this necessity, victims of the 'carceral state'. By carceral state and adapted from Foucault's notion of the 'carceral society', I mean the state that places more emphasis on its repressive apparatus to 'control' those who suffer from the excesses of the global neoliberal polices it accommodates (Mayo, in Simicevic, 2013). It is part of the process whereby the state organizes, regulates, 'educates' (the ethical state), creates and sustains markets, provides surveillance, evaluates (Gentili, 2005), forges networks and represses. One should underscore the role of the repressive factor as manifest by the state during this period. Behind the whole facade of consent lurks naked power which, in Mao Zedong's famous words, lies in 'the barrel of a gun'. Giroux uses the term 'carceral state' mainly in relation to schooling, with reference to 'the school-to-prison-pipeline' (Giroux, 2014a, 36) part and parcel of the 'carceral state' (ibid., 84) .

The state also provides a policing force for what can easily be regarded as the victims of neoliberal policies as well as related 'structural adjustment programmes' in the majority world. The migrants from SSA knocking on the doors of 'Fortress Europe' and who are contained in veritable prisons referred to as detention centres are among these victims. They live within the carceral framework which has been characterizing the life of many immigrants in Mediterranean shores of late, most notably in the aforementioned frontier islands.

The shifting of Southern populations against their will has been standard European imperialist policy.[2] Politics of this kind recur throughout history, repeating themselves over and over again, always ending in tragedies and never in farce.[3] Southern and oppressed populations can be moved at will to suit imperial interests. It happened with Africans during the slave trade periods; with the 1948 Nakba (Masalha in Gargour, 2009; Masalha, 2012) and, later, with Palestinians uprooted from their homeland; it happened during 'operation bootstrap' involving the uprooting and dislocation of Puerto Ricans (Darder, in Borg and Mayo, 2007); it certainly happens with people from sub-Saharan and North Africa today. All are pawns in a game of chess played by predominantly Western powers, conditioned by the long-term and deep-rooted legacies of their carefully engineered colonial, pre-independence and postcolonial moves.

This legacy of colonialism and its effect on the migratory movements from the South Mediterranean to the North Mediterranean and beyond reflects the similar colonial situation discussed by Gramsci. In his case, the colonial situation was of an 'internal' nature. Italy's North colonially dominated the country's Southern regions and islands. Gramsci discussed this in his writings on the Southern Question (Mayo and Vittoria, 2017a) and his prison notes on Italian history. He calls for solidarity among subaltern people on both sides of the 'North'-'South' divide.

Equally relevant, in this context, is Gramsci's concept of 'national popular'. What is 'national' reflects the culture of hegemonic ethnic groups. It plays a key role in the structure of hegemony and its apparatuses. Hegemony is the key concept used by Gramsci throughout his prison notes.[4] And yet one would be hard-pressed to discover any systematic exposition of the concept by Gramsci (Borg, Buttigieg and Mayo, 2002, 1). We would interpret this concept as referring to a situation in which most arrangements, constituting a particular social reality, are conditioned by and tend to support the interests of a particular class or social grouping.[5] Hegemony incorporates not only processes of ideological influence and contestation but also, as Raymond Williams (1976, 205; 1977, 110) argues, a 'whole body of practices and expectations'.

Concepts such as 'national identity' and 'national culture' are thus challenged, to negotiate relations of hegemony. This entails the renegotiation of relations among different groups within a single nation state. Subaltern groups, such as the proletariat and peasants, in Gramsci's time, needed to form a firmly entrenched and deep-rooted *historical bloc* (this is not to be confused with simply an alliance, which can be ephemeral) to challenge the absolutizing concept of 'national'. They would thus transform the hegemonic relations embodied in this unitary concept. One therefore had to challenge misplaced alliances that occur as a result of the obfuscation of these hegemonic relations and the interests they serve, specific interests made to look universal in order to acquire popular consent, but which, on considering the impact of ideology and its underlying contradictions, turn out to be very partial. It helps retain the status quo in the interest of the dominant hegemonic groups.

Gramsci makes reference, in the Southern Question piece, to a proposed alliance involving the exploited Sardinian peasants and their offspring on the island and mainland[6] and the offspring of the exploiting Sardinian landowning class, regarded by Gramsci as the Sardinian overseers of capitalist exploitation. In this regard, he refers, in 'The Southern Question', to the eight communists' effort to thwart an attempt at forming the Giovane Sardegna, a sort of all-embracing movement of Sardinians, irrespective of different and opposing social class interests. Landowners and peasants are thus lumped together in what would have been a false alliance buttressed by the ideology of regionalism or Sardismo.

This disruptive effort proved successful, causing the postponement *sine die* of the coming into being of the proposed organization.

Then we have the episode involving the *Brigata Sassari* (the Sassari Brigade) and its engagement to quell industrial strife in the North. Gramsci touches on the issue of cultural and ethnic hybridization. He felt that solidarity between proletariat and peasants can be facilitated by an important relation between the two. The proletariat consists, for the most part, of descendants of the latter, given that much of the industrialization in Italy's North depended on internal migration from the South. Gramsci argues that bonding between the soldiers and strikers, resulting from conversations, led to a change in consciousness or perspective transformation. They were both members of the same exploited subaltern class. The brigade returned to Sassari. The themes of solidarity therefore and the struggle against misplaced alliances feature prominently in Gramsci's ruminations concerning the South, which he never romanticizes, highlighting its unsavoury and wayward aspects (Germino, 1990). 'The Southern Question' contains these kind of ruminations. It has been argued (Mayo, 2015) that they have great resonance with respect to the present-day Southern Question, viewed in the larger context of 'North'-'South'/'South'-'North' relations. We are writing about conceptualizing the Southern Question on a regional and transcontinental scale. In short, while Gramsci wrote about 'North'-'South' relations in the context of a single nation state, we write about these relations in a larger context, that of the Mediterranean and European-African relations.

Renegotiating Hegemony and the National-Popular

Gramsci argued that the North was an octopus that enriched itself at the expense of the South (Gramsci, 1975, 47). The same can be applied to Europe and its colonial centres vis-à-vis the larger South. Migrants, from SSA, attempt to reach the centres of Europe and often end up on the continent's periphery. The intermeshing of cultures that this brings about leads to hegemonic contestation, depending on how strong and well developed the lobbies representing migrants are. Old hegemonic arrangements are questioned. The concept of 'national popular' develops a new meaning in this context. Concepts such as 'national identity' and 'national culture' are called into question by those who derive their inspiration from Gramsci and others (the latter would include Edward Said who draws on Gramsci's 'Southern Question' in his work).[7] The greater the presence of multi-ethnic groups and the stronger their lobby, the greater their challenge to the established hegemonic arrangements. In short, migrants who establish themselves and hone their lobbying skills as an ethnic group or specific community would, in the long term, demand certain rights which can be obtained following a lengthy process of renegotiation, persuasion and activism. In doing so, they would be challenging established hegemonic relations. They would lobby for the right to build mosques, secured by Muslims, or synagogues by Jews, alongside the historically hegemonic Catholic churches in Southern European countries such as Italy and Spain.

Gramsci's insisted that Turin's communists had the task of bringing the Southern Question to the attention of the workers' vanguard. He went so far as to regard this as a key task for the proletariat (Gramsci, 1997, 181, 182). Furthermore, the national popular alliance of Italian workers and peasants, he advocated, echoed in this regard by Piero Gobetti (ibid., 204), assumes a broader and global 'North'-'South' significance at a time of 'South' to 'North' mass migration. Bringing the southern issue to the forefront of political debates would be a key task for contemporary genuine socialist politics.

'North'-'South' Solidarity

This is to strengthen global working-class solidarity. It is also intended for the avoidance of misplaced alliances, often detrimental in the long run to subaltern class interests. One can include, as examples, much-called-for alliances between 'labour' and 'management' against 'the competition'. Hegemonic neoliberal globalization has engendered misplaced alliances involving and exacerbating racist, labour market segmentation. Workers are segregated on ethnic, national and religious lines, and of being refugees, Black, asylum seekers, Muslim, Arab, 'economic migrants' or, worse, 'illegal migrants'.[8] They are otherized, with the local autochthonous workers said to assume 'positional superiority', in Said's (1978, 1994) terms, in their regard. In this respect, especially where Arabs and Muslims are concerned, Egyptian writer Nawal El Saadawi (1992, 137) states:

> Perhaps the problem of the world has always been the 'objectification', the nullification, of the 'other'. For the West or the North, the South is the other which exists only as an object to be exploited and oppressed. Christianity or Western culture sees Islam and Arab culture as the other. And in all religions, all that does not belong to God is seen as emanating from the devil. The problem

of our world is to ignore, to dismiss, to destroy the other. To do this, the other must be satanised.

We would argue that an educational anti-racist programme, in concert with other types of action (education is not an independent variable) can only be effective when grounded in political economy and an understanding of colonialism. Gramsci sought to infuse his analysis of the Italian Southern Question with these elements. He combined political economy with an historical understanding of Italy's process of 'North'-'South' 'internal colonialism'. This is most evident in 'The Southern Question' and the notes concerning Italy's post-Risorgimento state (see Notebook 1 of the *Prison Notebooks*). In these works, he gives both economic and cultural historical reasons for the subordination of the 'South'. Economic historians such as Luigi De Rosa (2004) support this view. Gramsci mentions the 'Northern' economic protectionist strategies undermining the Southern economy. De Rosa (2004) mentions the process of deindustrialisation of 'Southern' economies such as those surrounding Naples, famous for the production of locomotives, among other things. The protectionist strategies include the Tariff wars with France that impacted negatively on 'southern' Italian agricultural life (Gramsci, 1975, 45). Furthermore, a point made earlier, economic power blocs such as the European Union adopt economic and agrarian 'closure' policies that are detrimental to African and other 'tricontinental' regions' economic development. Almost daily, wealthy countries provide billion-dollar subsidies to their farmers. Agricultural workers will find it hard to survive and maintain their families. They simply cannot compete and therefore feed their children and the rest of the family. Migration therefore appears to provide the only way out, often at terrible human costs.[9]

Interethnic solidarity necessitates work of an educational nature to contribute to improving the situation. Providing effective anti-racist education, predicated on an understanding of colonialism and neocolonialism, and grounded in both cultural understanding and political economy, is one of the greatest challenges facing those committed to a socialist, anti-neoliberal politics in the Mediterranean and elsewhere. The work would be as broadly educational as was the work in which Gramsci was engaged when attempting to generate a revolutionary working class consciousness in his country. In Gramsci's view, education is central to the workings of hegemony (Borg, Buttigieg and Mayo, 2002, 8). And the kind of educational work in which one must engage, in the contemporary context, is a lengthy one. Without an educational strategy of this sort, working-class people, living in a state of precariousness, stand a better chance of adhering to the populist right-wing and often neo-fascist discourse that plays on their fears (see Hall, 1987a,b). This situation would alas lead to greater segmentation among workers on ethnic lines. Again, misplaced alliances facilitate this and, once again, we encounter the mystification of the common fate shared by workers of different ethnicity: being subaltern and victims of a ruthless process of 'racialization', a callous form of 'divide et impera'. One-time socialist or Labour parties have been accused of having done nothing over the years to broaden the meaning of international as opposed to national solidarity, since 'socialism', the appropriate word in this context, has become passé in these parties' discourse. If anything, the target of any anger, where vulnerable working-class employees are concerned, should be those unscrupulous employers who prey on a destitute 'reserve army' to considerably cut down labour costs. If one goes by hearsay, they often completely do away with these costs, at best paying the migrant a pittance.

Unless these aspects of the migration issue are tackled systematically and backed by robust research by those whose historical function was that of leading the working class through a sustained process of an inclusive workers' education program spanning different media and settings, we are more likely to see a swing towards the right. And by this, we mean the emergence of not only right-wing parties but also former leftist parties veering towards right of centre.

Few, if any, attempts were made, over the years, to raise consciousness in the rank and file regarding the pitfalls of racism and a comprehensively inclusive, including gender-inclusive, notion of workers' solidarity. The term 'working class' has also become passé despite the presence of whole swathes of societies worldwide suffering from precarious living conditions rendering many sectors déclassé. With many members of what we would call the new working class (including those déclassé sectors) feeling vulnerable, in this age of constant layoffs, and downsizing and economic meltdowns, it is likely that they misguidedly pursue the route of xenophobia and racism.

It is not surprising to see racism towards people of colour and Arabs, as well as the Roma, being rife in Europe. The swing to the right is typical of many countries worldwide, large or small, in the context of increasing immigrant labour, including the *gastarbeiter* (guest worker). It would certainly be writ large in small frontier countries, with respect to North Africa, which are first port of call for many SSA and MENA migrants. A classic example would be the island of Malta, the country in which one of us lives, with a small land mass and around officially four hundred thousand inhabitants. The criminalization[10] of immigrants serves to fan the flames of racism and xenophobia. The marginalization of immigrants with no access to citizenship rights and social benefits, especially rejected asylum seekers, leads them to eke out a living at the very margins of society, in the 'underworld' if need be. There is a thriving crime organization among immigrant groups. This furthers the construction of irregular migrants as given to criminality, promiscuity and so forth rather than being victims of a systemic oppressive and ultimately racist structure that encourages abuse of their vulnerability.

How often do we see one-time socialist parties shunning their responsibility of fostering interethnic solidarity among workers? They are often accused of acting this way because they fear losing electoral votes. We have argued that this situation highlights the limits of bourgeois democracy in generating a genuinely socialist politics involving workers' solidarity across different identities, including ethnic ones (see Mayo, 2007, 105). The lengthy process of consciousness raising would exceed the usual five-year term of office of an electoral period, and five years are a long time in bourgeois representative democratic politics.

While hope springs eternal with regard to political parties' involvement in anti-racist education, focused on the quest for international workers' solidarity (Gramsci himself had a party, a Modern Prince, at the heart of his political strategy), there is a greater chance that this work is carried out, in the present scenario, by other agencies. We would include here progressive social movements, or alliances of these movements, who have been making their presence felt in the various rallies taking place in, say, England against UKIP and the BNP with regard to UK and European elections, actions such as ¡*Democracia Real Ya!* in Spain, various *indignados* and 'Debtocracy' rallies in Greece, the occupy activities in various international cities, the occupy Gezi Park in Istanbul (Gezgin, Inal and Hill, 2014) and such forums as the World Social Forum where Gramsci is a constant source of reference. There seems to be greater potential for progressive change in these grassroots movements than in certain 'socialist' parties of yore. It might well be argued that, in the words of Mark Fisher, they have easily adapted to and accommodated 'capitalist realism', operating within the bourgeois consensus politics framework marked by a swing to centrist or right-of-centre politics. One should, however, not tar all parties with the same brush, in this context, as there have been powerful voices for interethnic solidarity among the SNP, Plaid Cymru and the Green Party in the 2015 UK Elections televised debates and also among a variety of emerging progressive parties in Greece and elsewhere. It remains to be seen to what extent these parties can and will provide educational platforms and projects to combat misplaced alliances that exacerbate workers' or prospective workers' segregation on ethnic, racist lines.

Part Four

Popular Education, Social Movements and the Struggle for Independence

10

Amilcar Cabral and Paulo Freire: The Struggle for Independence and Popular Education in Guinea-Bissau

with Amilcar Araujo Pereira*

Amilcar Cabral's thought and action were objects of great admiration for Paulo Freire. It is not the first time that the ideas of both feature alongside each other in a comparative analysis. Reference ought to be made here to Portuguese scholar, from the Universidade do Porto, Luiza Cortesão. She reminds us, when confronting both figures, that they belong to two worlds that are similar but, at the same time, give rise to different preoccupations. *In primis*, according to Cortesão, Cabral was engaged in and dedicated to the struggle to obtain and render concrete his country's independence. Cortesão writes that, as a political actor in an age of modernity, Cabral is primarily dedicated to the construction, with real people, of a nation state. Freire, for his part, is described by Cortesão as a political figure, philosopher and pedagogue, in tune with the postmodern condition and who therefore revealed great sensibility and respect for minority cultures. According to the same scholar, he acknowledged the potential that existed in the commitment to work *with* and *in favour of* people belonging to these minority groups (Cortesão, 2011, 265). This partly explains their different positions regarding Guinea-Bissau's literacy issue, Cabral favouring Portuguese (a postcolonial *lingua franca* opening on to a part of the rest of the world) and Freire opting for Creole (a *lingua franca* mixture of Indigenous and non-Indigenous languages), as we shall see later on.

Freire was fascinated by Cabral particularly for his ability to wed revolutionary practice with the people's education. This rendered him not only an authentic revolutionary but also a *pedagogue of* revolution, teaching and learning with his people. Cabral conducted the process of emancipation from the Portuguese colonizers through not only an everyday political struggle but also an educational one. Freire dedicated his 1978 book *Pedagogy in Process: Letters to Guinea-Bissau* (original: *Cartas da Guinea-Bissau*) to him. In this book, Freire reflects on his literary experience in the African nation state. In the book's dedication to Cabral, Freire defines him as an *educator who learned from his people* (Freire, 1978). He declares that he shares with Cabral a particular interpretation of Marxism, which, in the Cold War climate, does not follow Eurocentric, orthodox and mechanistic positions but, to the contrary, denotes autonomy and independence, as indicated at a conference addressed by Freire in 1985. Freire declares that, for him, Cabral was a fine Marxist who provided an *African reading* of Marx, not a German or nineteenth-century reading of the same author. He states that Cabral provides a twentieth-century reading of Marx from an African perspective and that it was no surprise that, in a speech in Havana, he refuted the view that the class struggle is the motor of history. Freire underlines the fact that Cabral made this point in Soviet-backed Cuba, framing the question in Havana with great independence of thought. He stated that the reason for this position is that he cannot accept the view that Africa had no history prior to the advent of class struggle. According to Freire, Cabral posed two epistemological questions: what occurred before the class struggle and resistance? What happens afterwards … the end of history? This second question struck Freire as being more searching: would the socialist revolution, with its suppression of the antagonistic classes, mark the end of history? Freire concluded, tongue in cheek, that he would not wish this to occur as 'I like history' (Freire, A.M, 2005, 113).

Freire compares Cabral with Antonio Gramsci. With respect to Gramsci and Cabral, Freire appreciates the disposition to identify, understand and reveal the cultural basis of politics and the political basis of culture. Politics, understood as people's movement, consists of cultural action, in the same way that culture is a political necessity. Freire speaks of a cultural factor when describing Cabral's cultural-political actions and precepts. He argues that someone like Cabral should be studied along the extraordinary person that is Gramsci, admitting that he has no awareness of whether the African revolutionary ever studied Gramsci. Freire declares that Cabral makes no reference to Gramsci, in the same way, we would argue, that *Pedagogy of the Oppressed*, written in 1968, the year Marcela Gajardo introduced Freire to Gramsci's writings in *Letteratura e vita nazionale* (Literature and National Life) (Morrow and Torres, 1995), makes no reference to the Sardinian.

As for Cabral, Freire admits, this was no deliberate avoidance on his part as Gramsci's works were translated at the time when Cabral was fighting in the forest. Freire informs us that the first works by Gramsci were translated into

Spanish when he (Freire) was already in exile. He goes on to point out, however, a remarkable affinity as both Gramsci and Cabral show sensitivity towards culture when faced by its presence, none of them, however, exaggerating its importance. Freire was convinced, we are told, that the study of their texts, either in isolation or side by side, would be of enormous importance and that this idea should be proposed to educators. Freire felt that one of the things missing among educators is precisely this comprehension of the politics of education and pedagogy (ibid., 114–15). This is interesting, we would argue, given, as we saw previously, the introduction in Brazil of the slogan 'Escola sem partido' (School without Party) or the confinement, during the Thatcher UK government, of much teacher education to schools, and not faculties of education, for fear of contamination by left-leaning or outright 'Marxist' sociologists or philosophers. One ought to note that Don Milani used Gramsci's texts at the School of Barbiana (Martinelli, in Borg and Mayo, 2007) and Minister Luigi Berlinguer had proposed the *Quaderni* (Prison Notebooks) for the school curriculum in Italy, which led to the usual chorus of 'no propaganda in schools' – accusations levelled by the opposition in parliament. This was during the D'Alema government in 1998.

African Decolonization

Freire indirectly drew close to Cabral. When Freire initiated the literacy programmes in Guinea-Bissau and Cape Verde, Cabral had been dead for a year, his demise being the result of an assassination. In exile from Brazil, as a result of the 1964 coup, Freire, after periods in Chile and the United States, was ensconced in Geneva, where his daughter still lives. Freire was working for the World Council of Churches. This was after his two-year stint at Harvard, where he had *Pedagogia do Oprimido* (Pedagogy of the Oppressed) (Freire, 2013) translated into English. The Churches' Council carried out projects in a variety of contexts roused for social change, including former Portuguese colonies in Africa, which were therefore officially Portuguese-speaking. Profoundly religious (avowedly Christian and Roman Catholic, though subscribing to the Prophetic Church) and politically radical and autonomous, not connected to any rigidly 'ideological church' (political orthodoxy), Freire worked in an ecumenical context. The principles were religious but the nature of work was quite independent and can be regarded as almost secular. He admits that his first preoccupation at the Council was the extent to which he would move at ease especially in a work context that was nominally faith-based, an ecumenical place. He, however, reveals that no one queried his religious denominational affiliation, if any, during the ten-year period at the Council. He claims to have not, at any moment, been called over by the secretary general and admonished for the tenor of any talks or writings – 'be careful' or 'tone it down'. Freire states that there was none of this and that he never felt so free, in his work, as he did when he was working for the World Council of Churches (paraphrased from Freire and Guimaraes, 2002, 55).

During this time in Geneva, he founded, under the aegis of the Council, the Institute of Cultural Action (IDAC) that promoted or showed a keen interest in popular education, especially targeting social marginalization, gender politics and the question of the working class, bringing all these to bear on his reflections on the school and on the 'false neutrality' of education. IDAC promoted conscientization as the vehicle for liberation in the interrelated processes of education, development and social change.

In 1975, Mario Cabral, Minister of Education in the Republic of Guinea-Bissau, by then already independent, sent a letter to IDAC inviting Freire and his work group to help give rise to a national adult literacy project. The government of Guinea-Bissau had just been installed after years of struggle for independence carried out by the PAIGC[1] under the leadership and inspiration of Amilcar Cabral. It had obtained its independence from Portugal in 1973. It was effectively a young government, developing its own political principles regarding independence and autonomy. The road to liberation and the establishment of autonomy necessitated a determined action to reinforce the social conscience of a people historically educated by colonial forces to accept its state of dependency, deep-seated feeling of inferiority and alienation from its own cultural roots. The political and educational challenge consisted of inverting the historical schemes of a colonial education and instead initiating a long process of cultural decolonisation.

The political reality of Guinea-Bissau led to its inhabitants living through a situation of internal contradiction: on the one hand, there was a deliberate institutional effort at independence from the colonial forces; on the other, part of the people's culture was still fettered by its colonial mentality. The latter leads to people living a reality common among societies undergoing a revolution: lacerated by the divide between the new policies of the institution and the widespread people's culture or cultures. In these contexts, the educational process becomes even more political and necessary for a revolution to be transformed from institutional to cultural, that is to say, rooted in popular consciousness. The literacy programme was intended for a people struggling to develop a political consciousness but that also had to come to grips with a high incidence of illiteracy. As Freire revealed, the illiteracy rate in Guinea-Bissau surpassed 90 per cent.

Colonizers and Colonized

The programme of popular education and literacy had to critically understand the barriers separating colonized from colonizers. It therefore took on a significant historical-political character involving social and existential qualities inherent in language, music, dance, beliefs, aesthetics and education. It was not enough to resist: it was necessary to reject models of colonization and have faith in the people's cultures. In this respect, critical popular education had a fundamental role to play to reveal the falsification of history as brought about by colonizing strategies. One required, therefore, an education furthering cultural decolonisation.

Freire wrote that the distorted view projected was of the history of colonized people starting with the arrival of the colonizers, with their 'civilizing presence', while the culture of the colonized was presented as a barbaric way of understanding the world. Culture, according to Freire, was presented as pertaining only to the colonizers while the music of the colonized, their rhythms, their dancing, the lightness of their bodies' movement, their creativity in general, was meant to count for nothing. All the attributes of the colonized, Freire continues, had to be repressed with the tastes of the metropole and its dominant classes being predominant. This recalls Macaulay's infamous statement about colonial education in India under the British Raj. It had to produce a people 'Indian in blood and colour, but English in taste, in opinions, in morals, and in intellect'.[2]

In Freire's view, the one redeeming feature of this alienating education is that, once they become independent and, we would add, gain consciousness of the true meaning of independence, the formerly colonized would reject and replace it. He goes on to argue that this will come to pass when, as people, with their own history, they immerse themselves in what Cape Verde President Aristides Perreira called the process of 'decolonizing the mind' – the title, we would add, of a classic on the politics of African literature by Ngugi wa Thiong'o (1986). Freire refers to the phrase coined by Cabral, the 're-Africanisation of the mentalities', to which we can add the New Jewel Movement's education slogan in Grenada, under Maurice Bishop: 'to Grenadise Grenadians'. For Freire, this entails a radical transformation of the education system inherited from the colonisers (paraphrased from Freire and Guimaraes, 2002, 20).

We shall return to this aspect of a decolonizing education in the subsequent chapter on Julius Kambarage Nyerere.

'Africa Exists': Which Education?

Colonization is a dramatic historical process. Complex in its patterns and devastating in its broad reach – culture, economy, language, religion, to name but a few – it is a form of violence bent on suppressing individual and a people's identities. It is a form of depredation and appropriation, leaving in its wake a gross sense of economic and cultural injustice including what Boaventura de Sousa Santos calls 'cognitive injustice' and cases of 'epistemicide'. It also causes fragmentation in people best captured by Frantz Fanon's phrase 'Black skin, white masks' (Fanon, 1952). At its best, it allows scope for hybridization, especially among those subjects with a penchant for critical appropriation and capable of navigating a bicultural existence (Darder, 2012). This often serves as a form of resistance and resilience among those who, while not losing sight of their own cultural roots, can take advantage of the colonizer's imposed culture to take their struggles into larger, international forums and therefore not remain on the margins of economic and political life. Freire himself wrote about this and so did Gramsci especially with regard to the uses or misuses of the 'standard' (in this case, read: colonial) language. The case of the PAIGC government insisting on using the colonial Portuguese language, in the literacy campaign, suggests a form of pragmatism along these lines. Of course, the best-case scenario would be learning both the Indigenous and the international colonizing languages in a problem-posing manner that makes the learner aware of the political ramifications of the two languages. This has been a recurring theme in postcolonial education politics, lest we adopt a facile view of languages which would, otherwise, always be complex in these particular settings. The discussion in the postscript on the Guinea-Bissau experience in Freire and Macedo (1987) is quite revealing in this regard. The key point, alongside that of a critical decolonizing appropriation of the dominant, colonial language, is the affirmation of the formerly subjugated knowledge/wisdoms/culture of the colonised.

If, as denounced by Cabral, the Portuguese dictator António de Oliveira Salazaar went so far as to declare that 'Africa does not exist', one must therefore affirm, as the point of departure, the *right of existence of Africa*. The denial of this existence is as outrageous as it is absurd. And yet these statements reveal the absurd lengths to which colonial arrogance can lead. People from Portuguese colonies represented Portugal and not their country of origin prior to independence. For this reason, Eusébio da Silva Ferreira, popularly known as simply Eusébio, born in Mozambique and one of the very first Africa-born[3] football superstars, had to play for Portugal and not for the former colony. This situation still recurs with regard to French colonies called *départements*.

The partition of African territories, on the part of European colonizers, drastically marked this continent's destiny in poverty, hunger, misery and war. No country, continent or territory is 'born poor'. It is rendered poor by arrogance and a false sense of superiority by others with a misplaced sense of entitlement and bent on rapacious greed. Global importance and supremacy have alas been frequently measured, throughout history, in these terms.

The issue addressed in Guinea-Bissau's literacy programme was that of superseding the colonial legacy and the development of an educational system that inevitably had to connect with the country's history: the history of a colonized people who had only recently achieved independence. This historical responsibility entailed the attaching of importance to literacy as not a mere technical skill but a means of critically understanding the social process involved in its specific geographical and communal contexts. In Freire's phrase, the title of a book that devotes ample space to the Guinea-Bissau literacy experience, it is literacy that entails *reading the word and the world* (Freire and Macedo, 1987), including, in this case, the world of the colonizer and colonized.

Freire wrote that this critical understanding was a key feature of adult literacy in a society such as that of Guinea-Bissau whose people were directly or indirectly engaged in a war of liberation. Freire quotes Cabral as regarding this war as 'a cultural matter and a matter of culture' and the people's political consciousness as an important feature of this struggle (Freire, 1984, 16–17).

This political consciousness is a major ingredient of this struggle for liberation from not only colonial occupation but also the colonial system and its imposed educational programme which helps perpetuate violence at the intellectual, cultural and social levels, and therefore at the levels of personalities and identities. The struggle against *direct* colonialism (i.e., in Edward Said's terms, getting rid of an occupying force) must be supported or followed by a process of decolonization of the 'mental universe' (Thiong'o, 1986) of the people. The colonization of the people's mental universe can prove to be the most enduring form of colonization which can survive deep into the post-independence period.

Colonialism availed itself of the school, where this was available, to manipulate one's acquired sense of reality, inculcating in people's minds and lives a condition of dependency on the foreigner, experiencing a kind of cultural duplicity. What often follows is a false ideological conviction of one's inferiority, inability and low self-esteem. What emerges from the metropole is made to be perceived as superior and the benchmark against which domestic efforts are measured. This is a losing game for the colonized who are judged by standards more suited to the culture and conditions of the metropole than that of the colony itself. The colonial subjects are encouraged to 'ape' the former and devalue practices born out of and suited to the colonized home country or territory. The school and other means of education are key instruments of colonial cultural imposition, often of histories and contexts at odds with the realities of the colonized who therefore suffer cultural alienation. One must, once again, never overlook forms of resistance that are present, overt and covert, especially among sensitive educators. They can undermine this process of cultural imposition and transmission in a variety of ways, stimulating questions regarding what is not said by texts, in addition to what is being said. In the latter case, they would pose questions regarding what is being said by whom, defending which interests at the expense of which other interests and whose interests in both cases, and so forth. These are the potentially dangerous WH questions accompanied by the 'How' *process* question. Who represents whom, how and from which vantage point? This is the basis of a problem-posing education. We would not rule out the possibility that this subversion of the dominant discourse occurs in different forms of education, often at great risk. This can apply to schools before independence in education, formal or non-formal, taking the form of Freire's 'cultural action for freedom' (Freire, 1985). It can occur in liberated zones, as in Guinea-Bissau (Freire, 1978), during protracted wars of independence. It can occur in the post-independence context. There are cases, however, when there seems to be a disconnect between the actual official status of an independent nation and its schooling, especially, in the latter case, when colonial legacies are still being taken on board uncritically. There is so much 'unlearning', as well as learning, to occur after official independence. This takes us back to Freire's point at the outset regarding the formal institutional change and persistence with old forms of being and living, including schooling, at the grassroots. The foreign culture, which has a lot that is worth salvaging and critically appropriating, as explained earlier, is quite comprehensive and can easily survive the change of government from colonial to 'independent'. There are cases, as reported by the Subaltern Studies group in India, when a popular struggle for independence is hijacked by a bourgeois elite which simply replaces the colonizer without changing the contradiction of opposites between oppressor and oppressed: 'English rule without the English', as Mohandas Gandhi once put it.

The residues of colonialism are difficult to remove. There is, after all, a sort of 'parallel realities' syndrome, a double binary which triggers a 'cultural schizophrenia'. The senses of belonging and identification are divided between one's genuinely native culture – a colonized one – and that of the colonizer. Cabral states how all Portuguese (colonial) education belittled African cultures and civilization and that African languages were forgotten in schools. He states that the white person was always present as a superior being and the African represented as an inferior one, with the colonial conquerors being glorified as saints and heroes. He also states that no sooner do they commence school than African children acquire a feeling of inferiority, learning to fear the white person and becoming ashamed of being African. He goes on to denounce colonial education for misrepresenting or overlooking/not mentioning African geography and culture while compelling the scholar to study anything in a manner that connects with the Portuguese reality.[4]

The School of Anti-Colonial Struggle in Guinea-Bissau

The popular education programme serving as an alternative to colonial education was born in the course of the political struggle for liberation. In other words, it had a clearly articulated political history, intentionality and orientation. Territorially, in Guinea-Bissau, the literacy schools were established in areas which had been recently liberated – liberated zones – consisting of communities and villages: they were open spaces.[5] In these spaces, young students, farmers and members of the armed forces used to meet to learn things relevant to individual and communal life. They learnt how to proceed with the struggle. These were unmistakably *militant schools* but also schools in which a people developed awareness of the importance of learning. Cabral harped on the importance of having to learn from and among their people. He stated that persons (he used the collective 'we') had to learn from books, from other people's experiments. In short, learning and education had to be a way of life (Freire, 1978, 15). The task at hand was to restore dignity to the Guinean people, preparing them for the struggle, helping them rediscover their history, traditions and identity. This was the dream regarding the revolutionary school. It had to destroy the myths propagated by the colonial culture and reconnect people with their own territory. Cultural transformation was a primary objective to help cultivate a democratic practice, a sense of criticality and self-critique. It was meant to instil in the people a sense of responsibility to manage their own lives, develop their own literature, establish their own schools and public health centres and form their own cadres of peasants and workers.[6]

The Language Policy

There was one burning issue: which language should be adopted in the literacy campaign intended to foreground themes connected to independence and autonomy, as well as emancipation and decolonization? Freire proposed Creole, which he regarded as closer to the people's reality. From the liguistic perspective and, we would add, the *praxis* perspective, he considered it absurd to teach Portuguese in Guinea-Bissau. He nevertheless had to bow to the conditions imposed by the government despite the fact that, as he wrote, the students in one cultural circle transferred the technique learned in Portuguese to Creole. Freire argued that progress in the official language of the country, schools and literacy campaign, namely, Portuguese, was extremely slow. This, he feels, made it clear that Portuguese was completely alien to the day-to-day social practice of villagers. He informs us that the inhabitants did not know Portuguese, despite its being the spoken language. Freire states that conversations among Indigenous groups and many other people, though not all, were in Creole. This linguistic mix is a dialect deriving from Portuguese but enhanced by traditional African linguistic influences. Portuguese was quite diffuse during the battle for liberation when it became an important means of communication among those engaged. It is for this reason that Portuguese is considered the national language of the country. On the other hand, Freire informs us that, for the inhabitants of the countryside, Portuguese is merely a foreign language they do not understand, a linguistic code impossible to decipher. It would thus prove useless to learn given its lack of relevance in their everyday life. This notwithstanding, a very encouraging development occurred in the cultural circles of Sedengal.[7]

Despite all the difficulties arising from their shortcomings when learning Portuguese, the participants gradually managed to understand and master the pattern of division of syllables, within words, and their reconstruction, when applying this technique to Creole. Freire states that, spontaneously and unexpectedly, some groups managed to develop brief stories in Creole and write down phrases in their own Indigenous language. Being somewhat vindicated, Freire reports that these experiences rekindled the debate around the linguistic choices of a country. He declares that the structure of Creole as a written language and its diffusion made it the better linguistic choice, also in view of the need to preserve the African cultural identity. This, for Freire, would have been in keeping with the original objective of the literacy effort: to render the population the target of social change.[8]

This account by Freire provides much food for thought regarding the contradictions underlying the independence process. The government required a unitary language which would also have been recognized internationally. It required a language of international currency as indicated earlier. Creole, on the other hand, had many variations, according to village and community. The choice of Creole would have probably penalized the other linguistic minorities and created conflict, something about which Freire might not have been aware. He was told, in no uncertain terms, not to meddle into the language issue, as reported in Freire and Macedo (1987). Freire's preferred choice of Creole would have caused divisions, instead of having forged unity. Despite his firmly held belief in Creole, Freire followed the government's directives. The literacy campaign came in for much criticism especially from Linda Harasim[9] in her University of Toronto (OISE) PhD thesis whose arguments were echoed by Blanca Facundo.

Adult Literacy Education as a Political Act: São Tomè e Principe

Accounts of experiences and contents concerning literacy projects in Africa, particularly São Tomè e Principe, are available in the Popular Culture Notebooks.[10] They are education notebooks that refer to political pedagogical work. On the one hand, they describe the projects' different phases – based on cultural circles and generative words – which involve learning to read and write in a manner that encourages one to discuss themes of interest to the people. On the other hand, they critically elaborate on the contents through a political reading and therefore critical analysis of the material. Of undoubtedly great historical relevance, in our view, is a letter from the first notebook, where one finds an in-depth discussion of themes that render literacy a political act and, consequently, an act of consciousness and social reconstruction.

We are told that the task was to provide opportunities to a large number of comrades in the countryside, and elsewhere, to read and write. We are reminded that this was prohibited under the colonial regime. This is regarded as a political act in itself. The very decision to spread literacy is such an act. We are told that one has to remain wary of insinuations, often done naively, but at other times astutely, to convince one and all that literacy is simply a technical and pedagogical matter which should not be mixed with politics. We are then reminded of the classic Freire affirmation that, in reality, there is no neutral education and that this applies to the entire field including literacy. Education is political, as Freire has always maintained. We are told therefore that, for this reason, we must be very clear about our political choices and coherent in the way we 'walk the talk'. We are also reminded that, being a political act, adult literacy education is also an act of consciousness. This means that in the relationship between the educator and educatee, there is always something at stake one must learn about. We are reminded that, in a colonial education, the educator, by and large, transmitted his or her consciousness to us and our task, as learners, was to devour that consciousness, in Freire's famous statement, as an empty receptacle to be filled. Added to this is the rider that, from the outset, our reality was distorted in the colonizer's interests. The colonial literacy teacher, we are told, provided statements which the learner had to memorize.

It is argued that the revolution in process at the time required, from people, a coherence, a mode of behaviour, at all levels of action, in tune with its spirit. It is for this reason, we are told, that the term 'Night Schools for Adults' was rejected and replaced by 'Cultural Circles'. We are also told that instead of illiterates, a new term was used that comes close to 'literacy learners' in English. The letter also reveals other changes in terminology: from literacy teachers to cultural animators and from lessons to debates. It is the people's own reality, reflected in the 'generative words' and represented by 'codifications', that is discussed. It is further stated, in the document, that, in the case of adult literacy, and in keeping with the principles that govern the revolutionary, independence movement, both cultural animators and literacy learners together read and write their own reality, think critically about their own world and, through critical consciousness, immerse themselves in the reality being transformed (Freire and Macedo, 1987, 1–10).

Cultural action was not limited to simply adult literacy but contributed to important developments in mathematics and health education, besides education for production, work and culture. The Fourth Notebook of Popular Culture contains references to physical well-being, nutrition, protection from insects, intestinal issues, vaccines, tetanus, epidemic and non-epidemic ailments, and so forth. Water and refuse are also tackled. It consisted of an education for national reconstruction and this historical process had a socialist, revolutionary and anti-colonial orientation.

Diversification and expansion of collective work in the fields were areas given major importance. These practical skills were greatly valorized: people, for example, learnt to make better use of seeds and fertilizers, how to monitor the conditions of land and water or plan sales of produce. It consisted of a programme of integrated learning combining literacy with popular education. Education was no longer considered a specialized activity, divorced from life and production, as with the neoliberal system. It was, to the contrary, an integral part of the social environment, an instrument of social and political elaboration. Where literacy had become possible, the main goal was to establish, through collective decision making and creativity, an active communal presence. This foregrounded cultural action, popular education and community politics.

Conclusion

We can consider the cultural dimension of politics as a point of convergence in Amilcar Cabral and Paulo Freire. Freire regards culture as a key element in a process of emancipatory education and finds, in Cabral's sensitivity to the cultural dimension of politics, affinities with the ideas of Antonio Gramsci. He even goes so far as to advocate a comparative reading of Gramsci and Cabral, which would be useful to teachers in their formation. When Cabral and Freire speak of culture, they are not using the term in a vague sense. They are referring to a people's culture, way of life and artistic expression. They are also referring to popular culture which, we would add, echoing Gramsci, contains 'common sense' that can, through a critical education, be distilled of its contradictory elements to be elaborated as good sense. The people's culture provides the existential situation at the basis of the struggle for liberation: this is very clear in Cabral's strategy. It is also quite clear that the struggle, a cultural act, further produces culture. It is, however, the people themselves who provide the instruments for this struggle. Otherwise it would be struggling *for* the people rather than a struggle *of* the people. Freire, for instance, wrote of a pedagogy *of* and not *for* the oppressed.

It is in the relation between the political struggle and the people's culture that one discovers the importance of a popular, communal education. This is where Paulo Freire's experience in Guinea-Bissau becomes historically significant. The valorization of popular culture has always been a key feature of Paulo Freire's conceptualization of a pedagogy of the oppressed. It is the leitmotif of his work. His participation in the Popular Cultural Movement in Pernambuco was an important factor in this regard. At the heart of his practical and theoretical work, intertwined as praxis, lies popular language and culture.

Another point of convergence is the commitment of both Cabral and Freire to work with both urban and rural workers. As agricultural and forestry services assistant, during the first agriculture census in Guinea-Bissau, Cabral began to understand the world and struggles of farmers. Freire, for his part, availed himself of popular education to render it a vehicle for dialogue with and among workers. He managed to rethink his educational philosophy as a result of this dialogue. He regarded popular education as a process of organization of work, a means of coordinating movements and as a crucial factor in an emancipatory political strategy.

Freire's admiration for Cabral indicates that the thrust of his professed educational approach is profoundly revolutionary, a point underlined by Jonathan Kozol in his endorsement of the first edition in English of *Pedagogy of the Oppressed*. 'This is truly revolutionary pedagogy,' we are told. This revolutionary stance is something concrete and tied to a historical process. It would indeed be reductionist to read Freire without considering the concrete historical processes that gave birth to and helped him elaborate his ideas. We cannot isolate our reading of Freire from these historical developments and an appreciation of their bearing on educational activity. In the same way, we cannot read Cabral without recognizing the very important educational and cultural dimension of the struggle for national independence from Portugal's colonial yoke. Both highlighted the cultural basis of action against oppression for the ushering in of a better world forged with their people. They both gave importance to a critical reading of the world and recognize the potential of a genuinely relevant education developed *together with others*, instead of one that is *imposed on others* (Cortesão, 2011, 263). Both suffered because of this, Cabral paying the ultimate price, as with many other revolutionary figures from what was one called the 'Tricontinental World' (Africa, Latin America and Asia).

Both provide ideas and ingredients for a social and community education at the furthest remove from that which is technicist, heartless, atomizing and decontextualized, alas the staple of the neoliberal project today.

11

Julius K. Nyerere's Signposts for a Postcolonial Education

Julius Kambarage Nyerere (1922–1999) has his detractors, as with all political leaders for that matter. Despite all this, he happens to be one of the most respected and, in certain cases, revered figures in African and world politics and especially with respect to his thinking on development and education. A practising Catholic, son of a village chief at Butiama (Northern Tanzania) and former teacher in a Catholic school, Nyerere had an eventful political life, full of significant political moments. He led Tanganika to independence in 1961, became this country's president and later became the first president of Tanzania following the unification of Tanganika and Zanzibar in 1964, after the latter became independent.

Ever so ready to lead by example, 'Mwalimu' (teacher in Kishwahili), as he has been reverentially called, remained at the helm of Tanzanian politics even after he resigned from being president. Until 1990, he was the head of *Chama Cha Mapinduzi* (Party of the Revolution), the party that emerged from the fusion between TANU (Tanganykan National Union) and *Afro-Shirazi*, the party that governed Zanzibar. Later, under the guidance of his successor as president, Ali Hassan Mwinyi, Tanzania changed from a one party to a multi-party state.

Many consider the brand of socialism, espoused by Nyerere, to have failed insofar as material results are concerned. One can say the same thing for many other African countries that followed the capitalist path, a point which Nyerere stressed in an interview with a US correspondent (Nyerere, 1996). Some expressed reservations regarding his socialist project's viability for Tanzania. Different political standpoints led to different evaluations. Many, however, recognized his stature as a statesman. The country distinguished itself from others in Africa for its peaceful political transition and lack of ethnic strife. He claims that the country succeeded in attaining racial integration soon after independence and that religious discrimination was brought to an end (Nyerere, 1968, 270).

During the last years of his life, Nyerere played an important role as mediator seeking solutions to the great conflicts around power in the Great Lakes region in East Africa. He was principal mediator in Burundi (Smith, 1999, 9) to avoid a communal catastrophe reminiscent of nearby Rwanda. He was very much involved in development politics, directing the South Commission and later the Intergovernmental Centre for the South in Geneva (ibid.).

There are those who feel that his vision of Pan-Africanism remains unparalleled among African leaders.[1] During his presidency, Tanzania provided support and shelter for a host of African freedom fighters, including African National Congress (ANC) activists and others combating Portuguese colonialism. Furthermore, Nyerere was one of the founding figures of the Non-Aligned Movement. He was also instrumental in the overthrow of Idi Amin in Uganda.

He had his problems on the international scene. There were problems with Western countries which had led to foreign aid cutbacks. These consisted of conflicts with the UK following the latter's recognition of the unilateral Declaration of Independence by white settlers in Rhodesia, conflicts with West Germany following Tanzania's recognition of the DDR and conflicts with the United States following accusations by Tanzania of CIA involvement in the East African country (Unsicker 1986, 232). Nyerere's particular brand of socialism appeared to have incurred the wrath of several communists, especially those from the Eastern Bloc (Okoh, 1980, 52). Capitalism was obnoxious to Nyerere, who is on record as having said, at one time, that he differed from Western socialists precisely on the grounds that they glorify capitalism as a mode of production that begets socialism (ibid.).

His writings on development, socialism, literature (he translated Shakespeare's *Julius Caesar* [*Juliasi Kaizari*] and the *Merchant of Venice* [*Mabepari wa Venisi*] into Kiswahili), education, African liberation, intellectuals, non-alignment and a host of other subjects constitute an often-cited corpus of postcolonial writing to come out of Africa.

One area in which Nyerere is often cited is that of *Education* (see Samoff, 1990; Kassam, 1994; Smith, 1999) and this is hardly surprising given the importance he attached to this domain of social policy and practice in his writings and work as leader of Tanzania.

Nyerere's overarching political concept was that of *Ujamaa* (familyhood), which represents an attempt by a third-world leader to apply socialism to the specific needs of an African community. It rests on three basic tenets, expressed in his famous tract on education, 'Education for self-reliance': 'equality and respect for human dignity; sharing of the resources which are produced by our efforts; work by everyone and exploitation by none' (Nyerere, 1968, 272). The Tanzanian African National Union (TANU) established these basic ideals in the national ethic as well as in 'The Arusha Declaration' (ibid., 231–50), the latter being the declaration of policy which the country had to follow. Towards the end of his life, Nyerere expounded on these socialist values which he considered still pertinent in an age in which we are swamped by neoliberalism and its concomitant ideology of the marketplace. According to the transcript of the 1996 interview, he stated:

> And those values are values of justice, a respect for human beings, a development which is people-centered, development where you care about people … you can say leave the development of a country to something called the market which has no heart at all since capitalism is completely ruthless … who is going to help the poor? … and the majority of the people in our countries are poor. Who is going to stand for them? Not the market. So I'm not regretting that I tried to build a country based on those principles. You will have to—whether you call them socialism or not—do you realize that what made—what gave capitalism a human face was the kind of values I was trying to sell in my country. (Nyerere, 1996)

The Nigerian scholar J. D. Okoh states that the first principle in the Arusha Declaration, that of respect for human dignity, was stressed in view of the fact that 'several decades of colonization had created in the African a deep-seated "inferiority complex", coupled with a crisis of identity' (Okoh, 1980, 54). Okoh refers to Nyerere's statement that it was once a compliment rather than an insult to refer to a person harbouring a European mentality as a 'Black European', a statement which is reminiscent of Frantz Fanon's (1952) 'Black Skin, White Masks'. This is typical of the colonial ideology which often involves, in Paulo Freire's terms, an internalization of the image of the oppressor (Freire, 1970a, 32). We would submit that this often takes the form of pathetically *aping* the demeanour and other attributes (including spoken language) of the colonizer.

The second principle in the Arusha Declaration, stressing the need to share resources, suggests the idea of communitarianism that is at the heart of Ujamaa. Nyerere regarded this as an attempt to recuperate what he regarded to be the traditional African experience which was destroyed by the colonial powers through their notorious policy of 'divide and rule'. Okoh quotes him as having placed emphasis on recuperating a mindset that gives one the security deriving from one's sense of belonging to a 'widely extended family' (Okoh, 1980, 52), even though the same author is quick to point out that many African scholars criticized Nyerere for romanticising precolonial African society. This notion of familyhood led many to regard his political credo as 'Christian Socialism'.

His concept of grassroots democracy revolved around Ujamaa or, more appropriately, in this case, *Ujamaa Vijijni* (village familyhood), which entailed a process of participatory democracy. Writing in *Freedom and Development*, a policy booklet published in 1968, Nyerere says:

> Everyone must be allowed to speak freely, and everyone must be listened to. It does not matter how unpopular a man's ideas, or how mistaken the majority think him. It does not make any difference whether he is liked or disliked for his personal qualities. Every Tanzanian, every member of a community, every member of a District Council, every Member of Parliament, and so on, must have the freedom to speak without fear of intimidation – either inside or outside the meeting place [*sic*]. (Nyerere, 1974, 30, 31).

In a very important evaluative document, published ten years after the Arusha Declaration, Nyerere took political leaders to task for not listening to the people. He states: 'They find it much easier to TELL people what to do. Meetings are often monologues, without much, if any, time being devoted to discussion; and even then the speech is usually an exhortation to work hard rather than an explanation to do things better' (Nyerere, 1977, 29). Moreover, in *Freedom and Development*, Nyerere states that people should not be forced into joining 'Ujamaa Vijijni' and stresses that the concept is based on the post-Arusha Declaration understanding that what Tanzania needs 'to develop is people, not things, and that people can only develop themselves' (Nyerere, 1974, 36).

The idea of a participatory communal being was in marked reaction to the very limited and elitist colonial education in place in Tanganyika and Zanzibar at the time of independence. In 'Education for self-reliance', Nyerere argues that colonial education 'was based on the assumptions of a colonialist and capitalist society. It emphasised and encouraged the individualistic instincts of mankind, instead of his co-operative instincts [*sic*]. It led to the possession of individual material wealth being the criterion of social merit and worth' (Nyerere, 1968, 269). The colonial educational provision was characterized by what Freire (1970b, 151) would call 'cultural invasion,' a process which undermined traditional indigenous values:

> Colonial education in this country was therefore not transmitting the values and knowledge of Tanzanian society from one generation to the next: it was a deliberate attempt to change those values and to replace traditional knowledge by the knowledge from a different society. It was thus a part of a deliberate

attempt to effect a revolution in the society; to make it into a colonial society which accepted its status and which was an efficient adjunct to the governing power. (Nyerere, 1968, 270)

At the time of Tanganyika's independence, there were few people with the necessary qualifications to strengthen the administration of government. The country was impoverished and the educational infrastructure was largely underdeveloped. It was a major effort to provide universal primary education, let alone secondary education for all. In fact, secondary schooling was provided for only a select few. It is for this reason that Nyerere argued that primary schooling should not be conceived of as a preparation for secondary schooling, since the majority would not benefit from the latter. The situation was rendered problematic by the fact that private secondary schools existed alongside state schools. These schools allowed those who could afford to pay for their education the chance of benefiting from secondary schooling (see Bacchus, 1973). Furthermore, with regard to state schools, it is an acknowledged fact (practically a truism), substantiated by a huge corpus of sociological research, that any process of selection based on 'meritocracy' in effect favours those with the greatest amount of resources and congenial *cultural capital*. In Tanzania's case, these were the children of those 'new elites' who, following independence, had obtained lucrative jobs in the civil service (ibid.). This situation must have had a deleterious effect on any attempt to create an egalitarian society (ibid.).

One of the major goals for Tanzania was the provision of universal primary education by the end of 1977. Pressure was placed on bureaucrats to expedite this process, the slogan being 'we must run while others walk'. As a result of this bold step, Tanzania witnessed a massive expansion in state education. Nyerere himself provides the following statistics:

A tremendous jump in the number of children attending primary schools has been the result. In 1967 there were about 825,000 pupils in Tanzanian primary schools. In 1975 the comparable figure was 1, 532, 000 pupils, and the numbers will continue to rise rapidly for some years to come. (Nyerere, 1977, 8).

Nyerere also advocated an education which provided students with a sense of self-reliance, the focus being mainly on the development of an agrarian economy. It had to be an education characterized by the fusion of learning and producing, both processes taking place simultaneously. Each school had to develop its own means of subsistence. This concept is very much in keeping with the socialist tradition. One can cite as examples here Karl Marx's notion of a polytechnic education, as propounded in the Geneva Resolution of 1866 (see Castles and Wustenberg, 1979, cited in Livingstone, 1983, 186, 187); Freire's advocacy of a fusion between education and production in his advice to the PAIGC leadership in Guinea-Bissau (See Letter 11 in Freire, 1978, 99–120); the introduction, in Malta, under Dom Mintoff's socialist administration, of the worker-student and pupil-worker schemes (5½ month period of study alternating with a 5½ month period of work) at sixth form and university levels (Baldacchino, 1999, 207, 208); the system in China under Mao Zedong which involved a 2-4-2-4 (two months working-four months studying-two months working-four months studying) process (Chu, 1980, 79). The following statement by Mao best anticipates the spirit of the education-work process which Nyerere advocated:

> Whoever wants to know a thing has no way of doing so except by coming into contact with it, that is by living (practising) in its environment. (Mao, cited in ibid.)

The idea of school farms was developed in Tanzania: 'Every school should also be a farm; that the school community should consist of people who are both teachers and farmers, and pupils and farmers' (Nyerere, 1968, 283). Nyerere also went so far as to stress that the pupils' welfare would depend on their farm's output very much the same way that the peasants' livelihood depends on the produce yielded by their land (ibid.). Nyerere did not mince his words: 'By this sort of practice, and by this combination of classroom work and farm work, our educated young people will learn to realize that if they farm well they can eat well and have better facilities in the dormitories, recreation rooms, and so on. If they work badly, then they themselves will suffer' (ibid., 284, 285). He even encouraged experienced farmers and agricultural officers to participate in the project:

> Life and farming will go on as we train. Indeed, by using good local farmers as supervisors and teachers of particular aspects of the work, and using the services of the Agricultural Officers and assistants, we shall be helping to break down the notion that only book learning is worthy of respect. This is an important element in our socialist development. (ibid., 283, 284).

The school was no longer to be the exclusive domain of professionally formed teachers. In keeping with the idea of a productive community school, the entire community was to be regarded as a learning resource. This concept is quite in tune with the literature on community schools (Parson, 1990) and the more progressive literature on parental and other community members' involvement in the education of children (Curtis, Livingstone and Smaller, 1992; Smyth, 1994). It is a literature which underlines the importance of people outside the teaching profession having a say in the development of the school and contributing to the education it provides. In this respect, it is a literature which raises an important question: who can effectively act as an educator within the community? (Smyth, 1994, 135).

Nyerere maintained that it was absolutely vital that the schools and their pupils were to be integrated into village life: 'The children must be made part of the community by having responsibilities to the community and having the community involved in school activities' (Nyerere, 1968, 287). He suggests that school work – terms, times and so forth – be organized in such a way that the children are allowed to participate, as family members, in the family farms, 'or as junior members of the community on community farms' (ibid.).

As far as school capital is concerned, Nyerere believed that school farms should derive no more assistance than would be available to an ordinary established cooperative farm where the work is supervised (ibid., 284). Through such means, the students could, according to Nyerere, learn the advantages of 'co-operative endeavour' especially 'when outside capital is not available in any significant quantities' (ibid.). Of course, the responsibility for upkeep was to be much stronger at the secondary level than at the primary level (ibid., 287). The problem, though, is that, according to a report published in the early 1970s, secondary schools were the least affected by the move to introduce farming in the schools (Bacchus, 1973). The report stated that the majority of secondary schools still placed their greatest emphasis on formal academic studies (ibid.). It also stated that, in primary schools, teachers with a very poor agricultural background placed the emphasis on physical work on the farm, at times to the detriment of the 'educative' aspect of the experience (ibid.). In order to ensure that the primary school children were old enough to engage in running the school farm, the educational authorities in Tanzania raised the primary-school entry age 'from 5 or 6 to 7 years' (Kassam, 1994, 252).

Nyerere sought to provide an education which 'decolonized the mind', once again to use a very popular term in Africa reminiscent of Frantz Fanon, Ngugi wa Thiong'o and the former Cape Verde president Aristides Pereira (with respect to the last mentioned, see Freire, 1985, 187). He states that the education provided must be 'for liberation', acknowledging that a 'liberated nation, in Africa or elsewhere, is not just a nation which has overcome alien occupation. That is an essential first part of liberation, but it is only the first. Liberation means more than that' (Nyerere, 1979c, 43). The country, as Aristides Pereira underlined with respect to Cape Verde, might have been decolonized, but now the task was to decolonize the mind. For Nyerere, this meant that Tanzania had to become a 'self-reliant nation' while its people had to overcome feelings of inferiority and be able to use circumstances rather than be used by them (Nyerere, 1979c, 43). For Nyerere and others, however, such a decolonizing or liberating process entails a valorization of that which is Indigenous. Kiswahili was established as the national language while educational institutions were to promote African culture. A firm believer in Indigenous cultures, Nyerere states: 'No longer do our children simply learn British and European history. Faster than would have been thought possible, our University college[2] and other institutions are providing materials on the history of Africa and making these available to our teachers' (Nyerere, 1968, 271). National songs and dances found their place in the postcolonial Tanzanian curriculum. Civics lessons gave secondary school pupils some understanding of the aims of the young Tanzanian state (ibid.). Furthermore, a national board was introduced to set and mark examinations (Samoff, 1990, 209), a postcolonial measure adopted by a number of other former British colonies (see Bray and Steward, 1998).

It is not only schools that had to forge a link with the community but also the University. In a speech inaugurating the University of Dar es Salaam on 29 August, 1970, Nyerere wrote: 'When determining whether a particular subject should be offered, the university should therefore be asking itself: "What contribution can a study of this subject make to Tanzania's future?"... "What knowledge of, or from, our own society is relevant to this matter?"' (Nyerere, 1979d, 41). The University was to provide materials for a genuinely postcolonial school curriculum, including materials in Kiswahili. While advocating the tailoring of University provision to the needs of the country, Nyerere still felt that the University must be allowed the freedom to experiment, to try out new courses and methods (ibid., 42). He argued that the staff must pose challenging questions to the students and the University must pose challenging questions to society at large (ibid.).

As for students, Nyerere states: 'The peasants and workers of a nation feed, clothe, and house both the students and their teachers, they also provide all the educational facilities used – the books, test-tubes, machines and so on. The community provides these things because it expects to benefit – it is making an investment in people' (ibid., 39). He even criticized the tendency among educated workers to place a price tag on themselves. In an address to the University of Liberia on 29 February 1968, Nyerere stated: 'Shall we, in other words, use the skills which society has enabled us to acquire, in order to hold that same society to ransom?' (Nyerere, 1974, 7).

Of course, Nyerere, in a manner recalling Mao's reaction against Confucian principles and the Mandarin class, stressed that there should be no distinction between 'educated' and 'uneducated', between 'intellectual' and 'manual' labour. One of the most popular pictures of the former president is that in which he is shown wielding an axe in a *shamba*, in the company of other toiling peasants. It would be naïve to ignore the obvious PR element involved here, the sort of ploy adopted by many politicians and, in particular, populist politicians ever so eager to appear 'close to the people' or, more appropriately, 'the masses'. It ought to be underlined, however, that farming was the activity to which Nyerere returned following his retirement from Tanzanian politics.

Like Freire and others, Nyerere warned against intellectuals and 'experts' underestimating the knowledge of peasants and workers. He points to the fact that, in Tanganyika, thirty-six million pounds were spent by colonialists on a Ground Nut scheme. It turned out to be an expensive failure since the 'experts' underestimated the knowledge of local farmers, who they dismissed as illiterate and so made their own decisions regarding rainfall regularity. They also assumed that it was simple indolence that made people reluctant to cut down all the trees when planting a *shamba*, 'So large areas were cleared – and few nuts grew, but erosion began!' (ibid., 10).

One area which was given a tremendous boost in Tanzania during Nyerere's presidency was adult education. Nyerere is a respected figure in the global adult education movement. Budd L. Hall, former secretary general of the *International Council for Adult Education* and former head of the Department of Research, Institute of Adult Education, Dar es Salaam, wrote:

> Among his many accomplishments was his role as the founding Honorary President of the International Council for Adult Education. He delivered the keynote address to the First World Assembly of Adult Education organized in Dar es Salaam, Tanzania in June of 1976. His vision created the national slogan for 1970 Adult Education Year, 'Elimu Haina Mwiso' … Learning Never Ends … that was used on the commemorative cloth printed specially for the 1976 ICAE World Assembly.[3]

That Nyerere is often cited in adult education circles is not surprising given his country's achievement of 'outstanding standards' (Bacchus and Torres, 1988, 322) in the area. Many of these achievements have been outlined in the literature (see e.g. Hall and Kassam, 1972; Hall et al, 1972; Hall, 1973a,b; 1975; Bhola, 1984;

Unsicker, 1986; Sumra and Bwatwa, 1988; Mayo, M., 1997). As Jeff Unsicker (1986, 231) reports in his detailed study of Tanzania's literacy campaign, it was stated in Tanzania's first five-year development plan that 'the nation cannot wait until the children have become educated for development to begin'. As with the process of universal primary education, the feeling again was that 'we must run while others walk'. At the above-mentioned ICAE World Assembly, Nyerere stated that adult education 'incorporates anything which enlarges' people's 'understanding, activates them, helps them to make their own decisions, and to implement those decisions for themselves' (Nyerere, 1979a, 51). One of the aims of adult education, as with all education, was to liberate the mind in a way that allows people to develop a strong sense of agency characterized by a belief in their ability to master circumstances. One of the major challenges for adult education, according to Nyerere, was to combat what he perceived as a traditional sense of fatalism among Tanzanian people:

> The importance of adult education, both for our country and for every individual, cannot be over-emphasised. We are poor and backward, and too many of us just accept our present conditions as 'the will of God', and feel that we can do nothing about them. In many cases, therefore, the first objective of adult education must be to shake ourselves out of a resignation to the kind of life Tanzanian people have lived for centuries past. (Nyerere, 1979b, 33).

The situation is similar to that described by Freire with respect to the oppressed of Brazil:

> They resort (stimulated by the oppressor) to magical explanations or a false view of God, to whom they fatalistically transfer the responsibility for their oppressed state ... A Chilean priest of high intellectual and moral caliber visiting Recife in 1966 told me: 'When a Pernambucan colleague and I went to see several families living in shanties [*mocambos*] in indescribable poverty, I asked them how they could bear to live like that, and the answer was always the same: "What can I do? It is the will of God and I must accept it."' (Freire, 1970a, 163)

It appears most appropriate that, at some stage, reference is made to Freire's ideas when discussing Nyerere's educational speeches or writings. Nyerere and Freire admired each other's writings, with the former having read *Pedagogy of the Oppressed* and the latter having been 'so impressed by the writings of Nyerere' that he told the Tanzanian president, on his visit to the latter's home 'on the outskirts of Dar es Salaam' in 1971, 'that he would like to organize a series of seminars where his speeches could be discussed and analysed in depth'

(Hall, 1998, 97). The similarities between Nyerere's and Freire's ideas appeared so strong to the Brazilian educator that 'he asked President Nyerere to provide support for an educational center in Tanzania based on the ideas of Freire and Nyerere', a proposal which never materialized, although Freire, together with Moacir Gadotti, eventually managed to establish the Instituto Paulo Freire in São Paulo in the latter stages of the Brazilian educator's life (ibid., 98).[4]

Arguably, the greatest similarity between Nyerere and Freire lies in their emphasis on listening to the learners and 'building on' the knowledge that they possess. It was important for Freire that one does not remain at the same level of knowledge (Allman et al., 1998, 11) and that the educator should be disposed to learn from the learner (Freire, 1970a, 67; Freire, 1985, 177). With regard to the second point, Nyerere states:

> Every adult knows something about the subject he is interested in, even if he is not aware that he knows it. He may indeed know something which his teacher does not know. For example, the villagers will know what time of the year malaria is worse and what group of people - by age or residence or workplace – are most badly affected [*sic*]. (Nyerere, 1979a, 53)

And yet, Michaela von Freyhold states, with respect to the Tanzanian literacy campaign, that these principles were not observed:

> After a visit by Paulo Freire to Tanzania there were some discussions on whether it would be advisable to make the primers more 'problem-posing' and open. In the end this suggestion was turned down. The planners argued that: 'If we allow the peasants to criticize the advice of the extension agent, we undermine his authority' [*sic*]. Nor should there be any discussion of the choice of crops: 'If peasants begin to discuss whether they want to grow cotton or not they might decide against it, and if they produce no cotton where are we going to get our foreign exchange from?' (von Freyhold, 1979, 166, cited in Unsicker, 1986, 241, 242)

Interesting strictures which raise the issue regarding the extent to which the imperatives of economic viability ran counter to the principles of a liberating education, a situation which was not unique to Tanzania (see Carnoy and Torres, 1990).

The immediate task, underlined by Nyerere, six years following the start of a much-documented mass literacy campaign in Tanzania, is enabling adults to 'acquire the tools of development the literacy, the knowledge of health needs, the need for improved production, the need to improve dwelling places and the basic skills necessary to meet all these needs' (Nyerere, 1979a, 55).

Important landmarks in the development of adult education in Tanzania were of course the setting up of the Institute of Adult Education at the University of Dar es Salaam, including an impressive correspondence school (Bhola, 1984, 154), and Kivokoni college, the latter being developed on the lines of England's Ruskin College (Mayo, M., 1997, 65). Ruskin College, a residential college for workers, fascinated Nyerere who 'invited one of the younger Ruskin organizers, Joan Wicken, to work with him in Tanzania' (Hall, 1998, 96). She eventually became 'President Nyerere's personal assistant and sometimes speech writer' (ibid., 97) and, together with the president, founded Kivokoni College (ibid., 96). Kivokoni College focused on providing 'political and ideological training of lower level government officials and party cadres in the regions' (Bhola, 1984, 154). Other colleges of this type were subsequently created in other zones of the country (ibid.). Of course, the extent to which this can be considered a genuine, critical political education or an exercise in partisan party indoctrination remains a moot point. Is there a fine line between the two?

The mass literacy campaign was a considerable success and won the UNESCO Literacy Award. Key figures such as Freire were associated, in an advisory capacity, with the campaign, although Freire's involvement in this particular instance has been described as 'peripheral' (Torres, 1982, 87). The literacy programme went on for many years, sustained by the Ministry and other agencies, including the Swedish International Development Agency (SIDA) and the United Nations Development Program (UNDP) (Mushi, 1994, 67). As with most literacy campaigns, many of the thousands of teachers employed were volunteers who, according to Unsicker, were trained in workshops and were paid a small honorarium of thirty shillings per month (Unsicker, 1986, 239). However, there were also primary schoolteachers who acted as adult educators (Mushi, 1994, 68). The usual problem in such instances, encountered also in other contexts (see Baldacchino and Mayo, 1995), is that some of them replicate with adults the approaches they use with schoolchildren (Sumra and Bwatwa, 1988, 268; Mushi, 1994, 68). We also wonder whether the use, as adult education centres, of primary schools (Mushi, 1994, 67, 68), which have not been restructured or built in such a way that they accommodate community members of different ages, contributed to this replication (see Baldacchino and Mayo, 1995, 1997). The process of mobilization in Tanzania involved various media including primers and radio broadcasts in a country where radio provided, in the rural areas, the only means of technological communication. There were also post-literacy programmes involving the study of a number of subjects. Even prior to the 1970 literacy campaigns, there had been Scandinavian-influenced experiments based on folk education, often involving radio study groups in different rural areas (Unsicker, 1986, 234). Folk Development Colleges (FDCs), inspired by the Scandinavian (more specifically, Swedish) Folk High Schools, were also set up as residential colleges for those who had successfully been through the literacy programme and who were selected by their village communities to attend residential courses intended to be of benefit to the community at large (Bhola, 1984, 154; Mayo, M. 1997, 64). The FDCs' programme 'was launched in 1975' and has seen to the provision of 'courses for village leaders (chairpersons, secretaries, bookkeepers, and village shop managers); leaders of women's organisations, household activities, and small scale industries; various groups engaged in implementing various self-reliance projects; and assistant field officers' (Sumra and Bwatwa, 1988, 264). These FDCs have survived for several years (Earth, 1998, 59).

All these developments placed Tanzania at the forefront of initiatives with regard to adult education in the 1970s. Certainly, many of the programmes depended to a large extent on foreign funding, a potentially contradictory situation, given that self-reliance was the declared goal. This funding diminished in the 1980s especially following the onset of neoliberal policies brought into place by such institutions as the International Monetary Fund (IMF) and the World Bank with their 'structural adjustment' programmes. There were disagreements between Tanzania and the IMF which were not resolved until 1986. These disagreements concerned the IMF's 'insistence on sharp cuts in public spending', particularly 'in the social services' and on 'a substantial devaluation' (Samoff, 1990, 218). Tanzania has, since then, embarked on a path of development which can be regarded as a far cry from the policies advocated by Nyerere. There are those who would no doubt argue that his ideas were largely out of touch with a world governed by the imperatives of technological development and 'competitivity'. Others regard him to have been more of a philosopher king, confronting the logic of capitalist and neocolonial development with alternative ideas rooted in Indigenous forms of practice. There are those who underline the difficulties that confront a state such as Tanzania undergoing transition through non-revolutionary means (ibid., 268).

In his last days, Nyerere often stated that he always carried with him two books, the Bible and the Arusha Declaration.[5] This attests to Julius Kambarage Nyerere's lifelong commitment to Christian-Socialist principles.

12

Social Movements and Critical Education in Brazil: From the Origins of Popular Education to the Struggle for Democratisation

with Roberto Leher[1]

Social Movements and Education

One of the key contexts for education and learning, especially of a non-formal and informal nature, is said to be social movements, given the vast amount of literature centring on this area. Movements not only provide the context in which such learning and education occur but are themselves said to be sources of learning. The learning dimension is an integral part of a social movement. Social movements are said to constitute learning sites (Welton, 1993; Foley, 1999; Hall and Clover, 2005, 2006; English and Mayo, 2012) 'Social movements' is a term which by and large is given positive connotations in the literature on education and society in general, as though we seem to overlook that they can be downright reactionary. Movements come in different types. There are fundamentalist religious movements just as there are movements which are presented as progressive. Some focus on specific issues while others focus on a specific issue which is connected with so many other areas that its area of concern becomes broader in scope, allowing room for greater intersectionality. Movements gravitating around sustainability or land reform, the latter a recurrent issue in Latin America, embrace a whole array of interrelated issues.

Furthermore, the contextual bases of what we call 'social movements' is wide enough for us to distinguish historically between Old and New social movements, with the labour movement worldwide often referred to as a classic example of the former and the LGBTQI movement as an example of the New social movements (NSMs). Some work hand in hand with established institutions of which they form part, such as the Labour movement and the Trade Union movement, the trade union itself being an institution, while other movements tread warily in their relations with institutions, being 'in and against' to preserve their autonomy. The same applies to relations with the state at whatever level, national, provincial or municipal (see O'Cadiz, Wong and Torres, 1998). There are those who have argued that governments in the West seek to exert control over movements either through funding mechanisms, 'heterarchical' modes of governance or anticipation of their existence by setting up national commissions in the area. It is the unpredictability of movement actions which is the cause of concern to governments.

Paulo Freire, a key source of influence in this chapter is on record stating that parties (he had the PT – Partido dos Trabalhadores – in mind) can learn by working *with* movements and can therefore 'grow' this way, but warned that they should do so without attempting to take over the movements. He claims that this relationship can also help movements make their struggles 'politically viable' (Freire, in Escobar et al., 1994, 40). His experience in dealing with movements in São Paulo is that the autonomy of some of the social movements is *sacrosanct*. More significantly, there are those movements, globally, which, though claiming to have a wide international (Global 'North' and Global 'South') reach and variety of challenges, project an overall image that is predominantly Western and possibly middle-class-oriented.

Subaltern Southern Social Movements

Others, and there are many of these, have been classified as 'Southern' and subaltern social movements (Kapoor, 2009). There is a wide variety in this regard, comprising Indigenous movements often connected with a particular territory or country. Leona English and Peter Mayo (2012), drawing on Dip Kapoor (2009), refer to the Ejercito Zapatistas in Chiapas, seen as a movement and not a party; the Chipko and Adivasi movements in India; the Ogoni movement in Nigeria; the Greenbelt women's movement in Kenya; the San people of the Kalahari in South Africa (ibid., 77); and Maori, Aborigines and First Nations movements. We should also include the dispossessed Palestinians as a movement. Dispossessed people, such as the landless peasants including the MST – Movimento Trabalhadores Rurais Sem Terra – in Brazil (Tarlau, 2017, 2019), to whom we shall devote much space in this chapter, and others just mentioned, struggle against loss of the means to reproduce their material existence, in rural ecological resource economies, as a result of globalizing colonial dispossession (English and Mayo, 2012, 121). Their struggle also has a 'specific mythico-religious' dimension since the movements' adherents claim to be tied, spiritually and historically, to a 'physical and existential location' (Kapoor, 2009, 79). Their action involves, among others (see ibid.), the basic human right of citizenship and the assertion and vindication of the sovereign right of minorities in 'pluri-national states as a precondition for protecting and sustaining peasant spaces' (ibid., 81; English and Mayo, 2012, 121). The one movement Kapoor (2009) has in mind here is the Adivasi movement of disposed Indigenous in India which total to no fewer than 85 million (ibid.; Kapoor, in English and Mayo, 2012).

Many of the issues concerning popular education and the subaltern, 'southern' social movements apply to the country being discussed in this chapter – Brazil. The country's struggles for democratization over the years foreground a variety of social movements, the sort of movements that always provided key educators/intellectuals such as Leonardo Boff, Florestan Fernandes, Frei Betto and Paulo Freire with rays of hope. Before his death, and therefore well before the onset of the right-wing Neo-Fascist return to Brazilian politics headed by Jair Bolsonaro, Freire waxed lyrical about the various movements, 'Old' and 'New', that were contributing to what was then the democratization of Brazilian society, exclaiming, as he stood before the television watching the MST march into Brasilia: 'That's it, Brazilian people, the country belongs to all of us! Let us build together a democratic country, just and happy!' (Nita Freire, in Borg and Mayo, 2007, 3). We reproduced this quote in its entirety in Chapter 7.

The struggle to build such a democratic country has been a long one in Brazil marked by hope, breakthroughs and counter-reactions in the form of *O Golpe* in 1964, *abertura* (opening), renewed hope and, more recently, the *Golpe Branco*, where symbols and manifestations of hope such as Freire as 'Patron of Brazilian Education' and the MST's higher education centre, the Escola Nacional Florestan Fernandez, are the target of state-sponsored attacks (Santos, 2017). It is the trajectory involved in Brazil's long and tortuous road to democratization that we trace in this chapter.

Popular Education in Brazil in the Early 1960s: The Political Context

In the early 1960s a set of unusual political convergences occurred in which the common denominator was national 'developmentalism'. It brought to the fore tensions between a pedagogy 'within the order' and the struggles to defend socialism and break with the political model in vogue at the time. Developmentalism favoured the domination of rural oligarchies and a process of industrialization that would give rise to an industrial and financial class, partly linked with the rural oligarchy, thus ensuring the bourgeoisie's political hegemony.[2]

The Brazilian Communist Party (PCB) directed its activists, unions and intellectuals to support governments considered 'progressive' and 'developmentalist'. And this was encouraged even though the governments in question might be led by right-wing, pro-imperialist parties, such as the National Democratic Union (UDN). The Brazilian Catholic Action movement, linked to the Catholic Church, which led the campaign against the National Education Guidelines and Bases Act (LDB), supported developmentalism, developing a program in tune with the latter's tenets. Sectors having an affinity with the Economic Commission for Latin America and the Caribbean (ECLAC) were also excited about the 'import substitution' policies introduced as part of the national developmentalism project. This position was shared by intellectuals at the Institute of Brazilian Studies (ISEB). In this ambivalent and contradictory environment, covering the ten years from 1955 to 1965, several popular education programs thrived in the country, the landmark being the work of Freire in Angicos, Rio Grande do Norte, in 1962–3. With regard to popular culture, the Popular Culture Centres (CPCs), organized in spaces belonging to the National Union of Students (UNE), stood out. These were forums in which artists and social activists promoted and engaged with the culture *of* the people and culture *for* the people in many ways. These included poetry, theatre, cinema and music. They also provided cultural backgrounds to strikes, demonstrations and clashes, as well as questioning grassroots reform, in agriculture, education, energy, banking and so forth, while highlighting advances and setbacks. In the 1960s, the main social programs for popular education were developed in the Brazilian Northeast. In this region the peasant movement had become radicalized, particularly through the Peasant Leagues, gathering over fifty thousand participants, especially in the states of Pernambuco and Paraíba (Stedile, 2006).

These popular education efforts were, however, not initiated by grassroots movements, nor were they aligned with their struggles. On the contrary, these educational programmes were organized by governments hostile to the radicalized peasant movement. They were also organized by the Catholic Church, which, until then, was hardly engaged in the grassroots struggle, despite the presence of Catholic radicals in Brazil (De Kadt, 1970). To understand these seemingly unlikely alliances between popular educators, 'progressive' governments (strictly speaking, most were linked to oligarchies) and the PCB, a brief summary is needed of the debate on the strategies that guided the great struggles of the period. These struggles culminated in the defeat of 1964, when the populist government of Joao Goulart was overthrown in a CIA engineered coup – more about this further on. The strategic conception of popular education in the early 1960s was related to not only workers' self-organization and collective self-emancipation (education for socialism) but also education for developmentalism.

To understand the outlook of the Brazilian left in the late 1950s/early 1960s it is important to emphasize the Communist Party's strategy at the time. It was known as bourgeois democracy. The PCB advocated that socialism presupposed a bourgeois-democratic step in which workers should engage with national-developmentalist sectors, aiming to strengthen capitalist industrialization and modernization as a precondition for the transition to socialism. The canons of historical materialism were ironlike, in the PCB's view, to adopt the metaphor used by a young Antonio Gramsci, in *'La Rivoluzione contro il Capitale* (The Revolution against *Das Kapital*), heralding the Bolshevik Revolution as having overthrown the hard-line Marxist critical schema (Gramsci, 1977, 43). The underlying PCB thesis was that the country still had pre-capitalist, feudal and semi-feudal regions that hindered the training of an advanced proletariat. One way to suppress the pre-capitalist residues would be to transform the peasants into wage labourers. The workers' support for the 'progressive' sectors was considered a ploy – a form of pressure – to force the bourgeoisie to undertake social reforms that, until then, it had not carried out. Thus, the workers would force the bourgeoisie to accomplish its bourgeois revolution. In the north-east, this political orientation was embraced by the 'Left Fronts'. They supported bourgeois factions, regarded as anti-feudal and anti-oligarchic, in elections for state and municipal government. A perfect example of such a candidate was landowner Cid Sampaio, affiliated to the UDN, who successfully ran for the state government. Others included Miguel Arraes from the Socialist Labour Party, who successfully ran for City Hall in Pernambuco, and Aluisio Alves, also UDN, who was also successful when contesting the Rio Grande do Norte election. As a result of this election, the government of the City of Natal was entrusted to socialist Djalma Maranhão. Governors Cid Sampaio and Aluisio Alves made concessions to left-wing sectors to stem the political growth of certain oligarchic sectors and, secretly, possible competitors in the left-wing fronts, such as the mayors of the state capital cities.

The Church, in turn, sought to block the independent peasant organization to maintain its own influence amongst workers in the field. The strategic design of the PCB, however, was criticized and confronted by Peasant Leagues. As pointed out by Clodomir dos Santos Morais, one of the foremost Peasant League leaders and then a PCB activist, many leaders of the Leagues had links with the PCB. The impasse on land reform and the systematic repression marked by the murder of Paraíba Leagues' Leader, João Pedro Teixeira,[3] were actions intended to undermine the Leagues. The Leagues actively supported the Cuban Revolution and, with others like Francisco Julião from outside of the PCB, confronted the Communist Party's National Directorate.

This confrontation challenged the PCB's strategy, which was to form the working class through a national-developmentalist project, rather than through immediate revolutionary action – an evolutionary approach based on the Western view that capitalism, seen as a result of a bourgeois revolution, is a begetter of socialism. This belief extended beyond Brazil into other former colonies where it has been said that, in the absence of an Indigenous entrepreneurial 'bourgeois' class, the state had to take on this historical class function to develop the level of industrialization necessary as a precondition for socialism (see Vella, 1989, with respect to Malta). This situation accounts for many contradictions regarding the actions and lifestyles, as well as policies, of the party and its members (ibid.). Brazil was no exception. Despite the political wrangling, such as that involving the Leagues and the PCB, the Bourgeois-Democratic strategy was hegemonic in the early 1960s. Popular education programmes were meant to prepare newly 'conscious' voters who appeared willing to support governments committed to these reforms (only literate workers had the right to vote). This strategy resulted in paradoxical situations such as support forthcoming from US agencies for these popular education programs. We had the Alliance for Progress, introduced by President JF Kennedy to curb revolutions on the Cuban model in Latin America and the United States Agency for International Development (USAID). Both programmes backed the literacy program led by Freire in Angicos, as will be discussed later.

The Historical Programs of Popular Education in Brazil

In this section, we present the educational proposals of some of these popular education initiatives in the context of the overall strategy – national developmentalism. The Popular Culture Movement (1960), founded by Germano Coelho and Miguel Arraes in Pernambuco, proposed a different relationship involving the popular classes and culture. A restless movement containing different currents, it was initially going to be called the 'Culture and People Movement', but the name 'Popular Culture' was eventually preferred to affirm the idea that the working classes would be the agents of change. The focus on popular culture would influence Freire's concept of the 'generative word', as will be shown further on.

The Basic Education Movement in Natal (1961–6) created a major literacy and rural education campaign through radio. Driven by the Catholic Church, it introduced important innovations – in educational materials and in respecting and valuing local culture – that distinguished it from the earlier radio project, which had been broadcast through radio soap operas. Its post-literacy program, featuring the book *Living and Fighting*, was a landmark in Brazilian popular literacy. Based on Popular Culture Movement material, it featured the history of the workers' struggle around an agrarian reform. Some experiences proved more significant, particularly those involving an alliance with popular culture groups and interaction with rural trade unions and peasant struggles. The Natal movement began a broader and deeper reflection on literacy and historical consciousness. It made significant inroads into church communities favouring socially progressive and innovative thinking and action. The project 'De pé no chão também se aprende a ler' ('With your feet on the ground you too can learn to read', 1961–4) implemented in Natal (Rio Grande do Norte) by Mayor Djalma Maranhão sought to extend primary schooling to working class areas on the city's outskirts.

In addition to literacy, which was increasingly influenced by the work of Freire, vocational schools were set up under the slogan 'De pé no chão também se aprende uma profissão' ('With your feet on the ground you too can learn a trade'). This major campaign placed education in peripheral areas at the top of the political agenda. It was argued that the fight against illiteracy would raise awareness of and foster a social understanding of economic and political realities. The revolutionary character of these programs was in conflict with the interests of the political and economic oligarchies. Supported by fascist and military organizations, the military regime, representing their interests, staged the 1964 coup. On seizing power, it arrested, tortured or exiled militants and leaders, Freire among them.

We have seen that Freire (1962–3) gained prominence before the coup through his literacy experiments in Angicos, which were distinguished by their innovations in the methodological and political fields. His approaches, enabling formerly illiterate people to not only 'read the word' but, at the same time, 'read the world' (Freire and Macedo, 1987) profoundly influenced contemporary popular education in Brazil and Latin America. They would have a wider global influence in not only adult education but also other fields. An entire philosophy of learning and knowledge was intimately connected with the process.

The Literacy Project in Angicos by Paulo Freire: Political Contradictions

The spread of social movements in Latin America, the growing number of strikes and the popular demands for basic reforms were perceived by the US State Department as a sign that further revolutions on the 1959 Cuban model could not be ruled out or, at least, that new nationalist governments hostile to imperialism might come to power. Kennedy's 'Alliance for Progress', an 'economic aid' program for the countries of Central and South America, was introduced with this concern in mind. It was intended to counteract potential and existing popular revolutionary movements by forms of poverty alleviation and the spread of adult basic literacy and education. Some would see this primarily as the provision of 'Band-Aid solutions'. The Alliance defended US geopolitical interests in the region, which involved fostering a positive image of American hegemonic leadership. Similar efforts had been carried out in post-war Western Europe through the setting up of 'American universities' in Rome and other cities, with a view to bolstering a positive US image in territories that, like Italy, could easily have fallen prey to communist elements in the various anti-Nazi-fascist resistance movements in what was, post-Yalta, a US sphere of influence. This situation was similar to Latin America, this area's politics governed by the Monroe Doctrine.

Among the measures to this end, its creators realized they would have to win over modernizing bourgeois governments, in Latin America, to the US side. These governments, in turn, reasoned that Alliance resources could support urgent reforms. In addition, establishing an agreement with the Alliance was a gesture of friendship toward the United States, which would soothe the more openly reactionary oligarchies. A US priority was the Brazilian Northeast region (Freire's own territory), embattled by struggles and conflicts in rural areas. Rio Grande do Norte had a school enrolment rate of about 20 per cent. The Aluisio Alves government established an alliance with SUDENE, the federal development agency for the Northeast of Brazil, with financial support from the Alliance for Progress, aiming to implement an ambitious literacy program. For the governing class, investing in literacy would also influence new voters interested in strengthening basic reforms. The Rio Grande do Norte program, funded by the Alliance for Progress, provided training for elementary teachers, restoration of elementary schools, construction of new classrooms, provision of food assistance and medical and dental care to all enrolled children. It also catered for the development of an adult literacy campaign targeting one hundred thousand people in the region.

After ten years of work at Social Service for Industries (SESI, 1949–59), Freire was, at the time, the head of the Cultural Extension Service (SEC) at the Federal University of Pernambuco and was engaged in the Recife Popular Culture Movement (MCP, 1959–60). As Director of the Research Division and Coordinator of the Adult Education Project within MCP, Freire established centres of culture: spaces that included public libraries, theatrical performances, sports and cultural circles. He had to temper his enthusiasm for initiating an adult literacy project in this Nord-Este region, plagued by poverty and social dependency, with a dose of tension and an uneasy feeling. These arose from the contradictions of coordinating a project sponsored by the Alliance for Progress and by a government supported by conservative groups.[4] The working group in Recife resisted several attempts at interference from the technicians of the Alliance. Freire, in turn, seeking to maintain the autonomy of the project, demanded that the local authorities should be its only interlocutors.

The Alliance for Progress itself was criticized by the right-wing press for being tolerant of communism. With the increasing polarization of Brazilian society between left-wing groups (including reformers, with support from the PCB) and allies of imperialism (with support from the large economic groups), the Alliance and USAID withdrew their support for Freire's projects, which they considered a 'factory of revolutions' (Paiva, 1980, 25). The dominant sectors expressed discontent with this form of pedagogy, which sought to encourage critical consciousness with a view to turning the undifferentiated mass of rural workers into conscious people aware of their legal social rights. Conscientization aside, the mere ability to render people literate in a short amount of hours was in itself a political act as it enabled them to vote, something which would single out Freire as a dangerous person later on when he would be summoned to carry out a nationwide programme on these lines. He was capable of changing the demographic electoral landscape of Brazil.

The Political-Methodological Rupture in the Literacy Process

Once the literacy campaign started, Freire promoted an epistemological revolution with his literacy methodology based on generative words arising from the everyday language of the community, in cultural circles. This occurred through a process that Freire defined as 'research into the vocabulary universe', that is, a knowledge of the community's linguistic expressions, which was acquired through dialogical encounters. The literacy workers forming the team led by Freire and the learners (formally designated in both cases as their roles of teacher-student were to become interchangeable throughout the literacy process) addressed issues relevant to people's lives, everyday matters, work and social rights under the Constitution. It was a form of citizenship education in many ways.

Everyday words, sayings and folk songs were part of the universe of knowledge, including the vocabulary. Prayers, parties, work meetings or union meetings provided occasions for research, which was conducted in a way that minimized the distance between the researchers and the community (Vittoria, 2011). Through critical analysis of existential situations, developed through immersion in existing problems (generative words and themes), workers broadened the process of investigating reality, providing a critical tendency.

Reality was observed not merely on the surface or in a mechanical way, but as a phenomenon with a deeper vital core linking the subjective condition of illiteracy to the social conditions that underlie it. Critical consciousness requires depth and helps one discover the world and oneself through processes of dialogic inquiry and questioning. It involves a problem-posing education, and therefore a pedagogy of the question, not a pedagogy of the answer. The whole process involves standing back from what one knows or thinks one knows to collectively and hopefully begin to see that reality in a different, more critical, light. The obtaining of this critical distance, often enacted in plays by Brecht and others, involves *praxis* (Mayo, 2004a; Vittoria, 2011), reflection upon action for transformative action, all three elements (action, reflection, transformative action) being not sequential but in a dialectical relationship (Allman, 1999).

Following the success of the Angicos programme, Freire was invited by the then president Joao Goulart to coordinate the national literacy plan. Freire embarked on this work in earnest but by then he and others were marked men. The interests of transnational capital were seriously threatened by a series of events under Goulart's populist leadership, and as with other populist leaders in Latin America, he and his government were ousted by a civilian-military coup. This sudden halt in a country seemingly roused for transformation brought, in its wake, arrests, murders and people banished from the country. Freire was one of the last mentioned. Many figures such as Freire's friend, Plinio Sampaio, trusted their politician's instincts and fled having earlier seen the writing on the wall.[5] Freire did not heed Sampaio's and other friends' advice and was targeted, together with other non-communist educators such as the Dewey-inspired-Anisio Texeira, and arrested. This goes to show that there were no significant bourgeois factions willing to lead a project of nationhood in confrontation with imperialism. The coup was carried out by bourgeois sectors linked to monopoly capitalism and quickly unified the main bourgeois fractions. The centres of national developmentalist thinking such as ISEB, all the left-wing forces, including labour movements, communists and socialists, though allied to bourgeois factions in the social order, were outlawed and brutally repressed. The same fate befell union movements and Peasant Leagues that did not embrace national developmentalism.

Repression certainly reached the above-mentioned popular education schemes and the CPCs. In late 1967, the dictatorship replaced the popular education programs with the Brazilian Literacy Movement (MOBRAL), relegating adult and youth literacy to a technical activity. It served as an apologia for the regime. Its organizers even had the temerity to throw around Freire's name when promoting the event, the very same Freire sent into exile for sixteen years by the regime that sponsored the programme, a clear case of unabashedly 'co-opting Freire'. It would be a mistake to assert that the history of popular education in Brazil remained frozen during the dictatorship's long winter of discontent. In exile, Freire discussed education in a context of emancipation and decolonization and moved closer to Marxist authors, inspired, among others, by fellow-exile Fernando Henrique Cardoso in Chile. Freire would later develop his understanding of popular education through the thought of Amilcar Cabral, analysing more carefully the relationship between work, the capitalist mode of production and education (Freire, 1978; Pereira and Vittoria, 2013).

Groups of land workers in Brazil continued to organize clandestinely with the support of the progressive Church, with its links to liberation theology and the Pastoral Land Commission. There were also political sectors of the resistance, including trade unions within the framework of the National Confederation of Agricultural Workers (CONTAG), which in the 1980s gave rise to the Landless Workers Movement (MST).

In contrast to previous attempts, the MST was to prioritize the training of its militants in Marxism, leading it to discuss Latin American Marxist thinkers. The most outstanding of these was Florestan Fernandes, who was honoured after his death in 1995 with the naming of the movement's main training school: The Florestan Fernandes National School (Escola Nacional Florestan Fernandes) (Mayo and Vittoria, 2017a,b). The interpretation of Florestan's ideas on the formation of capitalism in Brazil, highlighting the uneven development of capitalism, the connections between local bourgeois fractions and hegemonic fractions, and the centrality of forms of worker exploitation and expropriation, was claimed to be of great political and strategic importance to the movement, despite the controversies within the MST about the nature of the alliances of the ruling classes in Brazil.

Dictatorship and the Exhaustion of the Bourgeois-Democratic Agenda: Florestan Fernandes's Analysis

In view of the failure of the political strategy pursued by the left, led by the PCB and the national-developmentalists in the ISEB and PTB (Partido Trabalhadores Brasileiro –Brazilian Workers' Party, or simply PT), a systematic and rigorous interpretation was urgently needed of the meaning of the civilian-military coup and especially the reasons preventing the anticipated bourgeois-democratic revolution. It was augured that this revolution would have brought a modicum of democratic reforms, erase any pre-capitalist traces and forge an organized working class willing to fight for socialism. Florestan Fernandes produced one of the most important theoretical works to explain the meaning of the civilian-military coup of 1964. He also forwarded reasons for the failure of the bourgeois-democratic strategy that had excited many on the Brazilian left and had largely served as a theoretical and political foundation for the popular education schemes of the early 1960s.

In 1968, he completed his famous book *Sociedade de classes e subdesenvolvimento* ('Class-Based Society and Underdevelopment'), which questioned the assumptions of the bourgeois-democratic strategy and examined in depth the formation of capitalism in Brazil. In his analysis, the national-developmentalist theoretical scheme, although apparently plausible, is misleading, as the dependent nature of Brazilian Capitalism rendered developmentalism and the strategies of the Bourgeoisie not viable. The genetic-evolutionary view of Marxism based on dialectical materialism blurred the reading of the capitalism that really existed in the country, undermining any meaningful analysis of the 1964 coup. Florestan's analysis of dependent capitalism resulted in a unique interpretation of bourgeois revolution in Brazil (Fernandes, 1975).

In contrast to Eurocentric and evolutionary social movement and education thinking, embraced by supporters of developmentalism and exponents of dialectical materialism, Fernandes concluded that the bourgeois factions in Brazil would not be able to perform a 'classical' bourgeois revolution, along the lines of the 1789 French Revolution. In fact, archaic and modern elements coexisted in the social-historical formation of Brazil, but that did not mean that the dominant local bourgeois factions were any less capitalist. Fernandes appropriated ideas from Lenin (the uneven development of capitalism and his analysis of the Prussian approach) and other Marxists. These included Trotsky (uneven and combined development, a concept incorporated in his dialogue with Hermínio Sacchettav (del Roio, 1988, 104)) and possibly Gramsci (in the 'Southern Question', his notes on Americanism and Fordism (Italy encumbered by a rentier parasite class) and his passive revolution thesis derived from Vincenzo Cuoco).[6]

Fernandes's strategic perspective did not foresee a mandatory step before the fight for socialism, in contrast with this theory supported by the PCB with its proposal of the Bourgeois Democratic Revolution. His strategy was directly socialist, requiring very special conditions for the subjective preparation of the workers for the transition from a social 'class against capital'[7] (Marx, in Marx and Engels, 1978, 218) to a *klasse für siche* (class for itself) (ibid.). Again, the influence of Lenin can be seen in his analysis in that he highlights the importance of training and education for the proletariat to achieve collective self-emancipation. In his conception, the political education of the working class required a specific form of relationship of the party with the masses that was not marked by dogmatism or the projection of theory onto the struggle of the people, but stressed a dialectical perspective: 'To drive the political process, that party would have to be in tune with the working class and the masses, following the development of their learning and their political socialization through the fluctuations of the class struggle' (Fernandes, 2012, 234).

The Context of Social Movements and Popular Education in Brazil in the 1970s and 1980s: From Resistance against the Dictatorship to the MST's Educational Leadership

After the outbreak of metalworkers' strikes, such as that in Osasco in 1968, and student protests for university reform and against the dictatorship in the same year, repression was intensified with the adoption of Institutional Act No. 5 and Decree No. 477/1969, which effectively 'legalized' the violent repression of democratic sectors of society. Therefore, the few remaining potentially democratic spaces – those not seen as threatening by the dictatorship – acquired prominence. They provided relatively safe spaces for popular education, in particular Freirean education. The spaces were found in Basic Ecclesiastical Communities (CEB), the Pastoral Land Commission, Workers' Pastoral Action Groups and residents' associations. In the late 1970s, the main left-wing organizations that remained underground, together with the CEB and other social movements, founded the Workers' Party (PT), which Freire joined in 1980.

In its early years, the PT criticized the bourgeois-democratic strategy, supporting an originally class-focused coalition, under the Popular-Democratic program advocating 'national' reforms of anti-imperialist orientation, involving capacity-building for the socialist struggle. Gradually, however, these strategic views (Bourgeois-Democratic and Popular-Democratic) were brought closer together due to the PT's electoral victories – which involved greater institutionalization of the party – and the broadening of the spectrum of alliances, as right-wing and centre-right parties propped up the coalition government (Leher, 2011; Leher and Trindade, 2012).

That shift had a significant effect on the PT's ideas about education. From being a defender of popular education and free, unitary public education, the party sought an alliance with the major economic groups and, practically, adopted the capitalist agenda for Brazilian education, the agenda of the 'All for Education' Movement (Movimento Todos pela Educação): use of standardized quality indicators, through centralized evaluation; establishment of performance goals;

public-private partnerships for the occupation of school space-time; conversion of policies for adult and youth education into workforce training programs focused on the 'poor' (Rummert, Algebaile and Ventura, 2012); and expansion of public subsidies for private for-profit enterprises through the 'University for All' Program (Universidade para Todos – PROUNI), a program which gives tax exemptions to for-profit educational institutions, and the Student Investment Fund (FIES), a student loan program subsidized by the public sector, a situation that has led to unprecedented control over higher education by the financial sector and equally unprecedented internationalization (Leher, 2010).

In an interview, Sergio Baierle of the non-governmental organization (NGO) Cuidade, stated halfway through the Lula-led, PT government mandate that 'what appears each time truer is the irreversibility of conservatism, as though new doors were closed at each concession to the international financial system' and confirms the above view regarding university students that the university 'reform is not different from measures traditionally proposed by the World bank and other international agencies' (Baierle, in Borg and Mayo, 2007, 147, 148).

MST: Beacon of Hope?

The beacon of hope is therefore provided by the MST, which can be traced back to the regrouping, from the 1970s onward, of the peasants' movements after the resistance struggles against the dictatorship carried out under the aegis of the Pastoral Land Commission and trade unions that formed the basis of CONTAG.

With the founding of the MST in 1984, the pedagogy of the movement was forged for the first time, in terms of scale and consistency, from within the social movement itself. This pedagogical orientation came into conflict with the PT, which in its early years had supported its struggles and demands, as explained above. As Roseli Caldart, militant and intellectual of MST claims (2004, 2012a), education was first included on the movement's agenda for a practical reason: the lack of schools in the settlements and, more acutely, in the camps of the families fighting for their land. It was inevitable that this would lead to criticism of rural education framed within the ideology of human capital. The problems of 'peasant' identity among children and young people and, more broadly, of political awareness are important dimensions within this educational issue.

In this context, the debate about socialist pedagogy led the MST to resume connections with the ideas of Freire and, gradually, other socialist educators, including Gramsci, Mariategui, Guevara, Pistrak, and Krupskaya, among others, not forgetting the essential precepts of the sociologist Florestan Fernandes. The MST's road to socialist pedagogy was paved largely by the Freirean tradition of popular education, based on ideas promoted by the Pastoral Land Commission and Liberation Theology. Other influences came through contacts with universities and, in particular, with the field of Marxist studies on the educational principle of work, in which Marx, Gramsci and the Russian theorists were important sources of reference. Rebecca Tarlau (2017, 2019) highlights important Gramscian educational and larger strategic principles (education was central to the working of hegemony in Gramsci: see Borg, Buttigieg and Mayo, 2002) in the MST's work. The strength of this influence was due largely to the intersections between Freirean and Marxist thought through the work of Gramsci.

The ideas of Gramsci and Freire converged strongly in the MST, especially in what Gramsci called the 'Philosophy of Praxis', meaning a philosophy that was not limited to a contemplative view of reality but had the intention of transforming social conditions to achieve a society without exploiters and exploited: action and reflection for social change. These confluences resulted in an important common ground between Gramsci and Freire, as indicated in great detail in a number of studies (Allman, 1999: Semeraro, 2007; Mayo, 2004b, 2019): the people-led struggle for the hegemony of the exploited and expropriated working class. As Freire suggested in the book *A Importância do Ato de Ler* ('The Importance of the Act of Reading'),

> the critical reading of reality, whether in a literacy process or not, related above all to certain clearly political practices of mobilization and organization can become an instrument for what Gramsci called counter-hegemonic action.[8] (Freire, 1982, 21)

The rereading of Marx by the two philosophers can be seen in the revolutionary character of their pedagogical ideas, as incorporated into the pedagogy of the MST. It can be seen in the vision of men and women as creators of culture and transformative beings, in the search for emancipation of the oppressed classes; in the value given to praxis as a driving force behind theoretical reflection and concrete action; in the deeply felt criticism of fatalistic interpretations of social processes; and in the strong link between education and politics.

Although influenced by Marx's thought, Freire rejected dogmatic interpretations of Marxism that would result in a mechanistic and deterministic view of history, what Gramsci called theories of 'grace and predestination' and Freire called a sense of 'liberating fatalism' (Gramsci, 1957, 75; Freire, 1985,

179). In these matters, there was a clear disagreement with those whom Freire calls orthodox Marxists (perhaps better termed 'evolutionists' or 'mechanists'), in that he opted for a reading of Marxism that differed from these trends typical of the Second International. The class struggle was seen not in the abstract, as often occurred in degenerate forms of Marxism, but as a contradiction of the mode of production (an original element in Marx's thinking). What seems more central in the development of Freire's thought, which became radicalized during his experience in Africa, is that relations between classes, the class struggle, could only be understood within the broader (and more complex) scope of the mode of production.

In this perspective, what mattered was changing the mode of production, without which class struggle would be meaningless. This would not be possible without popular education, or without forming a 'new man' and a 'new woman', as Che Guevara had stated, through the struggles and schools of the MST. The revolutionary struggle overflowed into the educational field, which thus cannot be delinked from political strategy. The relationship between the MST and Freire's thought expands to the field of Liberation Theology, which re-examines Christianity in defence of the exploited classes: the meek shall inherit the earth. This defence involves religious aspects and constraints deriving from the Church as an institution, but also a political and critical reflection on reality. It requires an analytic distinction between the Conservative and Modernizing Church, the Constantinean Church of Empire and the Prophetic Church (see Freire, 1985; West, 2006), the last mentioned (Prophetic Church) being the church with a 'preferential option for the poor' in Gustavo Gutierrez's memorable phrase.

The process necessarily involves a political, cultural, psychological, linguistic and economic analysis of the condition of oppression and, therefore, requires interpretative tools. One key to the reading of social inequality, which helps contextualize the conditions of poverty, hunger and exploitation as consequences of complex structures of capitalist society, rather than situations determined by fate, is Marx's thinking. We read in Paulo Freire:

> In my youth, I went to the peasants and workers of my city, driven by my Christian inclination. I do not disown it. On arriving there, the existential drama of the men and women that I started to talk to referred me to Marx. It's as if the peasants had said to me: 'Look here, Paulo, do you know Marx?' That is why I went to Marx. (Oliveira, 2003, 32–3).

In this sense, the Christian message in defence of the oppressed is supported by Marxist theories of social-political analysis of social classes. This dialogue between interpretations of Marx and a reinterpretation of Christian messages often attracted criticism and censure from the conservative sectors of Vatican, as in the case of Leonardo Boff, an intellectual who had always supported the MST's struggles, and outside Brazil, in Chiapas, Mexico, Bishop Samuel Ruiz.

For spreading its principles in his book *Church, Charism and Power: Liberation Theology and the Institutional Church* (Boff, 1985), Boff was sentenced to a year of 'obsequious silence' and removed from his editorial roles and religious teaching by the Sacred Congregation for the Defence of the Faith, a process that culminated in his resignation from the Church. In the 1970s and 1980s, liberation theology inspired popular education movements in Latin America and, as indicated, the MST. The incorporation of Marxism led to the movement's peasants' greater engagement in concrete struggles against exploitation and expropriation, as reflected in the extraordinary period of land occupations by the MST in the 1980s and 1990s. The labour issue became central – the settlements demanded that – and therefore education could not neglect labour as an issue to be problematized in the educational practices of the MST.

From the 1980s to the Present: The Role of Social Movements in Popular and Critical Education

In the long, stifling period of the civilian-military dictatorship there was a considerable expansion of the basic education offered by states and municipalities. In 1971, the first and middle stages of schooling, each lasting four years, were merged to form an eight-year period of compulsory education. However, paradoxically, the expansion of school provision and the extension of fundamental schooling did not, in practice, democratize scientific, technological, historical-cultural, artistic and social knowledge.

After the coup, publicly funded schools were left with poor infrastructure and teachers' employment conditions became precarious, due to both the lack of a decent career plan and the sharp decline in real wages. In practice, most public education came to be socially regarded as 'poor schooling for poor people'. Education as a whole was subordinated to crass educational technicism, based on the ideology of human capital, culminating in the obligatory vocationalization of the entire Brazilian high school system in 1971 (by Law 5692), a measure attenuated by Law 7044 in 1982. One of the few areas able to guarantee some intellectual and political autonomy for those educators who resisted the dictatorship was the emerging postgraduate sector, particularly from the late 1970s onward. A small group of Marxist researchers or, if not Marxist, scholars exposing educational reproduction, probably inspired by Pierre Bourdieu, gained strength in the new programmes.

Despite their theoretical pluralism, they converged in their defence of the unitary character of public schooling, confirming the Gramscian influence on Brazilian critical educational thought (Gramsci's writings in *Prison Notebooks* IV and XII on the Unitarian School – Gramsci, 1975). It is important to remember that Gramsci's work began to be translated into Portuguese by Carlos Nelson Coutinho in the mid-1960s, even before the French and US editions of the author's works came out. Marxist critical education (Morrow and Torres, 1995) was prominent in the debate about unitary schools (a concept adopted by the Allende government in Chile), particularly in the work of Dermerval Saviani (2003), a Gramscian intellectual who had a major influence in postgraduate education and, increasingly, in the MST, especially through such interlocutors as Gaudêncio Frigotto. Saviani made an important contribution to the organization of historical-critical education. Left-wing education in the 1980s emphasized the need for polytechnic schools, which were regarded as the one kind capable of ensuring that students mastered the scientific bases of the various technologies developed and perfected in the process of capital reproduction, while aiming to strengthen workers' resistance to the expropriation of their knowledge. The term must have been derived from Marx's address to the International Workingmen's Association in what is known as the Geneva Resolution of 1866. Marx's ideas are echoed by Freire in Cartas 11 to Guinea-Bissau where he focuses on the education-production nexus (Freire, 1978).

Socialist thought permeated the texts because the concept of the unitary, polytechnic school foregrounds experience in the world of labour as a fundamental pedagogical principle capable of overcoming the disjunction between thinking and doing, the core of socialist pedagogy, as advocated by Marx, Lenin and Gramsci. These contributions are widespread in the MST's current propositions for schooling. Workers' struggles, safeguarding public education in the Constitution of 1988, in the National Education Guidelines and Bases Act (LDB, 1988–96) and in the National Education Plan (PNE, 1996–2001), together with theoretical convergences between left-wing academics and trade unions, were consolidated within the National Forum in Defence of Public Schooling (FNDEP). With the trade union presence in FNDEP and the increasing use of typical working class protest forms (strikes, marches, actions of solidarity with other workers), the critical debate about education expanded beyond the postgraduate programmes' academic circle. The late 1990s saw the establishment of the first university courses congruent with the MST's demands.

In the same period, the state's neoliberal reform measures became more incisive, affecting public education as a whole, and therefore the struggles by the FNDEP and trade unions became more radical after a long period of decline. In a change to their form of organization, FNDEP entities closest to the unions convened a National Education Congress in 1996, repeated in 1997, which led to the drafting of an anti-neoliberal PNE to serve as counterpoint to the government plan. It was in this context in the late 1990s that the MST – influenced by Paulo Freire, Antonio Gramsci, and Florestan Fernandes – started defending public schooling more directly.

This political development was most clearly expressed in the organization of the Pedagogy of the Movement (Caldart, 2012b, 546), which included the MST's education policy for rural areas. Indeed, in the late 1990s, with anti-capitalist social struggles on the retreat and the counter-reforms undertaken by the government of Fernando Henrique Cardoso making headway, the two strands of critical thinking drew closer. The historical-critical school, which had its major influence in universities and trade unions and focused primarily on public educational institutions, had to recover from a bitter defeat, because its National Education Guidelines and Bases Act (LDB) had been roundly rejected in the National Congress.

The educational school based on the works of Freire, more prevalent in social movements and NGOs, had been feeling the effects of the offensive against land reform, whereby land occupied by the movements was excluded from this reform. Meanwhile, NGOs became increasingly separated from the movements, lost resources from international foundations and gradually fell hostage to the direct funding of capital through corporations or even large public companies such as Petrobrás. Many had to soften the critical content of their educational projects, a process which, a decade later, would result in the complete submission of most NGOs to the Education for All Movement organized by the capitalist General Staff (Evangelista and Leher, 2012).

On the other hand, among the most important new syntheses resulting from convergences in left-wing and progressive thought, especially Marxist and radical Christian thought (e.g. Liberation Theology), there occurred certain developments in universities, such as the creation of courses at undergraduate (agronomy, rural education, law, veterinary medicine, geography, etc.), specialization and extension levels based on left-wing groups and collectives in conjunction with the MST–Via Campesina.

These courses were subsequently incorporated into the MST's main political training school: the Florestan Fernandes National School (Leher and Vittoria, 2015). These confluences between the two strands would not have been possible, at least because of what occurred in Brazil, without the MST. Recall that the Christian, militant strand of the Basic Ecclesial Communities and the Pastoral Land Commission always claimed Freire as its own, not least because of his connection with Catholicism (see Leopando, 2017). However, just as Freire is placed in dialogue with Gramsci, so are Liberation Theology and, particularly, the MST, conversant with the Marxist tradition. The interest of the MST in the Marxist extension courses, especially its education and training sectors, led to convergences between the two critical traditions.

In educational terms, the synthesis results from the convergence between popular education (pedagogy of alternation, mystical pedagogy, active schooling, pedagogy of the oppressed, praxis) and Marxist-inspired education (omnilateral education, polytechnic education, work as an educational principle, unitary schooling, hegemony, collective class intellectuals). Those engaged in Marxist educational thought, therefore, came to value social struggle as an effective process of political learning and consciousness formation. As expressed by Caldart (2012b, 551):

> The Pedagogy of the Movement recovers, reaffirms and, at the same time, continues—from a specific reality, with its particular subjects and at a particular time in history—the theoretical and practical construction of a concept of materialist, historical and dialectical basic education. ... It is also the heir of the Pedagogy of the Oppressed (Paulo Freire), which, as an embodiment of the same concept, brings to pedagogical reflection the formative potential of the condition of oppression, which humanly demands an attitude of seeking freedom and fighting those who oppress and put the oppressed in the potential position of subjects of their own liberation.

In contrast to a part of the popular education projects practiced in the 1960s, the focus of Pedagogy of the Movement is directly anti-capitalist struggle and socialism. The perspective that it upholds includes a strategy to promote public schooling, which, however, is not the only formative space, as can be seen from the existence of two specific sectors in the MST organizational set up: education and training. The relationship between the two is one of complementarity: this pedagogy has anti-capitalist goals, which requires training in the theoretical-practical 'doing' of class struggle.

It is not the Pedagogy of the Movement that fits the school but, to the contrary, the school fits the Pedagogy of the Movement. This is because of the role that it may have in its political and educational project. It can, however, only play that role if it develops a historicity not limited to itself (Caldart 2012b, 551–2). The MST's proposals on education have similarities to those of other Latin American movements that are also assuming responsibility for the political education of their militants and the education of their children and youth. The experiences of the Zapatistas with their Good Government Councils, the Assembly of the Peoples of Oaxaca (APPO) in Mexico and the National Coordination of Indigenous Peoples of Ecuador (CONAIE) reflect this trend. Popular education, as expressed in the Pedagogy of the Movement, is inseparable from social struggles.

The real education of people, honest-to-goodness working people, can never be separated from their independent political, and especially socially transformative (into a society governed by greater social justice and ecological sensitivity), struggle. Only through struggle does the exploited class become educated. Only through struggle does it begin to realize the magnitude of its own power, widen its horizons, enhance its abilities, clarify its mind and forge its will.[9]

Differences regarding political education however remain, particularly in the strategic debate on the formation of consciousness in the dialectic 'class against Capital' and 'class-for-itself' – which in objective terms involves the problem of 'conventional wisdom', 'common sense' and 'philosophical consciousness', to use Gramscian terms. Political education requires its own spaces, self-organized by the class that lives on its own work and is exploited, and a specific type of relationship between teachers and students. If there are no links between the educational space and the real, concrete movements that effectively carry out the struggles, education risks being dogmatic, as if it were a literary club of bourgeois dilettantes who do not work (Leher, 2012). These ideas were articulated by Gramsci:

> We are an organization of struggle and in our ranks one studies in order to improve, to sharpen the fighting ability of individual members and of the organization as a whole to better understand the positions of our enemy as well as our own so that we are better able to adapt our day-to-day action to these positions. Study of culture, for us, is nothing other than theoretical knowledge of our immediate and ultimate goals, and of the manner in which we can succeed to translate them into deeds. (Gramsci, *L'Ordine Nuovo*, 1 April 1925)

Every relationship of hegemony is necessarily a pedagogic relationship (Gramsci, 1971, 350), as can be seen in the forces that make up the nation (class struggles at national level) and in power relations at international level (Leher and Vittoria, 2015). This process involves material, cultural and aesthetic forms of production.

Conclusion

The above struggles are ongoing and those involved have been facing several attempts at undermining some of the breakthroughs made during the Lula and Dilma periods of administration. The interim and Bolsonaro governments, following the new coup known as the *Golpe Branco*, the modern means of toppling governments allowing for some measure of democratization and alleviation of poverty, have rendered the MST and its sources of education the target of relentless attacks. In the first place, there was an all-out attack on the figure of Paulo Freire. A deliberate attempt was made to deny Freire the title of Patron of Brazilian Education, bestowed on him by the former PT government. This created huge commotions with reactions from critical educators from all over the world. A new mantra of 'Escola Sem Partido' (School without Party) was introduced (Mayo and Vittoria, 2017a, 100–1). This is an affront to Freire and those many others, ourselves included, who maintain that education is politics and that there is no such thing as a neutral education (Mayo, 2019). The Escola Nacional Florestan Fernandes also became the target of attacks. Boaventura de Sousa Santos (2017, 409) states that, in the immediate aftermath of the White Coup against Dilma Rousseff, 'various police forces invaded the ENFF campus in an action of intimidation'. The MST and other progressive movements are bracing themselves for further attacks in light of the Neo-Fascist politics espoused by Jair Bolsonaro and his ilk. Brazil, as had been the case throughout this and the previous century, is entering a difficult period for the left. Social movements, especially the MST, seem to be keeping the flame of genuine freedom burning – freedom for the landless, the poor and the disenfranchised. It gains courage from, among other things, its huge international support, not least that forthcoming from dispossessed people throughout the world, including the dispossessed Palestinians. The MST-PLO solidarity relationship is symbolically represented in a famous photo featuring Joao Stedile and Yasser Arafat. In our view, its internationalist stance and innovative pedagogical approaches, conditioned by the demands from its rank and file, the landless peasants, allow the MST to offer great space for critical and popular education. It embodies the spirit of learning in social-justice-oriented social movements. It is a prominent example, from Latin America, of a subaltern southern social movement (SSSM), the other major one from the region being the Frente Zapatista in Chiapas. For this reason, it will continue to be targeted by the powerful whose response to human crises, for example, the massive Covid-19 fatal casualties among the Indigenous of Brazil, is, in Bolsonaro's words, a mere 'So what?'[10] This is diametrically opposed to Milani's 'I care', a motto we can attribute also to the MST and other SSSMs with similar commitments.

Epilogue

Throughout this volume, we have sought to contribute to further internationalize the discourse on critical approaches to education (Apple, Au and Gandin, 2012; Darder, Mayo and Paraskeva, 2015). We hope to have shed light on a selection of authors, movements and ideas that can serve to stimulate practitioners and policymakers in their approaches to an education that can never be neutral and is often shaped by the values one upholds. This is why education will always be a contentious issue. It entails an ongoing struggle over meaning and social constructions of reality. It is closely linked with issues concerning power. In short, education and politics are inextricably intertwined. We associate the issue of the non-neutrality of education with Paulo Freire (2018), but it has been a feature of the radical discourse of education for quite some time, well before the publication of Freire's most celebrated book *Pedagogy of the Oppressed* written in Chile in 1968 (Freire, 2013) but first published in English in 1970 (Freire, 2018). A lot of the literature, concerned with other movements that preceded Freire, emphasized this. Think of the Plebs League (Simon, 1990; Waugh, 2009) and the discussions across the movement of workers' education connected with it. As Colin Waugh reports, in his important text on the movement, an editorial in the May 1909 issue of *The Plebs' Magazine*, stated:

> The worker is either robbed or not robbed; Labour is either paid or unpaid. To ask the workers to be neutral is both insulting, and absurd. The 'impartial education' idea has its source in a very 'partial' quarter, and so long as the control of education comes from that quarter the working-class movement will be poisoned and drained. In this light, Ruskin College stands condemned … Working class education is the powerful stimulating force that alone can build up efficient working-class organisation, and to this end we must press forward. (As quoted in Waugh, 2009, 24)

There are no two ways about it, they are saying. Of course, the situations involved, regarding critical approaches to education, call for more nuanced approaches than might be the impression given by the above. The issue of 'powerful knowledge', posed by Michael Young and which somehow echoes Gramsci's musings in prison on the 'Unitarian School' (Mayo, 2015), warrants caution in not throwing out the knowledge baby with the ideological bathwater. No matter how ideologically slanted it is, this powerful knowledge needs to be learnt, albeit in a different manner than is conventionally the case, if one is not to remain on the margins of political life. Learning it differently entails laying bare its ideological biases. This is where Freire's work becomes useful, as would be the case with teaching language. While learning the standard language, one is also enabled to understand its centrality to a colonial process of, for example, Anglicization, as far as English colonies were concerned, and as a means of social stratification.

This has been the staple of some of our published writings both in this volume and elsewhere (e.g. Mayo, 2004a, 2015; Vittoria, 2011, 2016). We need not rehearse the ideas further at this concluding stage. This point has also been made, with different emphases, in a whole array of writings in critical education. What we sought to provide in this volume, its major contribution, we might say, is the mixture of insights from writers well referenced in the critical education domain, such as Gramsci and Freire, and equally searching reflections by other key practitioners and thinkers not that well known in the English literature on critical education. Italian thinking is of course given ample coverage here for the very simple reason that both of us know the language well. Paolo Vittoria is an Italian national from Naples, a European city which stands out for its *Meridione* (Southern) culture. The other, Peter Mayo, hails from the equally Mediterranean and Southern European island of Malta, in close proximity to Italy and North Africa. This is an island where Italian was studied and spoken, as virtually the country's third language, by Maltese people of his generation. We sought to write on what we know best.

The example from Italy (Chapter 3) provides an approach to feminism which, though well known in countries such as Spain and other parts of Europe, deserves, in our estimation, wider resonance in the English-speaking world. Of course, the publication of works in English by Adriana Cavarero has done much to promote this perspective associated with the *Diotima* group of philosophers. In writing about the work of Anna Maria Piussi, a key figure in graduate studies in education in Italy, and Antonia De Vita, we sought to shed light on this perspective and the equally important grassroots educational and organizational work around *social creation* and a *social solidarity economy* far removed from the basic premises of the all-pervasive neoliberal paradigm that shapes not only economic production and distribution but wider subjectivities.

The latter we sought to expose and critique in our chapter on lifelong learning (LLL), arguing for an alternative approach or approaches, against the background of not one democratic utopia but democratic heterotopias (we sought, in this book, to promote ideas for social justice deriving from various decolonizing contexts grappling with different issues). LLL is part of the dominant *doxa* in education these days, certainly in Europe but continuing to be spread beyond this continent. There should be a huge debate in and around this, especially now that it is being touted as a key element in realizing the United Nations' much-trumpeted Sustainable Development Goals. As we argued, for LLL to be successful in this regard, the discourse must rid itself of its 1990+ economistic, production-consumption baggage. It also needs to eschew exclusively Eurocentric viewpoints and embrace multicentric perspectives in a quest for 'another world that is possible', to adopt the mantra of the World Social Forums.

It would do well to draw on the strong tradition of popular education, distilled of its wayward elements in the same way that 'common sense', in Gramsci's articulation, is to be rendered more coherent and therefore 'good sense' through systematic engagement with its contradictions. We widened the discussion here, drawing on our research interests, beyond Gramsci, whom we availed of to discuss the ever-burning issue of migration and misplaced alliances in the Mediterranean and not just Southern Italy, and Freire, on whom we both published widely (Paolo lived, published and taught in Brazil for several years). We sought to bring new faces to an international readership in English. Lorenzo Milani and the Schools of Barbiana and San Donato di Calenzano are important sources of reference in their native Italy and Spain (the work of José Luis Corzo Toral is key there as is the movement of Milani educators – *Movimiento de Educadores Milanianos*). Milani ought to be a household figure, much like Freire, in critical education circles elsewhere (Darder, Mayo and Paraskeva, 2015) but we suspect that he has not been as well known internationally. Some of his best known work, *L'Ubbidienza non é piú una virtú* (Obedience Is No Longer a Virtue, included in Burtchaell, 1988) and the book with which he is strongly associated, *Lettera a una Professoressa* (Letter to a Teacher), have been published in different languages, including English, though his masterly sociological text *Esperienze Pastorali* (Pastoral Experiences) has yet to be made available to an Anglophone readership. Despite its use in certain international quarters, and through the influence of Italian communities in Melbourne, as one of us had occasion to learn when delivering a seminar there, the *Lettera*, it is fair to state, does not seem to have had the kind of impact which, say, Ivan Illich's *Deschooling Society* or Freire's *Pedagogy of the Oppressed* had. All this seems to be the case, despite its anticipation, in the form of a compelling narrative, first published in 1967 (Scuola di Barbiana, 1967), of much of what was later to be written in sociology of education, critical pedagogy, critical education and the whole gamut of a critical discourse around schooling. The parallels of ideas in this book with those of Pierre Bourdieu are remarkable. The style of the *Lettera* is simple and direct, with the authors not pulling any punches. It has none of the turgid writing typical of a lot of contemporary social theory. Roger Dale, a key exponent of a critical sociology of education, underlines, however, that it was a key reading text/resource in an Open University course on Education and Society (Dale, 2014) in the 1970s. This goes to show its importance as a sociological text in critical studies in education. It seems to have been forgotten since. With a spate of written and annotated books about it in English in recent years (Borg, Cardona and Caruana, 2013; Batini, Mayo and Surian, 2014), it is due a revival. Unlike Freire's work, the book did not inspire a movement of writers ensconced in the United States and what Freire's or Gramsci's detractors would call an 'industry' to boot.

Other authors deserve to be better known outside their immediate firmament in critical social studies or education. We gave importance in this volume to Gabriela Mistral and Ada Gobetti, two critical voices in Latin America and Italy, respectively, who, in our view, deserve to be better known in critical education circles throughout the world. There are others but we limited ourselves to a handful in this single volume. Mistral, as we have seen, combines poetic language and therefore imagery with sound practical concerns regarding the alleviation of poverty and structural injustice through her writings, speeches and actual 'on the ground' work on and in education. While Freire probably remains the most heralded popular educator from Latin America, there is, as he would be first to admit, more to this continent's contribution to educational and social thought than him. Mistral is definitely one great contributor. Florestan Fernandes, the sociologist, is another. We have seen his influence on the Movimento Trabalhadores Rurais sem Terra (MST) which named its major school after him. We can also include Frei Betto (Friar Albert; actual complete name: Carlos Alberto Libânio Christo OP) and his work (Betto and Freire, 1986) concerning education for social leadership in various localities in Brazil. There are many others.

The rural educator, educational policymaker, Nobel laureate poet and diplomat, Mistral is, as we hope to have shown, an inspirational and much-travelled figure. Like Pablo Neruda, she is a writer and thinker of the people. She would make a good 'person to think with' in terms of rural and popular education. So is Gobetti from Italy, one of the country's leading critical educators, together with *noblesse oblige* Don Lorenzo Milani, Danilo Dolci, Aldo Capitini of 'grassroots education for democracy' fame, Alberto Manzi of literacy fame in Italy and Latin America,[1] Don Zeno Saltini and his work in the Grossetano (Tarozzi, 2017, 9)[2] and Maria Montessori. Capitini, Gobetti and Montessori's ideas stand diametrically opposed to the authoritarian 'regime of truth' fostered by Nazi-Fascism. Once again, before one starts questioning Montessori in this regard, we would remind readers that she fled Italy for France, as did Ada Gobetti's husband Piero much earlier, when she saw the writing on the wall. Initially singing her praises because of her international acclaim, thus regarding her as a net contributor to the 'glory of the nation', the Fascist regime eventually closed her schools. What she helped nurture was anathema to the sense of obedience to the national cause which the fascists sought to instil. They even drew on their interpretation of Catholic precepts (foremost was that of obedience) for this purpose, a position subsequently and vehemently denounced by Don Milani and his students when reading history 'against the grain' (Grech and Mayo, 2014, 41). At what price freedom? At what price critical education?

We live in an age when fascist politics surface in places such as the United States, Brazil, Hungary and elsewhere. Right-wing populist, xenophobic and downright neo-fascist politics is often triggered, in the areas in which we both live, by the phenomenon of mass migration, as we had occasion to demonstrate in this book, focusing on the central Mediterranean route. The pedagogical writings and accounts of action by Gobetti and Mistral become quite pertinent. They, together with classic pieces by the likes of Hannah Arendt and Theodore Adorno (e.g. 'Education after Auschwitz'), become ever so relevant, not least to confront a different kind of collectivity from that advocated by Freire and promoted in this book. This alternative sense of collectivity, associated with right-wing populism, is more reminiscent of Satan's 'Building of Pandemonium', exhibitionism and grandiloquence in Milton's *Paradise Lost* (see David Daiches's classic on this and the parallels he draws with the Nuremberg Rally: Daiches, 1966) than the rallying call for a collective effort for social justice and structural change. Mass hysteria is characteristic of this warped sense of collectivity. This critique is the staple of critical education in recent years. We would refer here to the recurring work of Henry A. Giroux, especially his exposure of the dangers of Trumpism, to which we add our consenting voices.

We also scour writings reflecting voices from outside the mainstream of critical education in the English language. Included here are ideas from Africa, and sub-Saharan Africa at that. We explored first, with UFRJ[3] academic Amilcar Araujo Pereira, the decolonizing ideas of Amilcar Cabral, who, together with Patrice Lumumba, Augusto Cesar Sandino, Carlos Fonseca Amador, Emiliano Zapata, Maurice Bishop and others, paid the ultimate price for anti-Imperial commitments. We then considered the ideas of Julius Nyerere. Nyerere's ideas concerning education, in the contexts of national and rural development, though difficult to survive in the murky world of *realpolitik*, furnish us with insights for a decolonizing politics. It also demonstrates how ideas inspired even by European countries can be reinvented to suit an Agrarian African context. Tanzania under Nyerere was one of the many international contexts where the Folk High School concept was reinvented (Highlander in Tennessee was another) to fit, in this case, a specific agrarian African context. The relevance here is for a critical gleaning of concepts in a manner that provides an antidote to cultural and educational imperialism. *Reinvention* is a key concept in critical education. We can once again echo Freire, writing about Guinea-Bissau, that 'experiments cannot be transplanted; they must be reinvented' (Freire, 1978, 9). Critical appropriation becomes the operative word in this regard. Just as colonizers appropriated and patented subaltern ideas from the colonized, making them their own ('cognitive injustice' in Boaventura de Sousa Santos's terms, or 'primitive knowledge accumulation'), so can colonizers appropriate ideas from above (from the colonizers) and make them their own, giving them an Indigenous imprint, relating them to a whole new 'way of life', in Raymond Williams's terms (Williams, 1982, 239). The use of the colonizers' language in the Caribbean by a people denuded of its African roots, giving a whole series of cultural production a Caribbean identity, is a case in point. Hybridization is a two-way process, as Gramsci and Williams argued and demonstrated with respect to working-class culture.

The ideas, appropriated or not, are, of course, the product of not only and necessarily single writers but often of emerging currents, old but repressed traditions and, of course, social movements. Much has been written about social movements in the critical education literature. We are referring here to social-justice-oriented social movements. Our focus in the final chapter, co-written with Brazilian scholar and former UFRJ rector, Roberto Leher, was on subaltern social movements in the 'South'. Drawing on previous studies on and from Brazil, we drew on various movements (see Muraca, 2019, with regard to the *Movimento de Mulheres Camponesas* (Movement of Women Farmers) in Santa Catarina) but most notably the large internationally supported movement popularly known as the *Sem Terra* (landless or, in its full name, *Movimento Trabalhadores Rurais Sem Terra*). We have just seen how the MST is engaged in large-scale social organization that transcends the limits of capitalist and neoliberal society while being rooted in the existential situation of landless peasants in Brazil. We have also just seen that this movement extends its reach across and beyond Brazil connecting with other landless people's movements in different parts of the world, including the stateless Palestinians. Its echoes of such figures as Gramsci (see Tarlau, 2017, on this) and Freire (Tarlau, 2019) and southern epistemologies (Santos, 2017) makes it the subject of a fitting finale to this book. We have seen that, unlike many non-governmental organizations (NGOs) in Brazil that have been drawn to organizations of capital, the MST remained steadfast to its racial politics drawing from Marxist and radical Christian thought (Liberation Theology, the Christian Base Communities (CEBs), Pastoral Land Commission, etc.) in contrast to the soft imperial politics of US-driven Evangelist thought. Its school, a form of higher education, named after a leading Brazilian sociologist, Florestan Fernandes, encapsulates many of the fine ideas of critical education espoused throughout this volume. Once again, we must heed the important proviso of these ideas' contextualization and the necessity of their reinvention in the borrowed context. While, once again, no culture is to be romanticized, and a critical education involves tackling and weeding out its contradictions, turning 'common sense' into a more coherent sense, the ideas contained here hopefully take us beyond Freire and Gramsci. Valuable ideas for social justice can emerge from different parts of the world, be it 'Southern' or 'Northern' Europe, islands or mainland, subaltern groups and their experience of organization or mainstream ones and the Global 'South' in addition to the Global 'North'. This volume has been more partial to ideas and action emerging from the Global 'South'. There is potential for this to continue. The flow of people migrating from 'South' to 'North' has potential for 'portability of cultures', including learning traditions, wisdoms and knowledge in general (Mayo, 2019). Might this process and vision of migrants continue to find its place in the discourse of critical education. People have always migrated but perhaps not on the scale witnessed today. This raises messy and perhaps disturbing issues which require confrontation, once again, echoing Freire, by people who are different but not antagonistic. We argue, once again, that people who migrate and their offspring are not to be seen simply as transporters of labour power, the way the capitalist system encourages us to view them in its quest to continue to segment the labour market on ethnic, national and stereotypical grounds – hence the misplaced alliances, tackled in the chapter on Gramsci.

And yet we live in an age when even the labour power we possess, and which partly defines our identity as people belonging to a specific international class, is being lost. It is being lost not only in terms of an appeal to individualistic struggle for survival, as opposed to a progressive collective struggle, but also through the lack of assurance regarding the right to work.

Looking to the future, we sardonically ask whether we can plan ahead in our lives when the conditions of or prospects for work are not reassuring but, to the contrary, generate insecurity. How does one separate the promises of education and education itself from work? While a recurring critique in our volume is levelled at a reductionist economistic rendering of education and learning, we would not go as far as to deny the formative/educational character of work, a dimension which manifests itself in various ways. What we argued is that work is just one dimension, albeit an important one, of our multiple subjectivities. We are multidimensional persons, with often shifting identities.

This is far from saying that work considerations should be discarded. On the contrary, we think about work as not only the production of the means of subsistence but also a process of making and remaking, including consciousness and other forms of sociality. The separation of workers from the product of their own actions constitutes alienation or estranged labour, as explained by Karl Marx and Friedrich Engels. Under neoliberalism, this aspect takes an additional disconcerting turn. Not only is there a separation between the worker-subject and the product-object but this is accompanied by uncertainty regarding the continuing guarantees and rights of workers. It is these rights that give people a sense of solidity from which to frame their own cultural values. We are referring here to the situation of the precariat. What does precarious living mean in this context?

The kind of alienation rooted among the precariat is partly caused by contracts with fixed times (hours and project duration), flimsy contracts that represent the commodification of work and its social relations. Profit before people is a key capitalist mantra that is still forcefully being put across during these perilous times of Covid-19. Those who reaped massive profits, through tax rebates, increasing lowering of labour costs, lay-offs, tax evasion, production relocation, dispersal and community devastation, massive bonus payoffs for tackling self-induced crises and so forth have the temerity to seek state assistance. They still play the victim, unabashedly, with an arrogant sense of entitlement to boot.

Meanwhile, the ranks of the precariat continue to swell. The areas of schooling and university education are not immune to this scenario. To the contrary, precarious living and work, mediated by ideological-linguistic somersaults, have been couched and sold to us as 'flexibility', a form of Orwellian double-speak or plain euphemism. This recalls a memorable scene from the 1970s' BBC sitcom 'Yes Minister' in which Humphrey's predecessor as Cabinet Secretary provides, with regard to a potentially malleable candidate for Prime Minister (Jim Hacker, played by Paul Eddington), the acceptable adjective to sugar-coat the more 'down to earth' one (e.g. malleable=flexible). Following in Ettore Gelpi's footsteps, Bruno Schettini, the Neapolitan scholar who did much to promote Gelpi's work, floats the idea of work as an educational process when arguing: there has been a play on words, exploiting the semantic-lexical ambiguity surrounding 'flexibility'. It has come to mean that the right to work throughout one's life is untenable, thus presenting this guarantee as a shortcoming in the workers' bill of rights (paraphrased from Schettini, in Mayo and Vittoria, 2017a, 20).

The ambiguity surrounding flexibility-precarious work suites dominant financial interests at the expense of workers' interests. This reduces not only economic-productive possibilities but clearly also future prospects. It undermines states whose constitutions, as in the cases of the authors' respective countries (Italy and Malta), foreground the basic principle of a Republic based on Work. This all sounds hollow in the context of the present scenario. It is at best part-time work in which women consistently find themselves in the majority (Power, 2019).

As a result of rapid global transformations, the new forms of subordination and oppression are predicated on the existence of a precariat, individualism, atomization, fierce competition and isolation. There is *double entendre* also with regard to the education-work nexus. A neoliberal interpretation would affirm the right to invade the educational sphere. That which stands opposed, namely, the social-justice-oriented and ecologically sensitive critical educational interpretation, echoing Gramsci, Gelpi and others, affirms the need to bridge manual and intellectual work – echoes of Gramsci's proposed Unitarian School, a non-class-divided school. A good critical pedagogical approach, as demonstrated by the likes of D. W. Livingstone (2002) and co-researchers in Canada, would not accept that the only work that is valorized is salaried work, the kind of work that is typical of capitalist society. This society comprises a class that privately owns the means of production, a mediating managerial class that controls it and a working class that possesses only its labour power. This type of exploitative relationship reaches its lowest depths when, as a result of precarious conditions, workers have no certainty of holding on to their labour power and any indication of how to realise it in practice.

It becomes more difficult to think of work as the means to subsistence, the illusory chimera that serves to justify all kinds of exploitation. This mentality is alas diffused throughout the specific education sector in which we are both employed, that is to say, those one-time venerated institutions of higher learning we call universities. The illusory view justifies the exploitation of the majority by a minority, precisely in that place which should, in our view, serve as a beacon of democratic work relations echoing the theories it produces in some (alas not all) of its sites. In fact, debates around and denunciations of the commodification of higher education make their presence felt in the contemporary critical educational literature (Giroux and Searls Giroux, 2004; Giroux, 2007, 2014a; Connell, 2019; Mayo, 2019).

Praxis

The issues of dialogue, the education-work nexus and the kind of social relations that influence education, foreground, as indicated in this volume, *praxis*. We have seen how this recurring concept is central to a critically engaged education and popular education of Freirean, Milanian and Gramscian inspiration, together with movements that draw on their and kindred spirits' influence. We have seen, in the conclusion to the preceding chapter, how it characterizes the work of the MST and its school, the Escola Nacional Florestan Fernandez. Recall that it concerns the relationship between theory and practice, involving the point made earlier regarding the relationship between action, reflection (this includes recourse to theory), research and transformed action (which entails revising theory). The theory-practice relationship renders the view of the educational setting as not idealist but grounded in existential situations.

The criticism levelled at the neoliberal model and its iniquities and contradictions, including the commodification of education, would suggest a struggle for its opposite – an education having a broad democratic popular reach. This is where the common thrust in the ideas of Mistral, Freire, Gobetti, Milani and other movements lies. It is one wherein the cultural values of different contexts are valorized and where the educational projects allow concrete participation by people as subjects. This is a key task for education of different groups within migratory contexts. It calls for a pedagogical vision that extends well beyond 'assistencialismo'.[4] People would be encouraged to relate what is learnt to the communities to which they belong, to connect, once again, with their 'way of life'.

This is where popular education becomes instructive. A critical and popular education is characterized by a clear and direct relationship between theory and practice. An education and particularly a school estranged from the world of practical activity (hence social realities and quotidian experiences and preoccupations) is a sealed-off space. It is located in the community's geographical space but it is not *of* the community, not acting *with* it. It is perceived by community members as 'not being ours' and is, as a result, often the target of vandalism by members of this community, as indicated by Freire with regard to the situation in São Paulo when he commenced his work as Education Secretary for the municipality (Gadotti, Freire and Guimarães, 1995; O'Cadiz, Wong and Torres, 1998). Being aloof from concrete experiences, this education does not fully develop a critical stance and constitutes an easy target or corpse for the vultures of marketization and commodification to encircle it. One other element in a theory-practice dichotomy is educational work devoid of any relationship with quotidian experience, divorced from the terrain of social and human-earth relations. It would be shorn of elements that capture the popular imagination and give rise to collective and singular creativity and that paradoxically also trigger social conflicts. With respect to the last point, conflict, lived in a non-violent manner, can lead to the evolution of thought based on the coming together of different entities acting in a mature manner – 'without contraries is no progression', the eighteenth century poet William Blake once asserted. Neoliberalism thrives on schools or other educational settings concerned not with a strong theory-practice rapport but with developing environments where students and teachers become credit conscious and concerned with the attainment of competences and positional educational goods. It would be more inclined towards improving time on task, metrics and climbing league tables.

Rendering a tight connection between theory and practice, with the starting point of education being one's existential situation and moving beyond that, represents not only an educational option but also the taking of a strong political stance. Once again we highlight, in this regard, the relationship between action, research, reflection and transformed action – the movement between all four being dialectical and not necessarily sequential.

Praxis is, lest we forget, not to be confused with practice, which is simply one component of praxis. This broader term involves theory, it involves reflection, it involves action but one without the other does not constitute praxis, hence our quibble with the often used phrase 'from theory to praxis' unless the reference is to theory devoid of the rest of the four dimensions.

The long and short of the above – the conceptual nucleus of this book – is that we did not limit ourselves to educational and cultural orientations of a technical-rational nature or simply a technicist approach to education and knowledge acquisition, that is to say, 'what works' within the current neoliberal system. Critical education would, in our view, aspire to engender a profound critical reflection on practical concerns to offer alternatives to totalizing and paradoxically dispersive (they do not serve to connect things) thought processes that are symptomatic of a homogenizing culture and construction of reality typical of neoliberalism, with its underlying old Thatcherite mantra of TINA – there is no alternative. Critical education, in its scouring of liminal spaces to explore a range of alternatives, based on the learning or unearthing of different knowledges and learning traditions, offers a challenge to those who resign themselves to what the late Mark Fisher (2009) called 'Capitalist Realism' – getting used to the idea that 'a change is not going to come'. We hope that the material we offered in this book, borne out of different contexts, grappling with different issues, provides much grist for the mill in an education praxis that transcends capitalist realism. Hope spring eternal. There are so many engaged in struggle for further democratization of work, education and society, such as the MST and those who earlier placed their lives on the line for this, to give up on Hope.

Notes

Foreword: 'Alternative Ways to Think and to Do Critical Theory and Pedagogy Alternatively'

1 S. Žižek, 'Broken eggs. But no omelette', *In These Times*, 7 July 2014. Available online: https://inthesetimes.com/article/broken-eggs-but-no-omelet (accessed 5 October 2020).
2 U. Eco, *Como reconhecer o Fascismo: Da Diferença Entre Migrações e Emigrações* (Lisboa: Antropos, 2017).
3 F. Cusset, *How the World Swung to the Right* (South Pasadena. Semtiotext(e), 2018), 17.
4 D. Harvey, *Senior Loeb Scholar Lecture*. Graduate School of Design, Harvard University, 2016. Available online: www.youtube.com/watch?v=pm_UgX-ef8&t=927s (accessed 5 October 2020).
5 Global Footprint Network: Advancing the Science and Sustainability. Available online: www.footprintnetwork.org.
6 C. Walsh, 'Insurgency and decolonial prospect, praxis and project', In *On Decoloniality: Concepts, Analytics, Praxis*, ed. C. Walsh and W. Mignolo (Durham: Duke University Press, 2018), 33–56; Also, M. De La Cadena and M. Blaser, eds, *A World of Many Worlds* (Durham: Duke University Press, 2018).
7 P. Virilio, *The Administraton of Fear* (Los Angeles: Semiotext(e), 2012).
8 Z. Bauman, *Globalization. The Human Consequences* (London: Blackwell, 1997).
9 G. Loury, *Race, Incarceration and American Values* (Cambridge: MIT, 2008).
10 L. Wacquant, *Punishing the Poor: The Neoliberal Government of Social Insecurity* (Durham: Duke University Press, 2009), xi.
11 X. Williams, 'Debt education: Bad for the young, bad for America', *Dissent*, 2006. Available online: www.dissentmagazine.org/article/debt-education-bad-for-the-young-bad-for-america.
12 M. Lazzarato, *Growing by Debt* (Amsterdam: Semiotext, 2015), 65.
13 A. Smith, 'School district votes to bring back paddling for disobedient students. Do you support this?', *American Web Media*, 2017. Available online: http://

theoklahomaeagle.net/2017/08/01/school-district-votes-to-bring-back-paddling-for-disobedient-students-do-you-support-this/ (accessed 30 March 2021).
14 E. Economy, *The Third Revolution: Xi Jinping and the New Chinese State* (Cambridge: Oxford University Press, 2018).
15 C. Enfu and D. Xiaoqin, 'A theory of China's miracle: Eight principles of contemporary Chinese political economy', *Monthly Review Press* 68, no. 8 (2017): 1–12, 1.
16 A. Touraine, *Carta aos Socialistas* (Lisboa: Terramar, 1995), 10.
17 C. Walsh and W. Mignolo, 'Introduction', in C. Walsh and W. Mignolo, *On Decoloniality: Concepts, Analytics, Praxis* (Durham: Duke University Press, 2018), 1–12.
18 A. Vanaik, 'India's two hegemonies', *New Left Review* 112 (2018): 29–59, 45; see also P. Patnaik, 'The fascism of our times', *Social Scientist* 21, nos. 3/4 (1993): 69–77.
19 A. Gudavarthy, *India After Modi: Populism and the Right* (London: Blomsberry, 2018), 10.
20 G. M. Tamás, 'Words from Budapest', *New Left Review* 80 (2013): 5–26, 26.
21 K. Borgo, *Cai a Noite em Caracas* (Lisboa: Alfaguara, 2019), 27.
22 A. Habib, *Suspended Revolution* (Athens: Ohio University Press, 2013).
23 A. Appadurai, 'O Cansaco da Democracia', in *O Grande Retrocesso. Um Debate International sobre as Grandes Questoes do Nosso Tempo*, ed. Heinrich Ginselberger (Lisboa: Objectiva, 2017), 17–31.
24 S. Žižek, 'Slavoj Žižek on Yellow Vests. How to watch the news. A short video series', RT Production, 29 December 2018. Available online: www.youtube.com/watch?v=TrdPchnAR60.
25 B. Santos, *If God Were a Human Rights Activist: Human Rights and the Challenge of Political Theologies* (Stanford: Stanford University Press, 2015).
26 J. Paraskeva, *Curriculum and the Generation of Utopia* (New York: Routledge, 2021).
27 M. Horkheimer, *Critical Theory* (New York: Continuum, 1999), vi.
28 N. Wolf, *The End of America: Letter of Warning to a Young Patriot* (White River: Chelsea Green, 2007).
29 N. Fraser, *The Old Is Dying and the New Cannot Be Born* (London: Verso, 2019), 19.
30 Paraskeva, *Curriculum and the Generation of Utopia*.
31 F. Pessoa, *The Book of Disquiet* (New York: Penguin, 2002), 31.
32 B.-C. Han, *A Expulsão do Outro* (Lisboa: Relogio D'Agua, 2018).
33 G. Arrighi, *The Long Twentieth Century: Money, Power and the Origins of Our Times* (London: Verso, 2005).
34 Paraskeva, *Curriculum and the Generation of Utopia*; J. Paraskeva, *Curriculum Epistemicides* (New York: Routledge, 2016); see also B. Santos, *Epistemologies of the South: Justice against Epistemicide* (Boulder, CO: Paradigm, 2014).

Paraskeva, *Curriculum and the Generation of Utopia*; Paraskeva, *Curriculum Epistemicides*.
35 B. Santos, *The End of the Cognitive Empire* (Durham: Duke University Press, 2019).
36 Han, *A Expulsão do Outro*.
37 Ibid.
38 Z. Leonardo, *Race Frameworks. A Multidimensional Theory of Racism and Education* (New York: Teachers College Press, 2013).
39 Santos, *Epistemologies of the South*.
40 Paraskeva, *Curriculum and the Generation of Utopia*; Paraskeva, *Curriculum Epistemicides*.
41 Han, *A Expulsão do Outro*, 9.
42 Ibid., 13.
43 Ibid., 17.
44 Ibid., 21.
45 Ibid., 22.
46 Ibid., 30.
47 B.C. Han, *The Burnout Society* (Stanford: Stanford University Press, 2015), 2.
48 Ibid.
49 T. Eagleton, *Hope without Optimism* (London: Verso, 2015), 99.
50 Han, *The Burnout Society*, p. 4.
51 Santos, *Epistemologies of the South*.
52 Han, *A Expulsão do Outro*, 34.
53 J. Gil, *O Imperceptivel Devir da Imanencia* (Lisboa: Relogio D'Agua, 2008).
54 Han, *A Expulsão do Outro*, 18.
55 Adapted from W. Benjamin, *On the Concept of History*, 1940. Available online: https://www.sfu.ca/~andrewf/CONCEPT2.html (accessed 5 October 2020).
56 B. Santos, *Democratizing Democracy. Beyond the Liberal Democratic Canon* (London: Verso, 2005), vii.
57 H. Geilselberger, *O Grande Retrocesso: Um Debate International sobre as Grandes Questoes do Nosso Tempo* (Lisboa: Objectiva, 2017), 10.
58 A. Honneth, *The Critique of Power: Reflective Stages in a Critical Social Theory* (Cambridge, MA: MIT Press, 1991), 37.
59 F. 'B.' Berardi, *The Uprising: On Poetry and Finance* (Los Angeles: Semiotext(e), 2012), 8.
60 Santos, *The End of the Cognitive Empire*, ix.
61 Paraskeva, *Curriculum and the Generation of Utopia*.
62 The Invisible Committee, *The Coming Insurrection* (Los Angeles: Semiotext(e), 2009), 14.
63 Han, *The Burnout Society*, 2.

64 S. Harding, *Sciences from Below: Feminisms, Postcolonialities and Modernities* (Durham: Duke University Press, 2008), 23.
65 A. Quijano, 'Colonialidad y Modernidad/Racionalidad', *Perú Indígena* 29, no. 1 (1992): 11–21.
66 W. Mignolo, 'The invention of the human and the three pillars of the coloniality matrix of power', in C. Walsh and W. Mignolo, *On Decoloniality. Concepts, Analytics, Praxis* (Durham: Duke University Press, 2018), 153–76.
67 G. Thernborn, *From Marxism to Post-Marxism* (New York: Verso, 2010), 59.
68 F. Fanon, *The Wretched of the Earth* (New York: Grove, 1963), 239.
69 M. Battiste, *Indigenous Knowledge and Pedagogy in the First Nations Education: A Literature Review with Recommendations* (Ottawa: Indian and Northern Affairs, 2002), 4.
70 B. Santos, 'Beyond abyssal thinking: From global lines to ecologies of knowledges', *Review* 30, no. 1 (2007): 45–89, 45.
71 B. Santos, J. Nunes and M. Meneses, 'Open up the cannon of knowledge and recognition of difference', in *Another Knowledge Is Possible*, ed. B. Sousa Santos (London: Verso, 2007), ix–lxii, ix.
72 M. Todorova, *Imagining the Balkans* (Oxford: Oxford University Press, 1997).
73 L. Smith, *Decolonizing Methodologies: Research and Indigenous Peoples* (London: Zed Books, 1999), 60.
74 S. Amin, *The World We Wish to See: Revolutionary Objectives in the Twenty-First Century* (New York: Monthly Review Press, 2008), 156.
75 Paraskeva, *Curriculum and the Generation of Utopia*; Paraskeva, *Curriculum Epistemicides*; also, Santos, *Epistemologies of the South*.
76 Amin, *The World We Wish to See*, 166.
77 Ibid., 88.
78 Santos, 'Beyond abyssal thinking', 49–50.
79 Ibid., 50.
80 Ibid., 52.
81 B. Santos, *Um Discurso sobre as Ciências* (Porto: Afrontamento, 1997); also Paraskeva, *Curriculum and the Generation of Utopia*; Paraskeva, *Curriculum Epistemicides*, 1.
82 b. hooks, *Teaching to Transgress: Education as a Practice of Freedom* (New York: Routledge, 1994).
83 Amin, *The World We Wish to See*.
84 L. Jorge, 'É preciso criar um estado de alarme', *Público*, 23 February 2020. Available online: https://www.publico.pt/2020/02/23/politica/entrevista/lidia-jorge-preciso-criar-estado-alarme-1904892 (accessed 5 October 2020).
85 G. Agamben, *The State of Exception* (Chicago: University of Chicago Press, 2005).
86 W. Streeck, 'How will capitalism end?', *New Left Review* 87 (2014): 35–64, 44.

87 Amin, *The World We Wish to See*, 111.
88 B. Santos, 'Porque é tão difícil construir uma teoria crítica?', *Revista Crítica de Ciencias Sociais* 54 (1999): 197–215, 220.
89 P. Freire, *Pedagogy of the Oppressed* (New York: Continuum, 1990).
90 S. Žižek, *The Relevance of the Communist Manifesto* (London: Polity, 2019).
91 Santos, 'Porque é tão difícil construir uma teoria crítica?'.
92 M. Apple, *Ideology and Curruclum* (New York: Routledge and Kegan Paul, 1979).
93 P. McLaren, *Schooling as a Ritual Performance* (New York: Routledge, 1986).
94 H. Giroux, *Ideology, Culture & the Process of Schooling* (Philadelphia: Temple University Press, 1981).
95 Santos, 'Porque é tão difícil construir uma teoria crítica?', 197.
96 D. Kellner, *Critical Theory, Marxism and Modernity* (Baltimore: John Hopkins University Press, 1989), 2.
97 Santos, 'Porque é tão difícil construir uma teoria crítica?', 201.
98 K. Nkrumah, *Consciencism* (New York: Monthly Review Press, 1964).
99 Ibid., 12.
100 Kellner, *Critical Theory, Marxism and Modernity*, p. 12.
101 Santos, 'Porque é tão difícil construir uma teoria crítica?', 202.
102 Ibid., 200.
103 G. Lukács, *Lenin: A Study in the Unity of His Thought* (London: Verso, 2009).
104 Paraskeva, *Curriculum and the Generation of Utopia*.
105 M. Horkheimer, *Eclipse of Reason* (New York: Bloomsbury, 2004), 21.
106 Ibid., 22.
107 Santos, 'Porque é tão difícil construir uma teoria crítica?', 202.
108 Ibid., 203.
109 A. Darder, P. Mayo and J. Paraskeva, eds, *International Critical Pedagogy Reader* (New York: Routledge, 2016).
110 Ibid.
111 Santos, 'Beyond abyssal thinking'.
112 Paraskeva, *Curriculum and the Generation of Utopia*.
113 Santos, *The End of the Cognitive Empire*.
114 Paraskeva, *Curriculum and the Generation of Utopia*.
115 S. Grande, *Red Pedagogy* (New York: Rowman & Littlefield, 2004), 116.
116 A. Lorde, 'History as a weapon: The master's tools will never dismantle the master's house', *History is a Weapon*, 1979. Available online: www.historyisaweapon.com/defcon1/lordedismantle.html (accessed 5 October 2020).
117 B. Santos, *Towards a New Commons Sense* (New York: Routledge, 1995).
118 P. Mayo, 'Educação Critica e Desenvolvimento de uma Cidadania Multi-Étnica: Uma perspectiva a partir do Sul da Europa', *Revista Lusófona de Educação* 6 (2005): 17–54.

119 Santos, 'Porque é tão difícil construir uma teoria crítica?', 210.
120 Ibid., 203.
121 Paraskeva, *Curriculum and the Generation of Utopia*; Paraskeva, *Curriculum Epistemicides*; J. Paraskeva, *Conflicts in Curriculum Theory: Challenging Hegemonic Epistemologies* (New York: Palgrave, 2011).
122 Santos, 'Beyond abyssal thinking'.
123 K. Marx, *The Jewish Question* (New York: Norton, 1978).
124 Santos, 'Beyond abyssal thinking'.
125 A. Darder, *Decolonizing Interpretative Research* (New York: Routledge, 2018).
126 W. Mignolo, 'The geopolitics of knowledge and colonial difference', in *Coloniality at Large: Latin America and the Postcolonial Debate*, ed. M. Morana, E. Dussel and C. Jauregui (Durham: Duke University Press, 2008), 225–58.
127 Paraskeva, *Conflicts in Curriculum Theory*.
128 M. Couto, *Terra Sonâmbula* (Lisboa: Leya, 2008).
129 Paraskeva, *Curriculum and the Generation of Utopia*.
130 P. Henry, *The Caliban Reason* (New York: Routledge, 2000).
131 Nkrumah, *Consciencism*.
132 S. Machel, *Fazer da Escola uma Base para o Povo Tomar o Poder* (Maputo: Departamento de Trabalho Ideológico da Frelimo, 1979).
133 Ibid.
134 A. Cabral, *Unity and Struggle: Speeches and Writings* (London: Heinemann, 1980), 242–3.
135 A. Abdi, 'Eurocentric discourses and African philosophies and epistemlogies in education', in *The Dialectics of African Education and Western Discourses*, ed. H. K. Wright and A. A. Abdi (New York: Peter Lang, 2012), 12–26, 18.
136 J. Hatcher and M. Erasmus, 'Service-learning in the United States and South Africa: A comparative analysis informed by John Dewey and Julius Nyerere', *Michigan Journal of Community Service Learning* Fall (2008): 49–61, 52.
137 Ibid., 53.
138 Ibid., 52.
139 Ibid., 53.
140 Ibid.
141 Ibid.
142 Nkulu (2005), quoted in Ibid., 82–3.
143 P. Freire, 'Amilcar Cabral: Pedagogue of the revolution', in *Critical Pedagogy in Uncertain Times. Hope and Possibilities*, ed. S. Macrine (New York: Palgrave, 2009), 167–88, 185.
144 Ibid.
145 P. Freire, *Pedagogy of the Oppressed* (New York: Continuum, 2010).

146 C. Ngara, 'African ways of knowing: Rethinking pedagogy in Africa', in *The Dialectics of African Education and Western Discourses*, ed. H. K. Wright and A. A. Abdi (New York: Peter Lang, 2012), 129–47, 130.
147 Ibid., 42.
148 Ibid., 131.
149 Nkrumah, *Consciencism*.
150 Ngara, 'African ways of knowing', 132.
151 Ibid.
152 Ibid., 133.
153 E. Mondlane, *Lutar por Moçambique* (Lisboa: Sá da Costa, 1969).
154 Ibid., 59.
155 Ibid., 77.
156 W. Rodney, *How Europe Underdeveloped Africa*. 1973. Available online: http://abahlali.org/files/3295358-walter-rodney.pdf (accessed 21 March 2021).
157 E. Mondlane, *Eduardo Mondlane* (London: Panaf, 1978), 64.
158 Ibid., 68.
159 Ibid., 63.
160 A. Cabral, *Return to the Source: Selected Speeches of Amilcar Cabral* (New York: Monthly Review Press, 1973), 51.
161 Ibid., 63.
162 R. Rabaka, *Concepts of Cabralism: Amilcar Cabral and Africana Critical Theory* (Lanham: Lexington Books, 2014), 152.
163 Ibid.
164 A. Davis, 'Memories of Black liberation: Amilcar Cabral', in *Claim No Easy Victories: The Legacy of Amilcar Cabral*, ed. F. Manji and B. Fletcher (Ghana: CODESRIA & Dajara Press, 2003), 463–7, 446.
165 Machel, *Fazer da Escola uma Base*.
166 Ibid.
167 Ibid., 10.
168 Ibid.
169 Ibid., 23.
170 Ibid., 24.
171 Ibid., 25.
172 Ibid.
173 Ibid., 26.
174 Ibid., 116.
175 Ibid., 117.
176 Ibid., 118.
177 M. Boatca, S. Costa and E. Rodriguez, 'Introduction: Decolonizing European sociology: Different paths towards a pending project', in *Decolonizing European*

Sociology: Transdisciplinary Approaches, ed. E. Rodriguez, S. Costa and M. Boacta (Burlington: Ashgate, 2010), 1–10, 6.
178 K. Nkrumah, *Class Struggle in Africa* (London: PANAF, 2006), 55.
179 S. Machel, *Establishing People's Power to Serve the Masses* (Toronto: Toronto Committee for Liberation of Southern Africa, 1976), 5.
180 A. Cabral, 'The weapon of theory', in *Revolution in Guiné Bissau*, ed. A. Cabral (New York: Monthly Review Press, 1969), 90–111.
181 Nkrumah, *Class Struggle in Africa*, 55.
182 Ibid.
183 Cabral, 'The weapon of theory', 4. See discussion in Chapter 10 around this issue.
184 Ibid.
185 Nkrumah, *Class Struggle in Africa*, 13.
186 Ibid.
187 Cabral, 'The weapon of theory', 5.
188 Machel, *Establishing People's Power to Serve the Masses*, 16.
189 Nkrumah, *Consciencism*, 27.
190 Ibid.
191 C. L. James, *The Black Jacobins* (New York: Vintage Books, 1963).
192 Machel, *Establishing People's Power to Serve the Masses*, 10.
193 Nkrumah, *Class Struggle in Africa*, 27.
194 Ibid., 25.
195 Machel, *Establishing People's Power to Serve the Masses*.
196 Ibid., 16.
197 Ibid.
198 Ibid., 17.
199 Nkrumah, *Consciencism*, 3.
200 Mondlane, *Eduardo Mondlane*, 152.
201 F. Fanon, *Black Skin, White Masks* (London: MacGibbon and Kee, 1968), 120.
202 Nkrumah, *Class Struggle in Africa*, 38.
203 Ibid.
204 P. Lumumba, 'Lumumba speaks, part 1 (1958–1959)', in *The Speeches and Writings of Patrice Lumumba, 1958–1961*, ed. J. Van Lierde (Boston: Little, Brown, 1963), 54–142.
205 Ibid., 86.
206 Rodney, *How Europe Underdeveloped Africa*.
207 S. Adejumobi, 'State and civil society in local and global contexts: Colonial contact and bourgeois reforms among the Yoruba of Nigeria', in *Africanizing Knowledge: African Studies Across the Disciplines*, ed. T. Falola and C. Jennings (London: Transaction, 2002), 315–42.

208 S. Amin, *Eurocentrism* (New York: Monthly Review Press, 2009).
209 Rodney, *How Europe Underdeveloped Africa*.
210 Ibid.
211 J. Nyerere, *The Arusha Declaration (and TANU's Policy on Socialism and Self-Reliance)*. Marxists Internet Archives, 1967. Available online: https://www.marxists.org/subject/africa/nyerere/1967/arusha-declaration.htm (accessed 5 October 2020).
212 S. Machel, 'Samora Machel', in *Samora Machel. An African Revolutionary*, ed. B. Munslow (London: Zed Books, 1985), 28.
213 Ibid., x.
214 Nkrumah, *Class Struggle in Africa*, 78.
215 Lumumba, 'Lumumba speaks'.
216 Ibid., 92.
217 O. Carvalho, *Alvorada em Abril* (Lisboa: Divina Comedia, 2014); A. Spinola, *Portugal e o Futuro* (Lisboa: Editora Arcadia, 1974); and J. Veloso, *Memories at Low Altitude: The Autobiography of a Mozambican Security Chief* (Cape Town: Zebra Press, 2012).
218 E. Dussel, *Philosophy of Liberation* (Oregon: Wipf & Stock, 1995), 14.
219 Ibid.
220 Ibid.
221 Amin, *Eurocentrism*.
222 A. Cesaire, *Discourse on Colonialism* (New York: Monthly Review Press, 2000), 41.
223 F. Fanon, *Toward the African Revolution* (New York: Grove Press, 1964).
224 Ibid., 40.
225 Cesaire, *Discourse on Colonialism*, 36.
226 A. Memmi, *The Colonizer and the Colonized* (Boston: Beacon Press, 1991), 103.
227 Ibid.
228 Fanon, *Toward the African Revolution*, 36.
229 Ibid., 32.
230 Santos, *Epistemologies of the South*.
231 Machel, *Fazer da Escola uma Base*, 27.
232 Nkrumah, *Consciencism*, 70.
233 Ibid.
234 Ibid., 78.
235 Ibid.
236 Ibid.
237 Fanon, *Black Skin, White Masks*.
238 Fanon, *Toward the African Revolution*, 39.
239 Fanon, *Black Skin, White Masks*.
240 I. Wallerstein, *Utopistics: Or, Historical Choices of the Twenty-First Century* (New York: New Press, 1998).

241 Fanon, *Toward the African Revolution*, 179.
242 Cesaire, *Discourse on Colonialism*, 52.
243 B. Santos, 'Aquino de Bragança: Criador de Futuros, Mestre de Heterodoxias, Pioneiro das Epistemologias do Sul', in *Como Fazer Ciências Sociais e Humanas em África. Questões Epsitemológicas, Metodologicas, Teóricas e Políticas*, ed. T. Silva, J. Coelho and A. Souto (Dakar: CODESRIA/CLACSO, 2012), 13–62.
244 Paraskeva, *Curriculum Epistemicides*.
245 Santos, 'Aquino de Bragança'.
246 Ibid.
247 J. Martí, *On Education: Articles on Educational Theory and Pedagogy, and Writings for Children from "The Age of Gold"* (New York: Monthly Review Press, 1979).
248 Paraskeva, *Conflicts in Curriculum Theory*; also, C. Eliot, 'The report of the Committee of Ten', *Educational Review* 7 (1894): 105–10.
249 F. Fanon, *Em Defesa da Revolução Africana* (Lisboa: Sá da Costa, 1969).
250 S. Žižek, 'Introduction: The spectre of ideology', in *Mapping Ideology*, ed. S. Žižek (London: Verso, 1996), 1–33.
251 K. Marx, 'For a ruthless critique of everything existing', in R. Tucker (ed.), *The Marx Engels Reader*, ed. (New York: W.W. Norton, [1843] 1978), 12–15.
252 Santos, *The End of the Cognitive Empire*.
253 Pessoa, *The Book of Disquiet*.
254 L. Panitch and S. Gindin, 'Transcending pessimism: Rekindling socialist imagination', *Socialist Register* (2006): 1–29, 6.
255 Ibid., 6.
256 Paraskeva, *Curriculum and the Generation of Utopia*.

2 Lifelong Education/Learning: An Alternative Critical Approach

1 In Italy there is talk of an educating society or community (see Vittoria, 2017).
2 There are those such as Rosa Maria Torres (2013) who has presented LLE and LLL as a Western concept detrimental to the concerns of Latin American adult and youth education.
3 The reference here is to the 1973 coup in Chile against the democratically elected socialist government of Salvador Allende and the coup's bloody aftermath which set the stage for the large-scale experiment in neoliberal economics, pushed forward by the 'Chicago Boys' inspired by Milton Friedman and Arnold Harberge.
4 A classic case is the recent decision by the relevant body in Brussels to support the proposal for an International Erasmus Mundus International Master in Adult Education for Social Change (IMAESC), with its content very much focusing on social justice and in which Freirean pedagogy plays an important part. It

was accorded the largest allocation of funds from among the selected Erasmus Mundus International Master programmes: http://www.gla.ac.uk/postgraduate/erasmusmundus/imaesc/ (accessed 2 April 2021).

3 Philosophy of Differences and Social Creation: Anna Maria Piussi and Antonia De Vita

A section in this chapter developed out of a review of Antonia De Vita's book, *La Creazione Sociale* (Social Creation), by one of the authors, which appeared in the journal *Educazione Democratica* in 2011.

1. Her work is included in the general bibliography in the *International Critical Pedagogy Reader* edited by Antonia Darder, Peter Mayo and João Paraskeva (New York and London, 2016). This volume includes an essay by Ana Sánchez-Bello who refers prominently to Anna Maria Piussi, the feminism of differences and Diotima.
2. See 'What is a social solidarity economy?': http://www.ripess.org/what-is-sse/what-is-social-solidarity-economy/?lang=en (accessed 23 March 2021).
3. We are indebted to Professor Alessio Surian, from the University of Padova, for this point.

4 Gabriela Mistral: Poet of Education

We are indebted to Professor Carlos Alberto Torres and Professor Eugenio Enrique Cortés Ramires, professors at UCLA and Universidad de Castilla La Mancha at Cuenca, respectively, for having commented on an earlier draft of this chapter especially with regard to our direct translations from Spanish.

1. See the website of the International Educational Cinematographic Institute on the League of Nations portal: http://www.lonsea.de/pub/org/797 (accessed 14 September 2020).

5 Ada Gobetti: Education for Resistance and Reconstruction

1. https://www.raiplay.it/video/2016/12/Italiani-con-Paolo-Mieli---Ada-Marchesini-Gobetti-labitudine-allazione-8da69db6-7134-45c4-8ccd-020d64478647.html (accessed 11 August 2020).

6 Lorenzo Milani and the Schools of San Donato and Sant'Andrea a Barbiana

This chapter was originally published, with slight modifications, as P. Mayo, 'Italian signposts for a sociologically and critically engaged pedagogy: Lorenzo Milani (1923–1967) and the Schools of San Donato and Barbiana revisited', *British Journal of Sociology of Education* 36 (2015): 853–70.

1. One of us is indebted to Professor Mary Darmanin and Professor Michael Young, the former for exposing him to Young and Young and Muller's later work around the curriculum when co-teaching PGCE seminars in Sociology of Education with her, and the latter for making available some of his most recent research papers and for discussing epistemological curricular issues with him both electronically and at a meeting in London.
2. One of us is indebted to his good friend Professor Roger Dale for this information. On this issue, see Dale (2014).
3. The biographical account is summarized from information provided by Fallaci (1993), Pecorini (1998) and the Centro Formazione e Ricerca Don Milani, e Scuola di Barbiana, http://www.barbiana.it/biografia.html (accessed 17 March 2007). See also http://www.icareancora.it/ (accessed 24 March 2007). For Our translation from the original in Italian: http://www.chille.it/progetti-in-corso/progetto-don-milani-lettera-a-unaprofessoressa/ (accessed 5 January 2013).
4. Interview on Italian state TV station (Rai) with Pier Paolo Pasolini on the *Lettera a una Professoressa* captured on YouTube: https://www.youtube.com/watch?v=i7r9mgYmDfMb (accessed 26 March 2021).

7 Paulo Freire, Globalization and Emancipatory Education

This essay draws on material previously published in the following:
1. Chapters 3 and 4 of P. Mayo, *Liberating Praxis. Paulo Freire's Legacy for Radical Education and Politics* (Westport: Praeger, 2004a).
2. The entire section on neoliberalism in C. Borg and P. Mayo, 'The EU Memorandum on lifelong learning: Old wine in new bottles?' *Globalisation, Society and Education* 3, no. 2 (2005): 257–78; and in C. Borg and P. Mayo, *Learning and Social Difference: Challenges for Critical Pedagogy* (New York: Routledge, 2006), ch. 1.
3. The introduction in P. Mayo, *Gramsci, Freire and Adult Education: Possibilities for Transformative Action* (London: Zed Books, 1999a).

1. International guidelines for a market economy were introduced in Chile in 1975, with most of the influential members of the relevant ministry having been

products of the University of Chicago (they were referred to as the 'Chicago Boys') and having been strongly influenced by the ideas of Milton Friedman (Martin, 1997, 39).
2 We are indebted to Dr Margaret Ledwith for this point.
3 Carlos Alberto Torres (2005, 205) mentions two other types of globalization, the globalization of human rights and the globalization linked to the issue of security as the precondition of freedom.

8 Towards an Anti-Racist Education and Human Solidarity in the Mediterranean and in the Context of Migrations

This chapter is substantially based on an article by one of the two authors in the Italian journal *Quaderni di Intercultura* 1 (2009): 301–6. The two authors of this volume modified the content rendering the text up to date and deepened the argument carried forward.
1 Our translation from the Portuguese original.

9 Hegemony, Migration and Misplaced Alliances: Lessons from Antonio Gramsci

This chapter was previously published as P. Mayo (2016), 'Hegemony, migration and misplaced alliances: Lessons from Gramsci', in *Solidarity without Borders: Gramscian Perspectives on Migration and Civil Society Alliances*, ed. O. G. Agustin and M. B. Jorgensen (London: Pluto Press), 135–49.
1 It also has a strong influence on identity especially with regard to communities that have traditionally not been organized along individualist lines as has been the case with most Mediterranean and non-Western communities. Hegemonic globalization, as with other previous modernizing forces, seems to be at odds with the fundamentally religious way of life experienced in certain regions of the Mediterranean and also tends to destroy that sense of mystery so much cherished in several non-Western societies. This fundamentally religious life can create tensions with the influx of people holding onto a different religious belief with the same vehemence as that to which large swathes of the 'autochthonous' population cling to theirs. We are indebted to Michael Grech for this point.
2 See Hrvoje Simicevic's interview with Peter Mayo (Simicevic, 2013).

3 Due apologies to Karl Marx (1907) concerning his famous comment, in a different context and on a different matter, that history repeats itself, first ending in tragedy and later in farce.
4 It dates back as a concept to the ancient Greeks and was later used by revolutionaries such as Lenin and Plekhanov. It was also used in the linguistics debates to which Gramsci was exposed as a student in Turin where 'Philology' was his specialization in the old broad-based Italian *laurea* degree.
5 Because his writings contained in the *Prison Notebooks* are notes for a future work, are fragmentary and would probably have been subject to eventual revision, expansion and reorganization had Gramsci lived longer to bring this work to fruition, one comes across ambiguities regarding 'hegemony'. The ambiguities concern whether hegemony refers solely to the consensual aspect of power or also combines this aspect with the coercive element involved. These inconsistencies have given rise to different uses of this term by different writers and commentators. In short, hegemony is often said to refer to either one of the heads (consent) or both twin heads (coercion and consent) of Macchiavelli's Centaur: force (coercion) + consent or else force + hegemony (consent). We favour the more comprehensive conception of hegemony, that is, consent + coercion / force, since it is very much in keeping with Gramsci's notion of the 'Integral State' (Gramsci, 1971, 239), an all-encompassing state which combines aspects of consent and repression at the same time. The separations are delineated by Gramsci for simply heuristic purposes. In reality, one cannot separate the two since there is no 100 per cent repressive apparatus and no 100 per cent ideological apparatus, as Louis Althusser would point out. Schools, for instance, may appear prima facie to be ideological but they are also repressive at the same time, the degree of repression varying from state to state.
6 'Il continente' – the 'continent', as Sardinians refer to the Italian mainland.
7 See Said (1994, 56–9).
8 Maria Pisani (2012) points out that 'illegal immigrant' is a non-existent term in international law. It is bandied about by politicians to justify 'illegal legalities', that is to say, the trampling over human rights, basic ones at that (a person's right to asylum). It has unfortunately become part of the popular *doxa*.
9 One of us is indebted to the late Professor M. Kazim Bacchus, Professor Emeritus University of Alberta, Canada, for this point.
10 In the majority of cases, we have bona fide breathing human subjects being criminalized for sins not of their making – sins for which Europe itself has a lot to answer. All this attests to the legacies of colonialism in Africa and the Middle East and the Western powers' collusion in the creation of situations characterized by the presence of client tyrannical regimes.

10 Amilcar Cabral and Paulo Freire: The Struggle for Independence and Popular Education in Guinea-Bissau, *with Amilcar Araujo Pereira*

* Professor Amilcar Araujo Pereira, militant of the Black movement in Brazil and academic at the Federal University of Rio de Janeiro.
1 Partido Africano para a Independência da Guiné e Cabo Verde (African Party for the Independence of Guinea and Cape Verde).
2 'Macaulay's Minute on Indian Education', University of California, Santa Barbara. Available online: http://oldsite.english.ucsb.edu/faculty/rraley/research/english/macaulay.html (accessed 3 April 2021).
3 By this we mean people born and raised in Africa and not in another country outside Africa but of African descent, as in the case of the Afro-American or Afro-Brazilian.
4 Paraphrased from a transcribed speech by Amilcar Cabral, in Guinea-Bissau '79, *Learning by Living and Doing*. IDAC Document 18, p. 11.
5 This is indicated in illustrations reproduced in Freire (1978).
6 Amilcar Cabral, in Guinea-Bissau '79. *Learning by Living and Doing*. IDAC Document 18, p. 11.
7 A village in Guinea-Bissau involved in the literacy campaign.
8 Guinea-Bissau '79. *Learning by Living and Doing*. IDAC Document 18, pp. 42–3.
9 See Harasim (1983).
10 The popular Culture Notebooks can be accessed at the World Council of Churches Library. *A luta continua, Primeiro Caderno de Cultura Popolar* (The Ongoing Struggle. First Popular Culture Notebook). Republic of São Tomé e Principe. Ministèrio da Educação Nacional e Desporto. Departamento da Educação de adultos e alfabetização (Ministry of National Education and Sport. Department of Adult Education and Literacy.) São Tomè, 1980. *A luta continua, Terceiro Caderno de Cultura Popular: Nosso Povo, Nossa Terra. Trabalho, Produção e Conta* (The struggle continues, Third Popular Culture Notebook: Our People, Our Earth. Work, Production and Account). Ministerio da Educação Nacional e Desportos. Commissão nacional coordenadora dos circulos de cultura popular. (Ministry of National Education and Sport. National Coordinating Commission of Popular Culture Circles), São Tomé, 1978. *Quarto Caderno de Cultura Popular, Nosso Povo, Nossa Terra, trabalho, produção, cultura e saude* (Fourth Notebook of Popular Culture, Our People, Our Earth, work, production, culture and health). Democratic Republic of São Tome e Principe. Ministry of Health. São Tome, 1979. *A luta continua: praticar para aprender, caderno de exercicios* (The struggle continues: practice to learn, exercise book). Democratic Republic of São Tomé e Principe. Ministry of National Education and Sport. Department of Adult Education and Literacy. São Tomè, 1980. An elaborate

theorisation of the Notebooks of Popular Culture is provided by Paulo Freire in *A importanca do ato de ler* (The Importance of the Act of Reading).

11 Julius K. Nyerere's Signposts for a Postcolonial Education

1 One of us is indebted to Professor George Sefa Dei from the Ontario Institute for Studies in Education/University of Toronto for this point.
2 This was formerly a college of the University of East Africa. In 1970, it became the University of Dar es Salaam.
3 Tribute to Nyerere, following Mwalimu's death in October 1999, written and circulated by Budd L. Hall via email.
4 Nyerere and Freire, who were both ICAE honorary presidents, were to meet again, in Dar es Salaam, at this international organization's first World Adult Education Assembly in 1976 where they were both invited speakers (Hall, 1998, 98, 99).
5 One of us is indebted to Dr Suleman Sumra from the University of Dar es Salaam for this piece of information (email correspondence).

12 Social Movements and Critical Education in Brazil: From the Origins of Popular Education to the Struggle for Democratisation, *with Roberto Leher*

1 Roberto Leher, Professor of Public Policies in Education, Faculty of Education, Federal University of Rio de Janeiro (UFRJ), email: leher.roberto@gmail.com, https://orcid.org/0000-0002-5063-8753.
2 The economic policy of national developmentism, based on growth targets of industrial production and infrastructure and the consequent increase of consumption, was particularly criticized by Brazilian sociologist Florestan Fernandes. He denounced the relationship between this model and what he defined as 'dependent capitalism'. This is one where integration into the capitalist world occurs in a state of dependency on advanced capitalist countries.
3 Teixeira's murder was portrayed in Eduardo Coutinho's masterful documentary 'Cabra marcado para morrer', filmed in 1964, but because of the dictatorship it could only be completed after two decades.
4 This would not be the only time such feelings would be felt: when later in exile in Chile, he would be involved in an 'asentamiento' (settling down of campesiños) literacy programme, sponsored by a Christian-Democrat led government (Freire, 1985); how serious and radical was the Eduardo Frei government about agrarian reform?

5 Information provided to Peter Mayo at a meeting at the late Plinio Sampaio's residence in São Paulo in April 1998 and documented in Mayo (2004a).
6 Carlos Nelson Coutinho (2000) makes some interesting comments on this subject.
7 See Marx's exact words in English translation (1978, 218) in the anti-Proudhon passage, *The Poverty of Philosophy*.
8 In actual fact, contrary to Freire's statement, Gramsci never used the term 'counter-hegemony', perhaps to avoid binary thought: hegemony-counter-hegemony. Hegemony contains, within its own interstices, the possibility of challenging and transforming its constitutive relations. When challenging hegemonic arrangements, one is rarely, if ever, external to the hegemonic structure itself (see Mayo, 2015, 5).
9 V. I. Lenin, 'Lecture on the 1905 Revolution', January 1917. Available online: http://www.marxists.org/archive/lenin/works/1917/jan/09.htm (accessed 23 March 2014).
10 See J. P. Linstroth, 'Bolsonaro's continuous follies', *Counterpunch*, 7 August 2020. Available online: https://www.counterpunch.org/2020/08/07/bolsonaros-continuous-follies/ (accessed 16 August 2020).

Epilogue

1 Manzi was declared a 'persona non grata' in certain Latin American countries because of the political implications of his literacy work, especially among the Indigenous.
2 Massimiliano Tarozzi writes of Don Zeno's contribution to the development of a 'comunità educante' (educating community, see Vittoria, 2017, on this) among the marginalized and excluded.
3 Federal University of Rio de Janeiro.
4 External assistance through charity rather than a process enabling structural change (English and Mayo, 2019, 226).

References

Allman, P. (1988), 'Freire, Gramsci and Illich: Their contribution to radical education for socialism', in T. Lovett (ed.), *Radical Adult Education: A Critical Reader*, 85–113, London: Routledge.
Allman, P. (1999), *Revolutionary Social Transformation: Democratic Hopes, Political Possibilities and Critical Education*, Westport, CT: Bergin & Garvey.
Allman, P. (2001), *Critical Education against Global Capitalism: Karl Marx and Revolutionary Critical Education*. Westport, CT: Bergin & Garvey.
Allman, P., and Wallis, J. (1995), 'Challenging the postmodern condition: Radical adult education for critical intelligence', in M. Mayo and J. Thompson (eds), *Adult Learning Critical Intelligence and Social Change*, 18–33, Leicester: NIACE.
Allman, P., with Mayo, P., Cavanagh, C., Lean Heng, C., and Haddad, S. (1998), 'The creation of a world in which it will be easier to love …', *Convergence*, 31 (1&2): 9–16.
Apitzsch, U. (1995), 'Razzismo ed Atteggiamenti Verso gli Immigrati Stranieri: Il Caso della Repubblica Federale Tedesca (Racism and attitudes towards foreign immigrants: The case of the German Federal Republic)', *Quaderni dei Nuovi Annali*, 33: 67–76 (in Italian).
Apitzsch, U. (2016), 'Gramsci's "Philosophy of Praxis" and migration', in Ó. G. Agustín and M. B. Jørgensen (eds), *Solidarity without Borders: Gramscian Perspectives on Migration and Civil Society*, 36–52, London: Pluto Press.
Apple, M. (1990), *Ideology and Curriculum* (2nd edn), New York: Routledge.
Apple, M. (1995), *Education and Power*, New York: Routledge.
Apple, M. (2000), *Official Knowledge: Democratic Education in a Conservative Age* (2nd edn), New York: Routledge.
Apple. M. W., Au, W., and Gandin, L. A., eds (2012), *The Routledge International Handbook of Critical Education*, New York: Routledge.
Aprile, P. (2010), *Terroni. Tutto quello che è stato fatto perche gli Italiani del Sud diventassero Meridionali (People Who Work the Land: All That Was Made for Italians from the South to become Southerners)*, Milan: Piemme.
Araujo Freire, A. M. (1997), 'A bit of my life with Paulo Freire', *Taboo: The Journal of Culture and Education*, 2 (Fall): 3–11.
Aronowitz, S. (1993), 'Freire's radical democratic humanism', in P. McLaren and P. Leonard (eds), *Paulo Freire: A Critical Encounter*, 8–23, London: Routledge.
Aronowitz, S. (1998), 'Introduction', in Freire, P., *Pedagogy of Freedom*, Lanham: Rowman & Littlefield.
Bacchus, M. K. (1973), *Report on Recent Educational Developments in Tanzania*, Edmonton: University of Alberta.

Bacchus, M. K., and Torres, C. A. (1988), 'Framework for a comparative study of adult education policy implementation in Mexico, Tanzania, and Alberta', *The Alberta Journal of Educational Research*, 34: 320–9.

Bacon, D. (2008), *Illegal People: How Globalization Creates Migration and Criminalizes Immigrants*, New York: Beacon Press.

Baldacchino, G. (1999), 'Recent developments in higher education in Malta', *Mediterranean Journal of Educational Studies*, 4: 205–14.

Baldacchino, G., and Mayo, P. (1995), 'Multifunctionalism, volunteers and the school culture: Adult learning in the Maltese context', in J. Knoll (ed.), *International Yearbook of Adult Education*, 229–44, Bochum: University of the Ruhr.

Baldacchino, G., and Mayo, P. (1997), 'Introduction', in G. Baldacchino and P. Mayo (eds.), *Beyond Schooling. Adult Education in Malta*, xix–xxxii, Mireva: Msida.

Bartlett, L. (2005), 'Dialogue, knowledge and teacher-student relations: Freirean pedagogy in theory and practice', *Comparative Education Review*, 49 (3): 344–64.

Batini, F., Mayo, P., and Surian, A. (2014), *Lorenzo Milani, the School of Barbiana and the Struggle for Social Justice*, New York: Peter Lang.

Bauman, Z. (2005), *Liquid Life*, Oxford: Polity Press.

Bauman, Z. (2006), 'The crisis of the human waste disposal industry', in D. Macedo and P. Gounari (eds), *The Globalization of Racism*, 36–40, Boulder, CO: Paradigm.

Berry, T. J. (1999), 'Foreword', in E. O'Sullivan, *Transformative Learning: Education for the 21st Century*, xi–xv, London: Zed Books.

Betto, F., and Freire, P. (1986), *La Scuola Chiamata Vita*, Bologna: EMI.

Bhola, H. S. (1984), *Campaigning for Literacy: Eight National Experiences of the Twentieth Century, with a Memorandum to Decision-Makers*, Paris: Unesco.

Boal, A. (1993), *Theater of the Oppressed*, New York: Theatre Communications Group.

Boff, L. (1985), *Church, Charism and Power: Liberation Theology and the Institutional Church*, New York: Crossroad.

Borg, C., and Mayo, P. (2000), 'Reflections from a "third age" marriage: Paulo Freire's pedagogy of reason, hope and passion. An interview with Ana Maria (Nita) Araujo Freire', *McGill Journal of Education*, 35 (2): 105–20.

Borg, C., ad Mayo, P. (2005), 'The EU Memorandum on lifelong learning. Old wine in new bottles?', *Globalisation, Societies and Education*, 3 (2): 257–78.

Borg, C., and Mayo, P. (2006), *Learning and Social Difference: Challenges for Public Education and Critical Pedagogy*, New York: Routledge.

Borg, C., and Mayo, P. (2007), *Public Intellectuals, Radical Democracy and Social Movements: A Book of Interviews*, New York: Peter Lang.

Borg, C., Buttigieg, J. A., and Mayo, P. (2002), 'Gramsci and education: A holistic approach', in C. Borg, J. A. Buttigieg and P. Mayo (eds), *Gramsci and Education*, 1–23, Lanham, MD: Rowman & Littlefield.

Borg, C., Cardona., M., and Caruana, S. (2009), *Letter to a Teacher: Lorenzo Milan's Contribution to Critical Citizenship*, Malta: Agenda.

Borg, C., Cardona, M., and Caruana, S (2013), *Social Class, Language and Power: 'Letter to a Teacher': Lorenzo Milani and the School of Barbiana*, Leyden: Brill/Sense.

Boron, A., and Torres, C. A. (1996), 'The impact of neoliberal restructuring on education and poverty in Latin America', *Alberta Journal of Educational Research*, 42 (2): 102–14.

Boshier, R. (2005), 'Lifelong learning', in L. English (ed.), *Encyclopaedia of Adult Education*, 373–8, New York: Palgrave-Macmillan.

Bourdieu, P., and Passeron, J. C. (1990), *Reproduction in Education, Society and Culture* (2nd edn), London: Sage.

Bray, M., and Steward, L., eds (1998), *Examination Systems in Small States: Comparative Perspectives on Policies, Models and Operations*, London: Commonwealth Secretariat.

Burbules, N. C., and Torres, C. A., eds (2000), *Globalization and Education: Critical Perspectives*, New York: Routledge.

Burtchaell, J. T., ed. (1988), *A Just War No Longer Exists: The Teaching and Trial of Don Lorenzo Milani*, Notre Dame, IN: University of Notre Dame Press.

Braudel, F. (1992), *The Mediterranean and the Mediterranean World in the Age of Philip II*, vol. 1, London: Harper Collins.

Brown, P., Lauder, H., and Ashton, D. (2010), *The Global Auction: The Broken Promises of Education, Jobs, and Incomes*, Oxford: Oxford University Press.

Caldart, S. R. (2004), *Pedagogia do Movimento Sem Terra (The Pedagogy of the Landless Peasant Movement)*, São Paulo: Expressão Popular.

Caldart, S. R. (2012a), 'Educação do campo (Education in the countryside)', in R. S. Caldart, I. B. Pereira, P. Alentejano and G. Frigotto (eds), *Dicionário de Educação do Campo*, 259–67, Rio de Janeiro: EPSJV/Fiocruz.

Caldart, S. R. (2012b), 'Pedagogia do Movimento (Pedagogy of the Movement)', in R. S. Caldart, I. B. Pereira, P. Alentejano and G. Frigotto (eds), *Dicionário de Educação do Campo*, 548–55, Rio de Janeiro: EPSJV/Fiocruz.

Carnoy, M., and Torres, C. A. (1990), 'Education and social transformation in Nicaragua, 1979–1989', in M. Carnoy and J. Samoff (eds), *Education and Social Transition in the Third World*, 153–208, Princeton NJ: Princeton University Press.

Cedefop and Eurydice (2001), *National Actions to Implement Lifelong Learning in Europe*, Thessaloniki: CEDEFOP.

Chu, D. C. (1980), *Chairman Mao: Education of the Proletariat*, New York: Philosophy Library.

Castles, S., and Wustenberg, W. (1979), *The Education of the Future: An Introduction to the Theory and Practice of Socialist Education*, London: Pluto.

Coben, D (1998), *Radical Heroes: Gramsci, Freire and the Politics of Adult Education*, New York: Garland.

Connell, R. (2019), *The Good University: What Universities Actually Do and Why It's Time for Radical Change*, London: Zed Books.

Corradi, A. (2012), *Non so se Don Lorenzo…(I do not know if Don Lorenzo…)*, Milan: Feltrinelli.

Curtis, B., Livingstone, D. W., and Smaller, H. (1992), *Stacking the Deck: The Streaming of Working Class Kids in Ontario Schools*, Toronto: Our Schools/ Our Selves.

CEC (Council of European Communities) (2000), 'A Memorandum on Lifelong Learning, European Commission on Education and Communication, Brussels, Commission staff working paper.

Cortesão, L. (2011), 'Paulo Freire and Amilcar Cabral: Convergences', *Journal of Critical Education Policy Studies*, 9 (2): 260–7.

Coutinho, C. N. (2000), *Cultura e sociedade no Brasil (Culture and Society in Brazil)*, Rio de Janeiro: DP&A. Evangelista.

Cropley, A. J. (1980), 'Lifelong learning and systems of education: An overview', in A. J. Cropley (ed.), *Towards a System of Lifelong Education: Some Practical Considerations*, 1–15, Oxford: Pergamon Press.

Daiches, D. (1966), *Milton*, New York: W.W. Norton.

Dale, R. (2014), 'Preface', in F. Batini, P. Mayo and A. Surian (eds), *Lorenzo Milani, the School of Barbiana and the Struggle for Social Justice*, vii–ix, New York: Peter Lang.

Dale, R., and Robertson, S. (2004), 'Interview with Boaventura de Sousa Santos', *Globalization, Societies and Education*, 2 (2): 147–60.

Darder, A. (2002), *Reinventing Paulo Freire: A Pedagogy of Love*, Boulder, CO: Westview Press.

Darder, A. (2005), 'What is critical pedagogy?', in W. Hare and J. P. Portelli (eds), *Key Questions for Educators*, 90–4, Halifax: EdPhil Books.

Darder A. (2012), *Culture and Power in the Classroom* (20th anniversary edn), Boulder, CO: Paradigm.

Darder, A., Mayo, P., and Paraskeva, J. (eds) (2015), *The International Critical Pedagogy Reader*, London: Routledge.

Dave, R. H. (1976), 'Foundations of lifelong education: Some Methodological aspects', in R. H. Dave (ed.), *Foundations of Lifelong Education*, 15–50, Oxford: Pergamon Press.

De Kadt, E. (1970), *Caholic Radicals in Brazili*, Oxford: Oxford University Press.

De Rosa, L. (2004), *La provincia Subordinata – Saggio sulla Questione Meridionale (The Subordinated Province – Essay on the Southern Question)*, Bari: Laterza (in Italian).

De Vita, A. (2009), *La Creazione Sociale: Relazioni e contesti per educare (Social Creation: Relaions and Contests to Educate)*, Roma: Carocci.

De Vita, A., and Piussi, A. M. (2013), 'Social creation', in P. Mayo (ed.), *Learning with Adults: A Reader*, 293–306, Rotterdam: Sense.

Delpit, L. D. (1988), 'The silenced dialogue: Power and pedagogy in educating other people's children', *Harvard Educational Review*, 58 (3): 280–98.

del Roio, M. (1998), 'Sociologia e socialismo em Florestan Fernandes (Sociology and socialism in Florestan Fernandes)', in P. H. Martinez (ed.), *Florestan: ou o sentido das coisas*, 101–13, São Paulo: Boitempo.

Earth, B. (1998), 'Participatory research: Gender and health in rural Tanzania', *Convergence*, 31: 59–68.

El Saadawi, N. (1992), *The Nawal El Saadawi Reader*, London: Zed Books.
Elsheikh, M. S. (1999), 'Le Omissioni della Cultura Italiana' (The omissins of Italian Culture), in I. Sigillino (ed.), L'Islam nella Scuola (Islam in the School), 30–45, Milan: Franco Angeli.
English, L., and Mayo, P. (2012), *Learning with Adults: A Critical Pedagogical Introduction*, Boston: Brill-Sense.
English, L., and Mayo, P. (2019), 'Lifelong learning challenges: Responding to migration and the Sustainable Development Goals', *International Review of Education*, 65 (2): 213–31.
Escobar, M., Fernández, A. L., and Guevara-Niebla, G., with Freire, P. (1994), *Paulo Freire on Higher Education: A Dialogue at the National University of Mexico*, Albany: SUNY Press.
Evangelista, O., and Leher, R. (2012), 'Todos pela educacão e o Episodio Costin no mec A Pedagogia do Capital em acão na política educacional Brasileira' (All for education and the Costin episode in MEC A Pedagogy of Capital in Brazilian educational policy), *Trabalho necesario*, 10 (15). Available online: https://periodicos.uff.br/trabalhonecessario/article/view/6865/5148 (accessed 28 March 2021).
Fallaci, N. (1993), *Vita del Prete Lorenzo Milani: Dalla parte dell'ultimo (Life of the Priest Lorenzo Milani: On the Side of the Socially Least Positioned)*, Milan: Biblioteca Universale Rizzoli.
Fanon, F. (1952), *Black Skin, White Masks*, London: Pluto Press.
Fanon, F. (1963), *The Wretched of the Earth: The Handbook for the Black Revolution That Is Changing the Shape of the World*, New York: Grove Press.
Faure, E., Herrera, F., Kaddoura, A. R., Lopes, H., Petrovsky, A. V., Rahnema, M., and Champion Ward, F. (1972), *Learning to Be: The World of Education Today and Tomorrow*, Paris: UNESCO.
Fernandes, F. (1968), *Sociedade de classes e subdesenvolvimento (Class Society and Underdevelopment)*, Rio de Janeiro: Zahar.
Fernandes, F. (1975), *A revolução burguesa no Brasil: Ensaio de interpretação sociológica (The Bourgeois Revolution in Brazil: An Essay of Sociological Interpretation)*, Rio de Janeiro: Zahar.
Fernandes, F. (2012), *Marx, Engels, Lenin: a história em processo (Marx, Engels and Lenin: History in Process)*, São Paulo: Expressão Popular.
Field, J. (2010), 'Lifelong learning', in P. Peterson, E. Baker and B. McGaw (eds), *International Encyclopedia of Education* (3rd edn), 89–95, Amsterdam: Elsevier.
Finger, M., and Asún, J. M. (2001), *Adult Education at the Crossroads: Learning our Way Out*, London: Zed Books.
Fisher, M. (2009), *Capitalist Realism: Is There No Alternative?*, Winchester: Zero Books.
Foley, G. (1999), *Learning in Social Action: A Contribution to Understanding Informal Education*, London: Zed Books.
Fondazione Laboratorio Mediterraneo (1997), *Obiettivi e mezzi per il paternariato euromediterraneo: Il forum civile EuroMed*, Napoli: Magma.

Forgacs, D., and Nowell-Smith, G. (1985), *Antonio Gramsci, Selections from Cultural Writings*, Cambridge, MA: Harvard University Press.
Freire, A. M., ed. (2005), *Pedagogia da Tolerancia*, São Paulo: UNESP.
Freire, P. (1970a), *Pedagogy of the Oppressed*, New York: The Seabury Press.
Freire, P. (1970b), *Cultural Action for Freedom*, Cambridge, MA: Harvard University Press.
Freire, P. (1973), *Education for Critical Consciousness*, New York: Continuum.
Freire, P. (1978), *Pedagogy in Process: The Letters to Guinea Bissau*, New York: Continuum.
Freire, P. (1982), *A importância do ato de ler*, São Paulo: Cortez.
Freire, P. (1984), *Cartas A Guinea Bissau: Registros de uma experiencia em progresso*, São Paulo: Paz e Terra.
Freire, P. (1985), *The Politics of Education*, South Hadley, MA: Bergin & Garvey.
Freire, P. (1993), *Pedagogy of the City*, New York: Continuum.
Freire, P. (1994), *Pedagogy of Hope*, New York: Continuum.
Freire, P. (1997), 'A response', in P. Freire (ed.), with Fraser, J. W., Macedo, D., McKinnon, T., and. Stokes, W. T., *Mentoring the Mentor: A Critical Dialogue with Paulo Freire*, 303–29, New York: Peter Lang.
Freire, P. (1998a), *Pedagogy of Freedom: Ethics, Democracy and Civic Courage*, Lanham: Rowman & Littlefield.
Freire, P. (1998b), *Teachers as Cultural Workers: Letters to Those Who Dare Teach*, Boulder, CO: Westview Press.
Freire, P. (2000), *Pedagogia da indignação: Cartas pedagogicas e outros escritos*, São Paulo: UNESP.
Freire, P. (2004), *Pedagogy of Indignation*, ed. D. Macedo, Boulder CO: Paradigm.
Freire, P. (2005), *Conscientização, teoria e prática da libertação (Conscientisation. Theory and Practice of Liberation)*, São Paulo: Centauro.
Freire, P. (2013), *Pedagogia do Oprimido (o manuscrito) (Pedagogy of the Oppressed: The Manuscript)*, ed. J. Ferreira Mafra, J. E. Romão and M. Gadotti, São Paulo: Editora e Livraria Instituto Paulo Freire, Universidade Nove de Julho (Uninove), Ministério da Educação.
Freire, P. (2018), *Pedagogy of the Oppressed* (50th anniversary edn), New York: Bloomsbury Academic.
Freire, P., and Faundez, A. (1989), *Learning to Question: A Pedagogy of Liberation*, Geneva: World Council of Churches.
Freire, P., and Guimaraes, S. (2002), *A Africa ensinando a gente (In Africa Teaching People), Angola, Guinea Bissau, São Tome e Principe*, São Paulo: Paz e Terra.
Freire, P., and Macedo, D. (1987), *Literacy: Reading the Word and the World*, Westport, CT: Bergin & Garvey.
Freire, P., and Macedo, D. (1995), 'A dialogue: Culture, language and race', *Harvard Educational Review*, 65 (3): 377–402.

Gadotti, M. (1996), Pedagogy of Praxis: A Dialectical Philosophy of Education, Albany: SUNY Press.

Gadotti, M. (2005), 'Pedagogia da Terra e Cultura da Sustentabilidade', *Revista Lusófona de Educação*, 6: 15–29.

Gadotti, M., Freire, P., and Guimarães, S. (1995), *Pedagogia: dialogo e conflitto (Pedagogy: Dialogue and Conflict)*, ed. B. Bellanova and F. Telleri, Torino: Societa` Editrice Internazionale.

Galea, S. (2011), 'Min hi l-Għalliema fl-Ittra lil Waħda Għalliema mill-Iskola ta' Barbjana? Sehem in-Nisa fil-Professjoni tal-Għalliema (Who is the teacher in Letter to a Teacher by the School of Barbiana? Women's role in the teaching profession)', in C. Borg (ed.), *Lorenzo Milani: Bejn Ilbieraħ u Llum (Lorenzo Milani: Between Yesterday and Today)*, 227–43, Malta: Horizons.

Galeano, E. (2009), *The Open Veins of Latin America: Five Centuries of the Pillage of a Continent*, London: The Serpent's Tail.

Gargour, M. (2009), 'The Land speaks Arabic' (video documentary), YouTube. Available online: https://www.youtube.com/watch?v=nY3v-yht_6g (accessed 24 April 2015).

Gatt, A. (2014), 'Fair sharing of asylum responsibility within the EU: Addressing Malta's scenario', in P. Xuereb (ed.), *Migration and Asylum in Malta and the European Union*, 103–40, Malta: Malta University Press.

Gelpi, E. (1985a), *Lifelong Education and International Relations*, London and New York: Continuum.

Gelpi, E. (1985b), 'Lifelong learning and international relations', in K. Wain (ed.), *Lifelong Education and Participation*, 16–29, Malta: University of Malta Press.

Gelpi, E. (2002), *Lavoro Futuro: La formazione professionale come progetto politico (Future Work: Vocational Preparation as a Political Project)*, Milan: Edizioni Angelo Guerini e Associati SpA.

Gesualdi, S. (2007), 'Come e' nata "Lettera a Una Professoressa" (How the 'Letter to a Teacher' came about)', in M. Gesualdi (ed.), *Scuola di Barbiana, Lettera a Una Professoressa: Quarnt' anni dopo (School of Barbiana, Letter to a Teacher: 40 Years Later)*, 5–13, Florence: Libreria Editrice Fiorentina.

Gentili, P. (2005), *La Falsificazione del Consenso: Simulacro e Imposizione nella Riforma Educativa del Neoliberalismo (The Falsification of Consensus: Simulacra and Imposition in the Educational Reform of Neoliberalism)*, Pisa: Edizioni ETS (in Italian).

Germino, D. (1990), *Antonio Gramsci. Architect of a New Politics*, Baton Rouge: Louisiana State University Press.

Gezgin, U. B, Inal, K., and Hill, D. (eds) (2014), *The Gezi Revolt: People's Revolutionary Resistance against Neoliberal Capitalism in Turkey*, Brighton: Institute for Education Policy Studies.

Giroux, H. (1992), *Border Crossings: Cultural Workers and the Politics of Education*, New York: Routledge.

Giroux, H. (2001), *Public Spaces/Private Lives: Beyond the Culture of Cynicism*, Lanham: Rowman & Littlefield.
Giroux, H. (2004), *The Terror of Neoliberalism: Authoritarianism and the Eclipse of Democracy*, Boulder, CO: Paradigm.
Giroux H. (2007), *The University in Chains, Confronting the Military-Industrial-Academic Complex*, Boulder, CO: Paradigm.
Giroux H. (2008), *Against the Terror of Neoliberalism: Politics beyond the Age of Greed*, Boulder, CO: Paradigm.
Giroux H. (2011), *On Critical Pedagogy*, New York: Continuum/Bloomsbury.
Giroux H. (2014a), *Neoliberalism's War on Higher Education*, Chicago, IL: Haymarket Books.
Giroux, H. (2014b), 'Barbarians at the gates: Authoritarianism and the assault on public education', *Truthout*, 30 December. Available online: http://www.truthout.org/news/item/28272-barbarians-at-the-gates-authoritarianism-and-the-assault-on-public-education (accessed 24 April 2014).
Giroux, H. (2020), 'Global Thursday Talks: An interview with Henry A. Giroux on critical issues in education', YouTube, 13 April (Webcast). Available online: https://www.youtube.com/watch?v=tRA3ZMbPaDc&fbclid=IwAR3sIP-IkcJYEyi6rUgY6YnmjqAHvSYoIi5BXBiW7iPia4_MCMA0Or9jj38 (accessed 22 October 2020).
Giroux, H., and Searls Giroux, S. (2004), *Take Back Higher Education: Race, Youth and the Crisis of Democracy in the Post-Civil Rights Era*, New York: Palgrave-Macmillan.
Gobetti, A. (1943), *Alessandro Pope: Il poeta del razionalismo settecentesco (Alexander Pope: The Poet of 18th Century Rationalism)*, Bari: Laterza.
Gobetti, A. (1958), *Non lasciamoli soli: Consigli ai genitori per l'educazione dei figli (Let Us Not Leave Them Alone: Advice to Parents on Their Children's Education)*, Turin: La cittadella.
Gobetti, A. (1963), *Storia del gallo Sebastiano ovverosia Il tredicesimo uovo (Story of the Cock Sebastiano, or Rather the 13th Egg)*, Turin: Einaudi.
Gobetti, A. (1967), *Vivere insieme: Corso di educazione civica (Living Together: Course in Civic Education)*, Turin: Loescher.
Gobetti, A. (1982), *Educare per emancipare: Scritti pedagogici 1953–1968 (Educate to Emancipate: Pedagogical Writings 1953–1968)*, Manduria: Lacaita.
Gobetti, A. (1996), *Diario partigiano (Partisan Diary)*, Turin: Einaudi.
Gobetti, A. (2014), *Partisan's Diary: A Woman's Life in the Italian Resistance*, ed. and trans. J. Alano, Oxford: Oxford University Press.
Gobetti, P., and Gobetti, A. (1991), *Nella tua breve esistenza. Lettere 1918–1926 (In Your Brief Existence: Letters 1918–1926)*, Torino, Einaudi.
Gramsci, A. (1925), *L'Ordine Nuovo*, 1 April.
Gramsci, A. (1957), *The Modern Prince and Other Writings*, ed. L. Marks, New York: International Publishers.
Gramsci, A. (1971), *Selections from the Prison Notebooks*, ed. Q. Hoare and G. Nowell Smith, New York: International.

Gramsci, A. (1975), *Quaderni del Carcere: Edizione Critica (Prison Notebooks: Critical Edition 1V volumes)*, ed. V. Gerratana, Turin: Einaudi (in Italian).
Gramsci A. (1977), *Antonio Gramsci, Selections from Political writings (1910–1920)*, ed. Q. Hoare and J. Matthews, New York: International.
Gramsci, A. (1995), *The Southern Question*, ed. and trans. P. Verdicchio, West Lafayette, IN: Bordighera.
Gramsci, A. (1997), *Le Opere: La Prima Antologia di tutti gli scritti* (The Works: The First Anthology of All the Writings), ed. A. Santucci, Rome: Editori Riuniti.
Grech, M., and Mayo, P. (2014), 'What Catholic educators can learn from the radical Christianity and critical pedagogy of Don Lorenzo Milani', *International Studies in Catholic Education*, 6 (1): 33–45.
Gutierrez, F., and Prado, C. (2000), *Ecopedagogia e cittadinanza planetaria (Ecopedagogy and Planetary Citizenship)*, Bologna: E.M.I.
Hall, B. L. (1973a), *Wakati wa Furaha: An Evaluation of a Radio Study Group Campaign*, Dar es Salaam: Institute for Adult Education.
Hall, B. L. (1973b), *Voices for Development: Tanzania's Mass Education Campaigns*, Uppsala: Scandinavian Institute for African Studies.
Hall, B. L. (1975), *Adult Education and the Development of Socialism in Tanzania*, Nairobi: East African Publishing House.
Hall, B. L. (1998), '"Please don't bother the canaries": Paulo Freire and the International Council for Adult Education', *Convergence (Tribute to Paulo Freire)*, 31: 95–104.
Hall, B. L., and Clover, D. E. (2005), 'Social movement learning', in L. M. English (ed.), *International Encyclopedia of Adult Education*, 584–9, New York: Palgrave Macmillan.
Hall, B. L., and Clover, D. E. (2006), 'Social movement learning', in R. Veira de Castro, A. V. Sancho and P. Guimarães (eds), *Adult Education: New Routes in a New Landscape*, 159–66, Braga, Portugal: University of Minho.
Hall, B. L., and Kassam, Y. (1972), *Studies in Adult Education*, Dar es Salaam: Institute for Adult Education.
Hall, B. L., Mhaiki, P. J., Malya, S. T., and Maganga, C. K. (1972), *The 1971 Literacy Campaign Study*, Dar es Salaam: Institute for Adult Education.
Hall, S. (1987a), 'Gramsci and us', *Marxism Today*, June, 16–21. Available online: http://www.unz.org/Pub/MarxismToday-1987jun-00016 (accessed 7 August 2014).
Hall, S. (1987b), 'Blue election, election blues', *Marxism Today*, July, 30–5. Available online: http://www.unz.org/Pub/MarxismToday-1987jul-00030 (accessed 7 August 2014).
Hall, S. (2017), 'The empire strikes back', in S. Davison, D. Featherstone, M. Rustin and B. Schwarz (eds), *Selected Political Writings: The Great Moving Right Show and Other Essays*, 200–6, London: Lawrence and Wishart.
Harasim, L. M. (1983), *Literacy and National Reconstruction in Guinea-Bissau: A Critique of the Freirean Literacy Campaign*, PhD dissertation, OISE-University of Toronto.

hooks, b (1989), *Taking Back: Thinking Feminist, Thinking Black*, Toronto: Between the lines.

hooks, b (1993), 'bell hooks speaking about Paulo Freire. The man, his works', in P. McLaren and P. Leonard (eds), *Paulo Freire. A Critical Encounter*, 146–54, New York: Routledge.

Horton, M., and Freire, P. (1990), *We Make the Road by Walking: Conversations on Education and Social Change*, Philadelphia: Temple University Press.

Kane, L. (2001), *Popular Education and Social Change in Latin America*, London: Latin American Bureau.

Kapoor, D. (2009), 'Globalization, dispossession and subaltern social movements (SSM): Learning in the South', in A. Abdi and D. Kapoor (eds), *Global Perspectives on Adult Education*, 71–92, London: Palgrave Macmillan.

Kassam, Y. (1994), 'Julius Kambarage Nyerere (1922 -)', *Prospects*, 24: 247–59.

La Belle, T. J. (1986), *Nonformal Education in Latin America and the Caribbean: Stability, Reform or Revolution?*, Westport: Praeger.

Larrain, J. (1983), *Marxism and Ideology*, Atlantic Highlands, NJ: Humanities Press.

Ledwith, M. (2005), *Community Development: A Critical Approach*, Bristol: BASW/Policy Press.

Leher, R. (2003), 'O governo Lula e os conflitos sociais no Brasil (The Lula government and social conflicts in Brazil)', *Revista del Observatório Social de América Latina*, 4 (10): 81–96.

Leher, R. (2010), 'Educação no governo Lula: a ruptura que não aconteceu (Education in the Lula government: the rupture that did not happen)', in CORECON/SINDICON (eds), *Os anos Lula: contribuições para um balanço crítico 2003-2010 (The Lula Years; Contributions to a critical appraisal 2003-2010)*, 369–412, Rio de Janeiro: Garamond.

Leher, R. (2011), 'Projetos em disputa, eleições e dilemas da reorganização das lutas sociais (Disputed projects, elections and dilemmas when reorganizing social struggles)', *Revista del Observatório Social de América Latina*, 12 (29): 93–106.

Leher, R. (2012), 'Todos pela educação e o episódio Costin no MEC: a Pedagogia do capital em ação na política educacional brasileira (All for education and the Costin episode at MEC: The pedagogy of capital in action in Brazilian educational policy)', *Trabalho Necessário*, 10 (15):1–29.

Leher, R., and Trindade, A. (2012), 'O Brasil e a crise: setores dominantes avançam, trabalhadores empreendem lutas "dentro" da ordem' (Brazil and the crisis: Dominant sectors advance, workers engage in struggles 'within' the order), *Revista del Observatório Social de América Latina*, 13 (31): 181–97.

Leher, R., and Vittoria, P. (2015), 'Social movements and critical pedagogy in Brazil: From the origins of popular education to the proposal of a permanent forum', *Journal for Critical Education Policy Studies*, 13 (3): 145–62.

Lengrand, P. (1970), *An Introduction to Lifelong Education*, Paris: UNESCO.

Leopando, I. (2017), *A Pedagogy of Faith: The Theological Vision of Paulo Freire*, London: Bloomsbury Academic.

Leuzzi, C. (2015), *Ada Gobetti e l'educazione al vivere democratico. Gli anni cinquanta di Ada Prospero Marchesini (Ada Gobetti and Education for Democratic Living. The Fifties of Ada Prospero Marchesini)*, Rome: Anicia (in Italian).

Livingstone, D. W. (1983), *Class, Ideologies and Educational Futures*, London: Falmer Press.

Livingstone, D. W. (2002), 'Working class learning, cultural transformation, and democratic political education: Gramsci's legacy', in C. Borg, J. A. Buttigieg and P. Mayo (eds), *Gramsci and Education*, 219–40, Lanham, MD: Rowman & Littlefield.

Lutterbeck, D. (2012), 'From Malta to Mogadishu: Travel experiences of Somali migrants', in P. Xuereb (ed.), *Migration and Asylum in Malta and the European Union*, 61–79, Malta: Malta University Press.

Malabotta, M. R. (2002), 'Education for a multicultural Italy', *Journal of Postcolonial Education*, 1 (2): 69–79.

Mallia, P. (2012), 'The disembarkation of migrants rescued at sea: Where is the 'solidarity'?', in P. Xuereb (ed.) *Migration and Asylum in Malta and the European Union*, 81–101, Malta: Malta University Press.

Marshall, J. (1997), 'Globalisation from below: The trade union connections', in S. Walters (ed.), *Globalisation, Adult Education and Training: Impact and Issues*, 57–68, London: Zed Books.

Marx, K. (1907), *The Eighteenth Brumaire of Louis Bonaparte*, Chicago, IL: Charles H. Kerr.

Marx, K., and Engels, F. (1970), *The German Ideology*, ed. C. J. Arthur, London: Lawrence and Wishart.

Marx, K., and Engels, F. (1978), *The Marx-Engels Reader*, ed. R. Tucker, New York: W.W. Norton.

Martin, I. (2001), 'Reconstituting the agora: Towards an alternative politics of lifelong learning', *Concept*, 2 (1): 4–8.

Masalha, N. (2012), *The Palestine Nakba: Decolonising History, Narrating the Subaltern, Reclaiming Memory*, London: Zed Books.

Mayo, M. (1997), *Imagining Tomorrow: Adult Education for Transformation*, Leicester: NIACE.

Mayo, P. (1999a), *Gramsci, Freire and Adult Education: Possibilities for Transformative Adult Education*, London: Zed Books.

Mayo, P. (1999b), 'Towards a critical multiculturalism in the Mediterranean: Reflections on the conference 'Il Mare che unisce. Scuola, Europa e Mediterraneo (The Sea that Unites. School, Europe and the Mediterranean)', *Mediterranean Journal of Educational Studies*, 5 (1): 117–22.

Mayo, P. (2004a), *Liberating Praxis: Paulo Freire's Legacy for Radical Education and Politics*, Westport: Praeger.

Mayo, P. (2004b), *Gramsci, Freire E A Educação De Adultos: Possibilidades para uma ação transformadora (Gramsci, Freire and Adult Education: Possibilities for Transformative Action)*, Porto Alegre: Arte Medicas (ArtMed) Editora.

Mayo, P. (2005), 'Educação Critica e Desenvolvimento de uma Cidadania Multi-Étnica: Uma perspective a partir do Sul da Europa (Critical education and the development of a multi-ethnic citizenship: A perspective from Southern Europe)', *Revista Lusófona de Educação*, 6: 47–54.

Mayo, P. (2007a), 'Critical approaches to education in the work of Lorenzo Milani and Paulo Freire', *Studies in Philosophy and Education*, 26 (6): 525–44.

Mayo, P. (2007b), 'Gramsci, the Southern Question and the Mediterranean', *Mediterranean Journal of Educational Studies*, 12 (2): 1–17.

Mayo, P. (2015), *Hegemony and Education under Neoliberalism: Insights from Gramsci*, New York: Routledge.

Mayo, P. (2016), 'Hegemony, migration and misplaced alliances: Lessons from Gramsci', in O. G. Agustin and M. B. Jorgensen (eds), *Solidarity without Borders: Gramscian Perspectives on Migration and Civil Society Alliances*, 135–49, London: Pluto Press.

Mayo, P. (2019), *Higher Education in a Globalising World: Community Engagement and Lifelong Learning*, Manchester: University of Manchester Press.

Mayo, P., and Vittoria, P. (2017a), *Saggi di Pedagogia Critica. Oltre il Neoliberismo. Analizzando Educatori, Lotte e Movimenti Sociali (Essays in Critical Pedagogy. Beyond Neoliberalism. Analysing Educators, Struggles and Social Movements)*, Florence: Società Editrice Fiorentina (SEF).

Mayo, P., and Vittoria, P. (2017b), 'La Scuola Florestan Fernandes e la pedagogia del Movimento dei contadini Senza Terra (MST) in Brasile: dialogo con Rosana Fernandes (The Florestan Fernandes School and the pedagogy of the Landless Peasant Movement [MST]. A Dialogue with Rosana Fernandes)', *Lifelong Lifewide Learning*, 13 (30): 78–92.

McGinn, N. F. (1996), 'Education, democratisation and globalisation: A challenge for comparative education', *Comparative Education Review*, 40 (4): 341–57.

McGinn, N. F. (1997), 'The impact of globalization on national educational systems', *Prospects*, 27 (1): 41–54.

McLaren P. (1994), *Life in Schools: An Introduction to Critical Pedagogy in the Foundations of Education*, Sydney: Longmans.

McLaren, P. (1997), 'Paulo Freire's legacy of hope and struggle', *Taboo: The Journal of Culture and Education*, 2 (Fall): 33–8.

Milani, L. (1970), *Lettere di Don Lorenzo Milani. Priore di Barbiana (Letters by Don Lorenzo Milani. Prior at Barbiana)*, Milan: Oscar Mondadori.

Milani, L. (1977), *Esperienze Pastorali (Pastoral Experiences)*, Florence: Libreria Editrice Fiorentina.

Milani, L. (1988a), *A Just War No Longer Exists: The Teachings and Trial of Don Lorenzo Milani*, ed. J. Burtchaell, Notre Dame, IN: University of Notre Dame Press.

Milani, L. (1988b), 'Letter of Don Lorenzo Milani to the military chaplains of Tuscany who signed the communiqué' of 11 February 1965', in J. T. Burtchaell (ed.), *A Just War No Longer Exists: The Teaching and Trial of Don Lorenzo Milani*, 18–28, Notre Dame, IN: University of Notre Dame Press.

Milani, L. (1988c), 'Milani's letter to the judges', in J. T. Burtchaell (ed.), *A Just War No Longer Exists: The Teaching and Trial of Don Lorenzo Milani*, 52–77, Notre Dame, IN: University of Notre Dame Press.

Milani, L. (1991), *L'Obbedienza Non e' Piu' Una Virtù (Obedience Is No longer a Virtue)*, Florence: Libreria Editrice Fiorentina.

Milani, L. (1996), *La Parola ai Poveri: Rilettura di Una Esperienza e di Una Testimonianza (The Word to the Poor: Rereading of an Experience and a Testimony)*, Fossano: Editrice Esperienze.

Milani, L. ([1997] 2004), *Una Lezione alla Scuola di Barbiana (A Lesson at the School of Barbiana)*, Florence: Libreria Editrice Fiorentina.

Milani, L. (2011), *L'obbedienza nella Chiesa (Obedience in the Church)*, Florence: Libreria Editrice Fiorentina.

Milani, B. (2002), 'From opposition to alternatives: Post-industrial potentials and transformative learning', in E. O'Sullivan, A. Morrell and M. A. O'Connor (eds), *Expanding the Boundaries of Transformative Learning*, 47–58, Basingstoke, UK: Palgrave.

Misiaszek, G. W. (2021), *Ecopedagogy: Critical Environmental Teaching for Planetary Justice and Global Sustainable Development*, London: Bloomsbury Academic.

Mistral, G. (2015a), *Por la humanidad futura: Antologia politica (The Future Humanity: Political Anthology)*, Santiago del Chile: La Pollera ediciones.

Mistral, G. (2015b), *Poema de Chile (Chile Poem)*, Santiago del Cile: La Pollera ediciones.

Mistral, G. (2017a), *Manuscritos: Poesía inédita (Manuscripts: Unpublished Poetry)*. Santiago del Cile: Garceta ediciones.

Mistral, G. (2017b), *La lengua de Martí y otros motivos cubanos (The Language of Martí and other Cuban motifs)*, Santiago del Cile: Lom ediciones.

Morrow, R., and Torres, C. A. (1995), *Social Theory and Education: A Critique of Theories of Social and Cultural Reproduction*, Albany: SUNY Press.

Muraca, M. (2019), *Educazione e Movimenti Sociali: Un'etnografia Collaborativa con il Movimento di Donne Contadine a Santa Catarina (Brasile) (Education and Social Movements: A Collaborative Ethnography with the Women Farmer Movement at Santa Catarina [Brazil])*, Sesto-San Giovanni, Milan: Mimesis.

Mulenga, D. (1996), 'The impact of economic crisis and structural adjustment on education and training in Africa', in H. Reno and M. Witte (eds), *37th Annual Adult Education Research Conference Proceedings*, 228–33, Tampa: University of South Florida.

Murphy, M. (1997), 'Capital, class and adult education: The international political economy of lifelong learning in the European Union', in P. Armstrong, N. Miller and M. Zukas (eds), *Crossing Borders, Breaking Boundaries: Research in the Education of Adults, Proceedings of the 27th Annual SCUTREA Conference*, 362–5, London: Birkbeck College - University of London.

Mushi, P. A. K. (1994), 'Literacy as agricultural development strategy: The Tanzanian experience', *Canadian Journal for the Study of Adult Education*, 8: 65–72.

Nyerere, J. K. (1968), *Uhuru Na Ujamaa. Freedom and Socialism*, London: Oxford University Press.

Nyerere, J. K. (1974), *Man and Development Binadamu Na Maendeleo* [sic], London: Oxford University Press.

Nyerere, J. K. (1977), *The Arusha Declaration - Ten Years After*, Dar es Salaam: Government Printing.

Nyerere, J. K. (1979a), 'Adult education and development', in H. Hinzen and V. H. Hundsdorfer (eds), *The Tanzanian Experience: Education for Liberation and Development*, 49–55, Hamburg: UNESCO Institute for Education.

Nyerere, J. K. (1979b), 'Education never ends', in Hinzen, H and V. H. Hundsdorfer (eds), *The Tanzanian Experience: Education for Liberation and Development*, 33–7, Hamburg: UNESCO Institute for Education.

Nyerere, J. K. (1979c), 'Our education must be for liberation', in H. Hinzen and V. H. Hundsdorfer (eds), *The Tanzanian Experience: Education for Liberation and Development*, 43–8, Hamburg: UNESCO Institute for Education.

Nyerere, J. K. (1979d), 'Relevance and Dar es Salaam University', in H. Hinzen and V. H. Hundsdorfer (eds), *The Tanzanian Experience: Education for Liberation and Development*, 38–42, Hamburg: UNESCO Institute for Education.

Nyerere, J. K. (1996), 'Working for peace, transcript of interview, with Charlene Hunter-Gault', A News Hour with Jim Lehrer (Online News hour), 27 December. Available online: https://www.juliusnyerere.org/resources/view/j.k.nyerere_talks_with_charlayne_hunter-gault (accessed 27 March 2021).

O'Cadiz, M. (1995), 'Social movements and literacy tin Brazil: A narrative', in C. A. Torres (ed.), *Education and Social Change in Latin America*, 163–73, Melbourne: James Nicholas.

O'Cadiz, M., Wong, P. L., and Torres, C. A. (1998), *Education and Democracy: Paulo Freire, Social Movements and Educational Reform in São Paulo*, Boulder, CO: Westview Press.

Okoh, J. D. (1980), *Julius Nyerere's Social Philosophy and Its Implications for Education*, PhD dissertation, Department of Educational Foundations, University of Alberta.

Oliveira, I. A. (2003), *Leituras freireanas sobre educação (Freirean Readings about Education)*, São Paulo: UNESP.

Olssen, M. (2004), 'Neoliberalism, globalization, democracy: Challenges for education', *Globalization, Societies and Education*, 2 (2): 231–76.

O' Sullivan, E. (1999), *Transformative Learning. Educational Vision for the 21 Century*, London: Zed Books.

O'Sullivan, E. (2002), 'The project and vision of transformative education', in E. O'Sullivan, A Morrell and M. A. O'Connor (eds), *Expanding the Boundaries of Transformative Learning: Essays on Theory and Praxis*, 1–12, Basingstoke: Palgrave.

Paiva, V. (1980), *Paulo Freire e o nacionalismo-desenvolvimentista (Paulo Freire and Developmentalist Nationalism)*, Rio de Janeiro: Civilização Brasileira.

Pannu, R. S. (1996), 'Neoliberal project of globalization: Prospects for democratisation of education', *Alberta Journal of Educational Research*, 42 (2): 87–101.

Parson, S. (1990), 'Lifelong learning and the community school', in C. Poster and A. Kruger (eds), *Community Education in the Western World*, 24–32, London: Routledge.

Pecorini, G. (1998), *Don Milani: Chi era Costui? (Don Milani: Who Was He?)*, Milan: Baldini and Castoldi.

Pereira, A., and Vittoria, P. (2013), 'A luta pela descolonização e as experiências de alfabetização na Guiné-Bissau: Amilcar Cabral e Paulo Freire (The struggle for decolonisation and experiences in education in Guinea Bissau: Amilcar Cabral and Paulo Freire)', *Revista de Estudos Históricos*, 25 (50): 291–311.

Perina, R. (2008), *Per una pedagogia del teatro sociale* (For a Pedagogy of Social Theatre), Milan: Franco Angeli.

Pisani, M. (2012), 'The elephant in the room: A look at how policies impact the lives of female sub-Saharan Africa rejected asylum seekers living in Malta', in P. Xuereb (ed.), *Migration and Asylum in Malta and the European Union*, 217–36, Malta: Malta University Press.

Piussi, A. M. (2003), 'L'incerto crinale: Formazione e lavoro nell'esperienza femminile e nel lifelong learning (The uncertain ridge: Formation and work in the feminine experience and lifelong learning)', *Studium Educationis*, 2: 404–16.

Piussi, A. M. (2004), 'Aprovechar La Libertad Femenina: Darse en Cuerpo y Alma al Trabajo y la Formación en Tiempos de Postfordismo (Approving feminine liberty: Giving a body and soul to work and education in the time of post-fordism)', in A. M. Piussi, P. Mayo, D. Jover, S. Piera and R. Alcolel (eds), *Trabajo Futuro. La Formación como proyecto y el apredizaje permanente (Future work. Formation as Project and lifelong learning)*, 3–16, Valencia: Laboratori d'iiciatives i ciutadanes Ettore Gelpi.

Piussi, A. M. (2011), 'Il senso libero della libertà: La posta in gioco di una civiltà desiderabile (The free meaning of freedom: The stakes in a desirable society)', *Encyclopaideia*, 15 (29): 11–45.

Piussi, A. M. (2012), 'Più del potere, l'autorità (More than power, authority)', in A. Ascenzi and A. Chionna (eds), *Potere, autorità, formazione (Power, Authority, Education)*, 24–41, Bari: Progredit.

Polychroniou, C. J. (2020), 'If Trump had followed Vietnam's lead on COVID, U.S. would have fewer than 100 dead', *Truthout*, 22 August. Available online: https://truthout.org/articles/if-trump-had-followed-vietnams-lead-on-covid-us-would-have-fewer-than-100-dead/?eType=EmailBlastContent&eId=cb730a39-059b-476c-b030-20e7fe306664 (accessed 5 January 2021).

Pope Francis (2015), *Laudato Sí: On Care for Our Common Home*, Vatican City: Libreria Editrice Vaticana.

Power, N. (2019), *One Dimensional Woman*, Winchester, UK: Zero Books.

Rikowski, G (2002), *The Battle in Seattle: Its significance for Education*, London: Tufnell Press.

Rossatto, C. A. (2005), *Engaging Paulo Freire's Pedagogy of Possibility: From Blind to Transformative Optimism*, Boulder, CO: Rowman & Littlefield.

Rummert, S., Algebaile, E., and Ventura, J. (2012), 'Educação e formação humana no cenário de integração subalterna no capital-imperialismo (Education and human formation in the scenario of subaltern integration in captialist-imperialism)', in M. M. da Silva, E. M. Quartiero and O. Evangelista (eds), *Jovens, Trabalho e Educação: a conexão subalterna de formação para o capital (Youth, Work and Education: The Subaltern Connection of Formation for Capital)*, 15–70, Campinas-São Paulo: Mercado de Letras.

Said, E. (1978), *Orientalism*, New York: Random House.

Said, E. (1994), *Culture and Imperialism*, London: Vintage.

Samoff, J. (1990), '"Modernizing" a socialist vision: Education in Tanzania', in M. Carnoy and J. Samoff (eds), *Education and Social Transition in the Third World*, 121–39, Princeton, NJ: Princeton University Press.

Sánchez-Bello, A. (2015), 'Perspectiva teoricas de genero: status questionis del impacto en el sistema educativo (Theoretical perspectives on gender: Status questions of its impact on the educational system)', *Convergencia. Revista de Ciencias Sociales*, 22 (67): 111–27.

Santos, B. (2016), *Epistemologies of the South: Justice against Epistemicide*, New York: Routledge.

Santos, B. (2017), *Decolonizing the University: The Challenge of Deep Cognitive Justice*, Newcastle upon Tyne: Cambridge Scholars.

Saviani, D. (2003), *Pedagogia histórico-crítica: primeiras aproximações (Historical-Critical Pedagogy: First Approaches)*, Campinas-São Paulo: Autores Associados.

Schugurensky, D. (2002), 'Transformative learning and transformative politics: The pedagogical dimension of participatory democracy and social action', in E. O'Sullivan, A. Morrell and M. O'Connor (eds), *Expanding the Boundaries of Transformative Learning*, 59–76, New York: Palgrave.

Scuola di Barbiana (1996), *Lettera a Una Professoressa (Letter to a Teacher)*, Florence: Libreria Editrice Fiorentina.

Semeraro, G. (2007), 'From liberation to hegemony: Freire and Gramsci in democratization processes in Brazil', *Rev. Sociol. Polit.* (29): 95–104. Available online: http://dx.doi.org/10.1590/S0104-44782007000200008 (accessed 6 April 2021).

Shiva, V. (2009), *Soil, Not Oil: Climate Change, Peak Oil and Food Insecurity*, London: Zed Books.

Shor, I. (1987), *Critical Teaching and Everyday Life*, Chicago, IL: University of Chicago Press.

Shor, I., and Freire, P. (1987), *A Pedagogy for Liberation: Dialogues on Transforming Education*, South Hadley, MA: Bergin & Garvey.

Silwadi N., and Mayo, P. (2014), 'Pedagogy under siege in Palestine: Freirean approaches', *Holy Land Studies*, 13 (2): 71–87.

Simeone, D. (1996), *Verso la Scuola di Barbiana: L'esperienza pastorale educativa di don Lorenzo Milani a S. Donato di Calenzano (Towards the School of Barbiana: Don Lorenzo Milani's Educational Pastoral Experience at San Donato di Calenzano)*, San Pietro in Cariano (Verona): Il Segno dei Gabrielli Editori.

Simicevic, H. (2013), 'Migration across the Mediterranean: When will Europe see that too many people have died?' (Interview with Peter Mayo), *Truthout*, 9 December. Available online: http://truth-out.org/opinion/item/20474-migration-across-the-mediterranean-how-many-deaths-will-it-take-till-europe-knows-that-too-many-people-have-died (accessed 8 August 2014).

Simon, B., ed. (1990), *The Search for Enlightenment: Adult Education and the Working Class*, Leicester, UK: NIACE.

Simon R. I. (1992), *Teaching against the Grain: Texts for a Pedagogy of Possibility*, Boulder, CO: OISE Press.

Smith, M. K. (1999), 'Julius Nyerere, lifelong learning and informal education', infed.org. Available online: http://www.infed.org/thinkers/et-nye.htm (accessed 3 May 2000).

Smyth, J. (1994), 'Skejjel Miftuħin għall-ġenituri f'dinja f'reċessjoni' (Schools open to parents in a world of recession), in R. G. Sultana (ed.), *Ġenituri u Għalliema għal edukazzjoni aħjar.Gwida għal Sħubija Ġdida*, 126–38, Malta: Mireva (in Maltese).

Stedile, J. P. (2006), *A Questão agrária no Brasil (The Agrarian Question in Brasil) vol. 4 – História e natureza das Ligas Camponesas – 1954–1964 (History and Nature of the Peasant Leagues – 1954–1964)*, São Paulo: Expressão Popular.

Stromquist, N. (1997), *Literacy for Citizenship: Gender and Grassroots Dynamics in Brazil*, Albany: SUNY Press.

Suchodolski, B. (1976), 'Lifelong education – some philosophical aspects', in R. H. Dave (ed.), *Foundations of Lifelong Education*, 57–96, Oxford: Pergamon Press.

Sumra, S., and Bwatwa, Y. D. M. (1988), 'Adult education, literacy training and skill upgrading in Tanzania', *The Alberta Journal of Educational Research*, 34: 259–68.

Tarlau, R. (2017), 'Gramsci as theory, pedagogy, and strategy: Educational lessons from the Brazilian Landless Workers' Movement', in N. Pizzolato and J. D. Holst (eds), *Antonio Gramsci: A Pedagogy to Change the World*, 107–26, Cham: Springer.

Tarlau, R. (2019), *Occupying Schools, Occupying Land: How the Landless Workers Movement Transformed Brazilian Education*, New York: Oxford University Press.

Tarozzi, M. (2017), 'Prefazione (Preface)', in P. Mayo and P. Vittoria (eds), *Saggi di Pedagogia Critica: Oltre il Neoliberismo. Analizzando Educatori, Lotte e Movimenti Sociali (Essays in Critical Pedagogy: Analysing Educators, Struggles and Social Movements)*, 7–10, Florence: Società Editrice Fiorentina (SEF).

Taylor, P. V. (1993), *The Texts of Paulo Freire*, Buckingham: Open University Press.

Thiong'o, Ngugi wa (1986), *Decolonising the Mind: The Politics of Language in African Literature*, Nairobi: Heinemann Educational.

Torres, C. A. (1982), 'From the *Pedagogy of the Oppressed* to *A Luta Continua* – An essay on the political pedagogy of Paulo Freire', *Education with Production*, 2: 76–97.

Torres, C. A. (2005), 'Education and transformative social justice learning', *Lifelong Learning in Europe*, 4: 204–7.

Torres, R. M. (2013), 'Youth and adult education and lifelong learning in Latin America and the Caribbean', in P. Mayo (ed.), *Learning with Adults: A Reader*, 19–31, Leiden: Brill-Sense.

Tuijnman, A., and Boström, A-K. (2002), 'Changing notions of lifelong education and lifelong learning', *International Review of Education*, 48 (1/2): 93–110.

United Nations (2015), *Transforming our World: The 2030 Agenda for Sustainable Development*. Available online: https://sdgs.un.org/2030agenda (accessed 18 March 2021).

Unsicker, J. (1986), 'Tanzania's literacy campaign in historical-structural perspective', in R. F. Arnove and H. Graff (eds), *National Literacy Campaigns in Historical and Comparative Perspective*, 219–44, New York: Plenum.

Vella, M. (1989), *Reflections in a Canvas Bag*, Malta: PEG.

Vigilante, A., and Vittoria, P. (2011), *Pedagogie della Liberazione: Freire, Boal, Capitini, Dolci (Pedagogies of Liberation: Freire, Boal, Capitini, Dolci)*, Foggia: Il Rosone (in Italian).

Vittoria, P. (2011), *Narrando Paulo Freire: por uma pedagogia do diálogo (Narrating Paulo Freire: For a Pedagogy of Dialogue)*, Rio de Janeiro: Editora UFRJ (in Portuguese).

Vittoria, P. (2016), *Narrating Paulo Freire: Towards a Pedagogy of Dialogue*, Brighton: Institute of Education Policy Studies.

Vittoria, P. (2017), *L'educazione è la prima cosa! Saggio sulla Comunità Educante (Education Is the First Thing! An Essay on the Educating Community)*, Firenze: SEF EDITRICE.

Vittoria, P. (2018), 'Paulo Freire and Augusto Boal: Poetry, praxis and utopia', in K. Howe, J. Boal and J. Soeiro (eds), *The Routledge Companion to Theatre of the Oppressed*, 58–70, New York: Routledge.

Vittoria, P. (2019), *Paulo Freire and Augusto Boal: Revolutionary Praxis in Theatre and Education*, London: Institute Education Policy Studies.

Vittoria, P., and Mazzini, R. (2011), 'Augusto Boal: il teatro per la liberazione', in A. Vigilante and P. Vittoria (eds), *Pedagogie della liberazione* (Pedagogies of Liberation), 63–109, Foggia: Edizioni del Rozone.

Von Freyhold, M. (1979), 'Some observations on adult education in Tanzania', in H. Hinzen and V. H. Hundsdorfer (eds), *The Tanzanian Experience: Education for Liberation and Development*, 162–7, Hamburg: Unesco Institute for Education.

Wain, K (1987), *A Philosophy of Lifelong Education*, London: Croom Helm.

Wain, K. (2004), *The Learning Society in a Postmodern World: The Education Crisis*, New York: Peter Lang.

Waugh, C. (2009), *Plebs: The Lost Legacy of Independent Working Class Education*, Occasional paper, Sheffield, UK: Post 16 Educator.

Welton, M. (1993), 'Social revolutionary learning: The new social movements as learning sites', *Adult Education Quarterly*, 43 (3): 152–64.

West, C. (2006), *Cornel West on the Passion* (with T. Morrison), Audio visual on YouTube https://www.youtube.com/watch?v=fjifj_PZONo

Williams, R. ([1958] 1990), *Culture & Society*, London: Hogarth Press.

Williams, R. (1976), 'Base and superstructure in Marxist Cultural Theory', in R. Dale, G. Esland and M. Macdonald (eds), *Schooling and Capitalism: A Sociological Reader*, 202–10, London: Routledge and Kegan Paul.

Williams, R. (1977), *Marxism and Literature*, Oxford: Oxford University Press.

Williams, R. (1982), *Culture & Society*, London: Hogarth Press.

Williamson, W. (1998), *Lifeworlds and Learning: Essays in the Theory, Philosophy and Practice of Lifelong Learning*, Leicester, UK: NIACE, 1998.

Willis, P. (1977) *Learning to Labor: How Working Class Kids Get Working Class Jobs*, New York: Columbia University Press, 1977.

Wood Royo, A. J. (2007), *Gabriela Mistral. The Teaching Journey of a Poet*. A dissertation submitted in partial fulfilment of the requirements for the degree of Doctor of Philosophy in the Department of Romance Languages (Spanish-American Literature), Chapel-Hill: University of North Carolina.

Wright, H. K. (2009), 'Handel Kashope Wright talks to the project about interculturalism vs multiculturalism, youth in Canada, USA and Europe, his relationship with project founder, Joe Kincheloe and critical pedagogy's influence on his own work', webcast, University of British Columbia, June 10, Montreal: The Paulo & Nita Freire International Project for Critical Pedagogy, McGill University.

Wright, H. K. (2012), '"Is this an African I see before me?" Black/African identity and the politics of (Western, Academic) knowledge', in H. K. Wright and A. A. Abdi (eds), *The Dialectics of African Education and Western Discourses: Counter-Hegemonic Perspectives*, 180–91, New York: Peter Lang.

Xuereb, P., ed. (2013), *Migration and Asylum in Malta and the European Union*, Malta: Malta University Press.

Yarnit, M. (1980), 'The 150 hrs: Italy's experiment in mass working class adult education', in J. Thompson (ed.), *Adult Education for a Change*, 192–218, Kent, UK: Hutchinson.

Young, M., and Muller, J. (2010), 'Three educational scenarios for the future: Lessons from the sociology of knowledge', *European Journal of Education*, 45 (1): 11–27.

Young, M. (2013), 'Overcoming the crisis in curriculum theory: A knowledge-based approach', *Journal of Curriculum Studies*, 45 (2): 101–18.

Author Index

Adorno, T. xxx, 161
Allende, S. 30, 35, 151, 178
Alves, A. 138, 141
Arafat, Y. 155
Arraes, M. 137, 139

Bauman, Z. 11, 79, 92, 93, 169, 188
Berry, T. 18, 26, 188
Boal, A. 87, 187, 205
Boff, L. 135, 150, 188
Bolsonaro, J. xvi, 135, 155, 156, 185
Bourdieu, P. 54, 55, 151, 160, 189
Braudel, F. 92, 189
Bresciani, Fr 86
Buber, M. 59

Cabral, A xiv, xxv, xxvii, xxix, xxx, xxxii, xxxiv, 53, 105–18, 143, 162, 174, 176, 183
Caldart, R. 147, 152, 153, 154, 189
Cardoso, F. H. 143, 152
Carmichael, S. 3, 51
Cerdá, P. A. 35
Coleridge, S. T. 18, 24, 26

D'Annunzio, G. 29
Da Silva, L. I. (Lula) 71, 72, 147, 155, 196
Dave, R. 12, 190, 204
Davis, A. xxxii, 3, 175
De Rosa, L. 99, 190
Delpit, L. 7, 190
Dolci, D. 4, 23, 161, 205

Eusébio (da Silva Ferreira) 111

Fanon, F. xx, xxi, xxxvii, xli, xliii, 86, 110, 121, 125, 172, 176, 177, 178, 191
Fernandes, F. 135, 144, 145, 146, 148, 152, 153, 155, 160, 161, 163, 184, 191, 198
Fisher, M. 101, 168, 192

Foucault, M. 1, 3, 95
Francis of Assisi 26
Freire, P. xiii, xiv, xxiv, xxiii, xxix, xxx, 2, 3, 4, 6, 7, 13, 22, 26, 32, 36, 42, 49, 52, 53, 56, 57, 58, 59, 62, 65–76, 82–5, 87, 105–18, 121–30, 134–6, 138–44, 146–50, 152, 155, 158–64, 166–7, 173–5, 179–80, 183–5

Galdino, J. 82
Galeano, E. 85, 193
Giroux, H. A. xi, xxiii, 1, 6, 25, 47, 66, 68, 83, 84, 95, 162, 166, 173, 194
Gobetti, A. xiv, xxiv, xxv, xliv, 4, 6, 39–45, 160,
Gobetti, P. 4, 39, 40, 41, 98, 161, 166, 179
Gramsci, A xiv, xxiv, xxv, xxix, 3, 4, 6–8, 13, 23, 39, 42, 49, 52, 68–70, 72, 86–7, 91–102, 106–7, 110, 117, 137, 145, 147, 151–5, 158–60, 162–6, 180–3, 185
Gutierrez, G. 149

Habermas, J. 3, 13, 24
Hall, S. 3, 81
Harasim, L. 115, 183, 196
Hooks, b. 3, 22, 75, 172, 196

Jara, V. 33

Keats, J. 85
Kennedy, J.-F. 138, 140

Lancaster, J. 60
Lenin, V. I. 145, 151, 173, 182, 185, 191
Lombroso, C. 86
Lorca, F. G. 34, 87

Macaulay, T. B. 109, 183
Macedo, D. 7, 74, 85, 110, 111, 115, 116, 140
Maranhão, D. 138
Mariátegui, J. C. 147
Marti, J. 30, 34
Marx, K. xviii, xxvi, xl, xlv, 68, 106, 124, 145, 148, 149, 151, 164
Milani, L. xxiv, xxv, 3, 6, 7, 32, 47–64, 107, 156, 159, 161, 166, 180
Milton, J. 161
Mistral, F. 29
Mistral, G. xiv, xliv, 29–37, 51, 160, 161, 166, 179
Muraro, L. 3, 23, 24
Mwinyi, H. 119

Neruda, P. 30, 35, 161
Nikolakaki, M. 6
Nyerere, J. K. xiv, xxv, xxvii, xxviii, xxix, xxxviii, xxxix, 110, 118–31, 162

Obregon, A. 33

Pasolini, P. P. 49, 180
Passeron, J. C. 51, 55, 189
Perreira, A. 109, 125
Pinochet, A. 65
Pope, A. 39

Said, E. 7, 82, 85, 87, 97, 111
Sampaio, C. 137–8
Sampaio, P. 143, 185
Santos, B. de S xxii, xxiii, xxv, xxvii, xliii, xliv, 5, 7, 65, 67, 110, 135, 155, 162, 163, 170–4, 178
Santos, C. dos 138
Saviani, D. 151
Shakespeare, W. 120
Simon, R. I. 6
Stedile, J. 136, 155
Suchodolski, B. 12

Teixeira, J. P. 138
Texeira, A. 143
Torres, R. M. 16, 178
Trotsky, L. 145

Ugarte, E. 34

Vasconcellos, J. D. 33–4

Williams, R. 5, 33, 96, 162
Wood Royo, A. J. 37

Young, M. 7, 8, 58, 59, 62, 158, 180

Zamboni, C. 21

Subject Index

Aborigines 13, 134
Action Party 41
Adivasi 13, 134–5
adult education/learning 11–12, 15–17, 23–4, 60, 89, 127–8, 130–1, 140–1
Africa/n xiv, xvii, xxv, xxvii–xxix, xl, xlll, xliv, 13, 52, 79, 80, 82, 86, 88, 92–5, 97, 99, 100, 106, 107, 109–11, 113–15, 118–22, 125–6, 134, 149, 158, 162
Afro-American 3, 7, 51, 183
Afro-Shirazi 119
Agrarian xxviii, 32, 34, 35, 99, 123, 139, 162, 184
Agriculture xxxiv, xxxix, 118, 136
Aid 14, 67, 120, 140
alienation xxix, 108, 112, 164
alliance/s 64, 66, 72–3, 91–4, 96, 98, 100–2, 137–41, 144, 146, 159, 164, 181
American–Americanism, 1, 47, 140, 145
Angicos 136, 138, 140, 143
Apartheid 5
Arab xii, 2, 82, 88, 98, 100
art, artists, artistic 33, 48, 62, 82, 86, 117, 136, 150
Arusha Declaration xxxix, 121, 122, 131
authority 22, 74, 129
authoritarian/ism xvi, xvii, xviii, 2, 21, 22, 74, 161

Barbiana 3, 7, 32, 47, 48, 49, 50, 51, 52, 53, 54, 55, 56, 57, 58, 59, 60, 61, 62, 63, 107, 159, 160, 180
being xli, xliii
Biennio Rosso 39
Black–European 121
Brazil/ian 2, 36, 70, 71, 72, 82, 87, 107, 128, 129, 133, 135, 136, 137, 138, 139, 140, 141, 142, 143, 144, 145, 146, 150, 151, 153, 155, 156, 159, 160, 161, 162, 163, 183, 184
Burundi 120

Calabrian 86
Calenzano 48, 51, 61, 159
Campesino/a/camponesas 30, 37, 163
Cape Verde xxvii xxviii, 107, 109, 125, 126, 183
capitalism xviii xix, xxii, xxiii, xxxiii, xxxv, xxxix, xli, 65, 67, 79, 94, 120, 131, 138, 143, 144, 145, 172, 184
carceral 89, 95
Caribbean xxxvi, 136, 162
Catholic Action 136
CEB (Basic Ecclesial communities) 153
Chama Cha Mapinduzi xxvii, 119
Chile XIV, 29, 30, 31, 32, 33, 34, 35, 36, 51, 65, 73, 017, 128, 143, 151, 157, 178, 180, 184
Chipko 134
Christian XV, XVIII, XL, XLII, XLIII, 30, 35, 49, 54, 62, 70, 71, 81, 84, 98, 107, 122, 131, 149, 150, 152, 162, 163, 184
CIA 120, 137
cinematographic 35, 179
class xiii, xviii, xxxi–xxxii, xxxiv–xxxvi, xl, xli, 1, 3, 6–7, 16, 17, 21, 30, 32, 41–2, 47–8, 50–8, 60, 62, 67–8, 86, 91, 94–8, 100, 106, 109, 127, 134, 136, 138–9, 141, 144–6, 148, 149, 153–5, 157, 161, 164–5, 176–7
class-suicide 52, 53, 84
collective xiii, xiv, xvi, xxviii, xx, xxxiii, xxxv, 4, 6, 19, 22–3, 50, 54, 61–3, 113, 117, 137, 145, 152–3, 161, 164, 167
colonization (de) xii, 5, 7, 81, 107–11, 114, 121
common sense xix, xxiv, 11, 68, 86, 87, 117, 154, 159, 163
community xxviii–xxx, xxxv, xxxix, xliv, 4, 13, 16, 17, 19, 23, 25–6, 48, 56–7, 61, 86–7, 98, 115, 117–18, 120, 122, 124–6, 130–1, 140, 164, 167

conquistadores 34
conscientious objection 49
Constantinean 149
Coup 71, 107, 137, 140, 143–5, 150, 155, 178
Covid-19 xi–xii, xx, 5, 44, 156, 164
coyotes 92
creation xxiii, xxxi, 13, 19, 21–6, 159, 179
Creole 105, 114–15
critical consciousness 1, 3, 68, 116, 141, 142
critical pedagogy xiii–xiv, 1–2, 5–6, 47, 160
cultural capital 7, 52, 55, 123
Cultural Extension Service (SEC) 141
cultural studies 5
culture xii–xiii, xx, xxii–xxiii, xlii, 1, 2, 5–7, 19, 21, 23, 30, 34, 44, 46–7, 50, 55, 76, 80, 82–90, 96–8, 105–13, 115–18, 126, 136, 139, 141, 148, 154, 158, 162–3, 168
curriculum xix, xxii, xxvi, xlv–xlvi, 1–2, 6, 57–9, 63, 107, 126

Dar es Salaam 127–8, 130, 184
democracy/atisation xi, xviii, xxv, xxxii–xxxiii, xlv, 2–4, 23, 25, 41–3, 45, 47, 50, 71, 73, 83–4, 88, 101, 122, 133, 135, 137, 155, 161, 168, 184
development/alism xii–xiii, xvi, xx, xxii, xxviii–xxxix, xll, xliii, 1, 2, 14, 18–19, 23, 26, 35–6, 43–4, 52, 57, 60, 65, 67, 76, 84, 89, 94, 99, 108, 114, 116, 118–25, 128–31, 136–9, 141, 143–6, 149, 152, 159, 162, 184–5
dialectic/al xli, 3, 12, 17, 43, 73–4, 88, 90, 143, 145–6, 153–4, 167, 174–5, 193
diotima 22, 25, 158, 179

Economic Commission for Latin America and the Caribbean (ECLAC) 136
ecopedagogy 75
El Warsha 87
Escuela/Escola xxxii, 31, 35, 107, 134–5, 144, 155, 166, 174
European Union (EU) xvi–xvii, 11, 92–3 99
exotic/isation 85–6

fascism xv, xix–xx, xxxii, 4, 34, 39, 41–2, 161, 169
feminine 23, 31, 35
feminism xiv, 21–2, 30–2, 158, 172, 179
First Nations 18, 134, 172
Florence xiv, 48, 52
Folk High Schools 131
folklore 86
food xxix, xxxviii, 5, 18, 115, 141
forum/s 19, 26, 33, 36, 73, 76, 80, 84, 101, 110, 136, 141, 151, 159
FRELIMO xxvii–xxviii, xxx–xxxi, xl, xliii, 174
Frente Popular 35
Fuhrer 34

Geneva 91, 107–8, 120, 124, 151
Gezi xii, 6, 101, 151
Giornale dei genitori 39, 42–3, 51
girls 25, 32, 51
Global South xxi, xlv, 2, 5
Globalization 70, 180
Golpe Branco 72, 135, 155
grassroots xii, xiv–xxv, 4, 23, 101, 112, 122, 136–7, 155, 158, 161
greenbelt 134
Guinea Bissau xxvii, 7, 105–14, 117–18, 124, 151, 162, 183

having 56
health xii, 2, 5, 44, 55, 66, 76, 89, 114, 116, 129, 183
hegemony/ic xviii–xix, xxiii, xxiv, xl, xliv, 1, 3, 7, 11, 13, 17, 20, 23, 65–7, 69–70, 75, 86, 90–1, 95–9, 136, 138, 140, 144, 148, 153, 155, 181–3 185
historical bloc 96
history xvi, xviii, xxi–xxii, xxiv–xxxv, xxxvii–xxxix, xiii, 1, 6, 11, 13, 20, 29, 32, 42, 44, 51, 53–4, 59, 69, 87, 91, 95–6, 106, 109, 111, 113, 126, 139, 143, 148, 153, 161, 171, 173, 182
Hodgkin disease 49
human waste 79, 92–3
hundred and fifty hours (150 hours) 21–2
hybrid/isation 17, 58, 81–2, 97, 110, 162

ideology 23, 50, 61, 65–6, 68–9, 73, 75, 91, 94, 96, 121, 147, 150

independence xvii–xviii, xxxi, xlI, 40, 95, 103, 105–6, 108–9, 111–12, 114–16, 118–20, 122–3
Indigenous xxi–xxii, xxx–xxxi, xxxvi, 2, 7, 13, 24, 29, 30, 32, 34, 71, 85, 105, 110, 114, 122, 126, 131, 134, 135, 138, 154, 156, 162, 172, 185
Indignados 16, 101
industrialist/s 14–15
intellectuals xv, xxi, xxIv–xxxii, xl–xlv, 3, 4, 15, 21, 33, 35–6, 39–42, 45, 49, 62, 68, 73, 111, 120, 127–8, 135–6, 147, 150–1, 153, 165
International Monetary Fund (IMF) 131
Islam xl, xlii–xliii, 2, 81–2, 85, 98
Israel/is xvii–xviii, 88–9, 93

Jew/ish 48, 53, 98, 109
journalist/ism 33, 39–40, 48

Kalahari 134
Kishwahili 119
Kivokoni 130
Knowledge 52, 57–9, 61–2, 74–5, 83–5, 89, 105, 110, 122–3, 126–7, 129, 140, 142, 150–1, 154, 158, 162–3, 168, 172, 174, 177

La Barraca 34, 87
language xxx, xlv, 1, 5, 7, 12, 29, 30, 32, 34, 36, 39, 57, 59–60, 88, 105, 109, 110, 113–15, 118, 121, 126, 142, 158–60, 162
Latin America xiii, xxiv, xxxvi, 13–14, 16–17, 29–30, 32–7, 49, 58, 70, 72, 118, 133, 136, 138, 140, 143–4 150, 154, 156, 160–1, 178, 185
learning Society 12–13
legal/ities Illegal 82, 95, 98, 141, 146, 182
letter/s/e/a 3 39–40, 42, 76, 47, 49–51, 53–4, 57–8, 62–4, 106, 108, 115–16, 124, 159–60, 170, 180
liberation theology 144, 150
Libya 80, 92–9
lifelong education/lifelong learning xxiv, 11, 13–15, 17, 19, 20–1, 13, 26, 131, 159, 178, 180

Madres 23
Maori 134

markets'isation/place xi, xviii, xix–xxx, xxxv, 2, 9, 14, 15, 18, 22, 25, 66–8, 75, 78, 81, 95, 98, 121, 164, 167, 180
Marxism/ist xliv, 49, 106, 144–5, 148–50, 172–3
mass media 33, 84
Mediterranean xlii, xlv, xxv, 16, 76, 79–81, 85, 87–8, 91–3, 95, 97, 99, 158–9, 161, 181
Mexico 33, 35–6, 92, 150, 154
migration xii, xiv, xix–xx, xxv, 75–7, 79–81, 88–9, 91–5, 97–101, 159, 161, 181
military 2, 49, 53, 140, 143–4, 150
Millennium Development Goals 67
MOBRAL (Brazilian Literacy Movement) 143
modernizing 140, 149, 181, 202
Modern Prince 101
Movimento de Mulheres Camponesas 163
Mozambique xxvii–xxviii, xxxv, xliv, 111
multinational 14
Muslim 81, 82, 98

Nakba 95
nationalism xvi, xxiii, xliii, 91
national-popular 97
Nazi-fascism 4, 34, 39, 161
neoliberal/ism xi, xvi, xviii–xix, xxii–xxiii, xlv, 2, 5–6, 14, 18–19, 21–2, 65–8, 76, 90, 93, 95, 98–9, 117–18, 121, 131, 152, 159, 163–9, 178, 180
neutral/ity 6, 14, 45, 53, 87, 90, 108, 116, 155, 157
Nobel Prize 30, 36, 161
non-Aligned xliii

occupy 6, 16, 101, 111
OECD 14–15, 23
Omnicrazia 4, 23
One Life 18, 24
oppressed xiii, xviii–xxiv, xxiii, xxxii, xxxvi, xli, xliii, xlv, 2, 3, 48, 51, 53, 69, 87, 90, 95, 99, 106–7, 113, 117–18, 128, 148–9, 153, 158, 160, 173, 175
Ottoman 85

Paese Sera 39
PAIGC xxvii, xl, 108, 110, 124

Palestine/inians 5, 7, 81, 88–9, 93, 95, 134, 155, 163
parents xxviii, xxx, 16, 32–3, 43–4, 48, 50–1, 55, 64, 93
partisan 4, 39–42, 130
party xv, 35, 41, 49, 62, 71, 72–3, 101, 107, 119, 130, 134, 136–8, 144–6, 155, 183
Pastoral Land Commission 72, 144, 146–8, 159, 163
PCB (Brazilian Communist Party) 136–8, 141
PCI (Italian Communist Party) 49–50
Peasant leagues 136, 138, 143
peer tutoring 59–60, 63
Pernambuco 117, 136–9, 141
Plebs League xxiv, 157
poet/try 24, 29–37, 136, 160, 161, 167, 171, 179
Politica Prima 24
popular education xiv, 13, 24, 32–3, 36, 41, 103, 105–56, 159, 161, 166–7, 183–4
Portugal xvii, 76, 108, 111, 118, 177
Portuguese xx, xl, 3, 7, 65, 84, 105, 107, 110–11, 113–14, 120, 151, 181
pragmatist/sm 12–13, 110
Praxis xxiv–xxvii, xxxii, xliii–xliv, 17, 45, 73, 76, 90, 114, 118, 143, 148, 153, 166–70, 172, 180
problem posing 85, 110, 112, 129, 142
Prophetic 107, 149

Quaderni 107, 181

race/ism xiv, xxxvi, xli, xlii–xliii, 1, 30, 51, 80–3, 100–1, 169, 171
realism xi, 101, 168
Recife 128, 141
regimes of truth 2
reinvention xlvi, 13, 17, 76, 162–3
resistance xxv, xl, 4, 39, 40–2, 54, 56, 67, 106, 110, 112, 140, 144, 146–7, 151, 179
responsibility xi, xxiii, xxix, xxx, xxii, 15, 42–3, 61, 93, 101, 111, 114, 125, 128, 154
RIPESS 26, 179
Risorgimento 54, 99
Roman Catholic 30, 84, 107
rural educator 29, 32–3, 36, 37, 147, 152, 161

Sahara xvii, xxv, 80, 92, 95, 162
Sao Tome e Principe 74, 183
Sardegna/inia/ns 96, 106, 182
Sassari 97
self-reliance 120, 122, 123, 131, 177
slavery xxxi, xxxvi, xxxix, 79, 80, 82
social justice 2, 4, 23, 33, 35–7, 40–1, 45, 52, 62–3, 76, 87, 154, 159, 161, 163, 179
socialist xxiv, xxix, xl, 30–1, 35, 66, 98–101, 116, 119–21, 123–4, 137–8, 143, 145–8, 151, 170, 178
social Movements xiv, 5, 16, 19, 23, 25, 33, 67, 70–2, 90, 101, 103, 134–56, 162, 184
Social Service for Industries (SESI) 141
sociology xiv, 3, 48, 160, 176, 180
solidarity xiii, xl, 22–4, 26, 41–2, 48, 51, 76, 79, 83, 87–8, 90, 93, 96–101, 151, 155, 159, 179, 181
Southern Question xxii, 96–9
Spain/anish xvii, 21, 24, 34, 36, 47, 80–1, 85, 87, 98, 101, 107, 158–9, 179
state xi, xxiii, xxxvi–xxxviii, 4–5, 15, 22, 53, 64, 65, 67, 71–3, 89, 91, 93–9, 105–7, 119, 123, 126, 131, 134–5, 138, 152, 170, 173, 177, 182
structure of feeling 5
student xii, xvi, xxvii, xxxii–xxxiii, xliv, 3–5, 22–4, 37, 48–52, 54, 57–63, 70, 74, 84, 113, 123, 125–6, 136, 146, 151, 154, 161, 167, 169, 182
Sustainable Development Goals (SDGs) 18, 19, 26, 67, 159
Swedish International Development Agency (SIDA) 130

Tanzania xxvii–xxix, 119–31, 162
Teatro Giolly 87–8
transnational 14, 66, 143
Turkey 6, 81

Ujamaa xxv, xxviii, xxix, xxx, xxxi, 120–2
UNESCO 11–15, 18, 130
Unidad Popular 30
United Nations xiii, 12, 18, 36, 130, 159
United States Agency for International Development (USAID) 138, 141

Subject Index

university xii, xiv, xxxi, xxxvii, 15, 22–3, 34, 40, 47–8, 69, 115, 124, 126, 130, 141, 146–7, 152, 160, 165
Utopia/n xvii–xviii, xxvii, xlvi, 12, 68, 83, 159, 170–4, 178

women xviii, 21, 22–4, 26, 29–32, 34–5, 37, 42–3, 50, 71–2, 94, 131, 134, 148–9, 163, 165

workers xiv, xxxii, 15, 16, 22, 39, 42, 52, 59, 60, 70–2, 89, 91, 94, 98–102, 114, 118, 126–7, 130, 137–9, 142, 144–7, 149, 151, 157, 164–6
World Council of Churches 107, 108, 183

Zanzibar 119, 122
Zapatista/s 70, 134, 154, 156

www.ingramcontent.com/pod-product-compliance
Lightning Source LLC
Chambersburg PA
CBHW062134300426
44115CB00012BA/1919